Beyond Dalma

A Holistic Foray Into Odia Food

SWETA BISWAL

INDIA • SINGAPORE • MALAYSIA

ISBN 979-8-89067-766-2

ACKNOWLEDGEMENT

To everyone without whom this book would not have been possible.

To my mother, from whom I have inherited a minimalistic and conscious approach towards cooking.

To my late grandmother, from whom I imbibed a sense of pride for my culinary heritage.

To my mother-in-law, who helped me acquire the knowledge of a completely diverse cuisine.

To Sujata, my sounding board and go-to-girl with whom the idea of writing the book was first conceptualized.

To my brother, for helping me out with the Sanskrit texts and translations. Thank you for the valuable inputs.

To all the women who have been my cheerleaders throughout this journey. Thank you for egging me on with your subtle nudges and regular reminders.

To my husband and son for supporting me as I worked late hours to complete this book.

INTRODUCTION

Odisha – a state where most people begin their day with a trip to the local market. For them, only the freshest of vegetables and fish will suffice. No meal is considered complete without including a slice of conversation about the next one. It is a state where holy days are synonymous with a meal of *Arua-Dalma* and *Khatta,* and wedding feasts judged by the quality of mutton served to the guests. It is a serene land on the eastern coast of India where everyone, from the Gods to the poorest of the poor, relishes a bowl of *Pakhala.* Quite remarkably, it is a state where people crave *'Sagaw'* and *'Santula'* as much as they desire a serving of *'Chennapoda'* and *'Rasagola.'* And yet, all of the above dishes constitute a minuscule fraction of Odia cuisine, which is as vast as its geographic spread. It is a cuisine that draws inspiration from the dense forests, the mighty rivers, the expansive shoreline, and the glorious nuances put forth by the seasons. For understanding and appreciating the state's rich culinary heritage, it is crucial to study and analyse it from the perspective of history, caste or community, region, and season. The following paragraphs provide a brief overview of these facets that make Odia cuisine unique.

Historically, the region of Odisha, which was earlier known as Kalinga, has mostly existed as an independent territory, except for the brief period when it was ruled by the Nanda and Maurya empires. It finds a mention in many a religious Hindu text, notably the Mahabharata. Shaivism and Shakti worship have been the dominant influence on Odisha, except from the short but significant duration when Buddhism and Jainism prospered under Ashoka and Kharavela. Later, Vaishnavism gained prominence under the Ganga rulers and one observes the emergence of the Jagannath culture. Kalinga wielded substantial maritime clout in the early centuries of the Common Era and even established offshore colonies in the Indian Ocean. But sometime in the later part of the 15th century CE, this glorious state entered a period of decline. The control over the region passed to the Bengal Sultanate, then to the Marathas, and ultimately into British hands. While each of the phases has left its imprint on the state's cuisine, none of it is as pronounced as the decision of the British to divide Odisha into three administrative zones, namely the Bengal Presidency, Central Provinces, and Madras Presidency. Even today, one can find the echoes of the influence once exerted by these regions on the districts of Odisha that had been mapped to them.

Moving on to the regional distinctions within Odisha, the state can be classified broadly into five zones. The Northern districts of Mayurbhanj, Balasore, and Bhadrak share borders with West Bengal. Their cuisine reflects a shared culinary heritage with their poppy seed and fish-loving neighbours. The inclusion of *Mudhi*, almost as the last course of every meal, is a feature that one doesn't find anywhere else in the state. Dishes like *Patua*, *Mudhi-Mansa*, and fish-based preparations are some of the dishes traditionally prepared in this region. On the other end, the southern districts of Ganjam, Gajapati, and Koraput, have a cuisine with elements of the southern states. But it is unfair to stereotype it as such because it has evolved through the interaction of two cultures. I would put it as one can find Andhra food in Berhampur but not Berhampur food in Andhra Pradesh. Dishes like *Charu pani*, Mutton *Ambil*, Puri-Upma, a wide variety of finger-licking pickles, and wholesome tiffins are unique to this region. The eastern coastal belt has a cuisine that has evolved around the Jagannath temple and, specifically, the Mahaprasad. This region has an enviable list of incomparable dishes like Dalma, Rasabali, Chennapoda, *Nadia bara*, and poda pitha. Most foods of this have a characteristic sweet note. The Western districts of Sambalpur, Sundargarh, Deogarh, Balangir, and Bargarh have a cuisine that is the exact antithesis of the eastern cuisine. Savoury, sour, and rustic in character, it draws heavily from the forest produce and tribal food habits. Bamboo shoots, varieties of foraged tubers, leaves, and smoked fish are some of the unique foods consumed in this region. The central zone of the state consists of districts like Angul, Dhenkanal, and Boudh. These districts have a cuisine that lies in between that of eastern and western Odisha. Some famous foods from this region are *Bara*, *Magji* (a buffalo cheese delicacy), and *Badi*. Some of the districts like Mayurbhanj, Malkangiri, Kandhamal, Koraput, and Rayagada have a considerable tribal population, and each one of them has its own unique micro-cuisine which had remained isolated from the mainstream until a few decades ago. However, with the advent of urbanization and access to social media, most of this diversity is eroding swiftly.

Shifting our focus to the next aspect, caste divisions have always been a primary factor in shaping food habits. Brahmins, especially those under the patronage of kings and powerful landlords, had access to premium ingredients like fine rice, dairy products, coconut, and ghee. This is still evident from the dishes cooked in their homes even today. Furthermore, the women in Brahmin households had the luxury of time for honing their culinary skills as they were not allowed to step out for work. The relatively well-off *Karanas*, a creamy layer of the Kshatriyas, probably have the most evolved cuisine among all castes in the state. Well-travelled, and hence, more open to experimentation, they did not follow the numerous taboos observed in a Brahmin community. While they could afford the best ingredients, at the same time, they also had the means to employ the highly-regarded Brahmin cook. Thus, the Karanas, who constituted the ruling class, had the best of both worlds. The Chasas, who belong to the farming community, make up the demographic majority in the state. Their menu had relatively more pungent dishes or sides, which helped to ingest the large volume of carbs required to derive the energy to work in the fields. Their meals often included foraged ingredients as the women were required to contribute to farm work, and they often went to the fields and forests to collect firewood. The Gaudas, the cow and buffalo herders, have a distinct cuisine where dairy products are a part of everyday dishes. But as the caste system is steadily phased out, a certain homogeneity has crept into the cuisine of various communities. While equality results in access to better nutrition, the unfortunate fallout has been the loss of diversity.

The final and most worthwhile perspective to consider when exploring a cuisine is seasonality. This aspect is intricately coupled with the regional aspect as both are dependent on local flora and fauna.

Making a deep dive into the seasonal component of everyday meals makes one realize that it is the thread of commonality that binds various Indian cuisines and micro-cuisines. It is impossible to overlook the strong representation of the local and seasonal food in any festive menu. Odisha is no different in this aspect. There is a strong correlation between the food of the state and the agricultural cycle, which, in turn, moves in sync with the changing seasons. This relationship will be the primary focus of *'Beyond Dalma'* as it strives to decode Odia cuisine from a seasonal perspective while touching upon the others at various points during this book.

HOW TO READ THIS BOOK?

This book is intended to be a seasonal eating guide for Odia cuisine, and it traverses through the various months of the year, giving insights into the agricultural cycle, local produce, festivities and recipes mapped to them. It reiterates the belief that Mother Nature knows best and that the way to eat healthy is to find ways to accommodate seasonal produce on our plates while keeping open the possibility of reviving the eating habits of the older generation.

Undertaking this work is also an attempt to identify and focus on the commonalities in the cuisine across the state while trying to address regional and even community-based variations whenever possible. It is a daunting task, but I have attempted to do so without bias and keeping in mind the sole focus of not deviating from the common thread of an 'Odia' identity.

The chapters are arranged as per the Odia Calendar year, which begins with Baisakha and ends with Chaitra. It comprises 12 lunar cycles, and each cycle corresponds to a month. With the lunar cycle duration being 27 days, the additional days add up to an extra month called 'mala masa' every 32-33 months. The concept of 'mala masa' is identical to that of 'Adhik Mas,' a compensatory month added to keep the Lunar and Solar calendars in sync and to ensure that there is no significant deviation in the timings of the festivals which have a strong agricultural focus at their core. The foods, rituals and festivities are grouped into 12 months in this book.

Is this book aligned with Ayurveda?

Yes and No. This is a seasonal eating guide that draws from inherited folk wisdom and tribal resources and digs into the old Odia texts associated with indigenous festivals rather than following the guidelines laid down by Ayurveda. It leverages local and seasonal ingredients rather than going by the ones that are mentioned in Ayurvedic texts. However, references and certain terms related to Ayurveda have been made to keep the content relatable.

Coming to Ayurveda or rather, Ritucharya, a set of seasonal guidelines that go beyond food, it focuses on the three doshas and their cyclic nature of accumulation, aggravation and finally, pacification. It broadly outlines that the consumption of foods should follow a cycle that coincides with the period of the year during which their medicinal properties are at the peak and they help balance the doshas. It specifies ideal foods for the various seasons - foods that grow underground for winters, flowers for spring, old grains and preserved foods for monsoons, new leaves or shoots for the summers and things growing in mud for the autumn. Most of the regional cuisines in the subcontinent, including Odia cuisine, roughly adhere to the same guidelines and yet adapt themselves to the local climate and soil conditions. For example, the consumption of fermented parboiled rice (Pakhala) is common in the Eastern part of India during summer. But we do not come across a similar dish in the Northern parts of the country. Instead, one finds a lot of buttermilk and lassi on the menu. This is mainly due to the difference in local produce, climatic conditions, and cultural influences throughout history.

Another point of similarity with Ayurveda is the way certain food items are put together in the meal. The remarkable property of food to exhibit a different characteristic when consumed by itself, as opposed to its transformation when paired with other food items, has been committed to writing in Ayurveda. However, in Odisha, such knowledge has been passed on to the next generations in oral form by legions of women who practised awakened cooking and mindful eating.

GLOSSARY

Aghria	A group of Hindu settlers who migrated from Agra during the Mughal period
Ambula	Sun-dried green mango
Anukula	To begin something
Arua	Sun-dried and pared rice (not subjected to heat treatment)
Badi	Sun-dried black lentil dumplings
Baraw	Refers to the day of the week
Batibasa	A dish prepared by mixing finely chopped vegetables, oil and seasonings in one small bowl and cooking it on the embers. No mixing or stirring is done during cooking.
Bhaja	Pan fried or stir-fried; with or without oil (hot sand is used instead)
Bhoga	Offering made to Gods
Bhuiyan	An indigenous community found in Odisha, Chattisgarh, Bihar, Jharkhand, West Bengal, Uttar Pradesh and Madhya Pradesh
Brata	A sacred thread mostly worn by Brahmins. Brata is also a solemn pledge made to a god or goddess in lieu of the fulfilment of a wish.
Budha	Old man (but it is also used to refer to anything that is old)
Chakata	Mashed
Chakuli	A thick pancake made with rice and another ingredient (black lentil, Mahua, Finger millet, etc.)
Champuta	Sun-dried half-ripened mango
Chara	A small sweet-sour berry

Chasa	A sub-caste of Khandayat, primarily engaged in farming
Chaula	Rice, also referred to as *Tandula* in many books
Checcha	Crushed
Chuda	Flattened rice
Chuna	Powder, can also mean small
Dahi Chenna	A special kind of cheese found around Cuttack; it is prepared from the liquid residue after extracting the butter
Dehury	A non-brahmin priest in the Garhjat areas
Garhjat	Hilly areas of Odisha, which were largely autonomous under Mughal governance (present-day Sundargarh, Sambalpur, Deogarh, Jharsuguda, Angul and Keonjhar)
Ghadaghadiya Tarkari	A soupy winter vegetable stew that is served boiling hot.
Ghanta	Mixed vegetable preparation; a lentil or two is usually added
Gota	Whole
Habisa	Religious restrictions followed during the month of Kartika
Hendua	Dried and coarsely powdered bamboo shoots
Huduma	Roasted rice
Jagar	A tall conical shape made out of popped paddy or Khai. Also called 'Jugar.'
Jau	Rice is cooked to an extent where the grains start to disintegrate by themselves; it is always served warm
Jhunti/Chitta	Beautiful patterns or *Mandala* drawn on the floor, mud plastered walls or even on the mud and cow dung plastered lanes leading to the house

Kakara	A fried pita with stuffing
Kanji	A watery preparation that usually contains vegetables and a souring agent. Some have a hint of sweetness
Karadi	Fresh or fermented bamboo shoots
Khai	Popped rice
Khasa/Rasi	Sesame seeds
Khatta	A sour dish with/or without sweet undertones.
Khudaw	Broken rice
Kulita	A community of farmers in Western Odisha
Kumuti	A community of traders and money-lenders
Manda	A kind of pitha made by steaming or boiling
Manji	Seeds
MogulBandi	The fertile tract of the coastal plain that was under direct Mughal rule from 1590 to mid-1700s (present-day Cuttack, Bhadrak, Balasore, Jajpur, Jagatsinghpur and Kendrapada)
Mudhi	Puffed rice
Nua	New
Osa	Similar to a brata but less austere
Pagaw	A quick condiment that usually requires no-cooking, it is made and served immediately with meals.
Panaa	A sweetened drink meant to cool the body
Patua	Similar to batibasa, but the ingredients are cooked in a parcel made out of leaves.
Pej	The excess water drained out after cooking rice
Phesi	Flaxseed
Pithau	Rice paste or rice-lentil paste
Pitru	Deceased ancestors
Poda	Burnt

Sakara	A sweet dish with sour notes
Sasan	A village leased to the Brahmins by the Puri king
Sijha	Boiled or steamed
Sikar	Hunting
Sikka	A contraption for suspending food items. It consists of a circular base, supporting ropes and a hook for hanging from the ceiling.
Sukhua	Dried fish
Tanti	Weaver
Torani	The fermented rice water associated with pakhala
Usuna	Parboiled rice

CONTENTS

BAISAKHA (APRIL – MAY)

It is the first month of the Odia calendar year and naturally corresponds with the beginning of the agricultural year. As the sun continues its northwards trajectory during this month, the days get progressively hotter. Despite the scorching sun, this is a preparatory phase for the farming community. Ploughing or loosening of the soil and subsequent manuring take precedence. The first sowing of paddy takes place on the auspicious day of Akshaya Tritiya. Surrendering the first seeds to the earth's warm embrace is nothing less than a manifestation of faith. The farmer observes a fast, wears a new pair of clothes, carries the seeds in an aesthetically decorated bamboo basket and does a little ritual in the fields before planting the seeds. This occasion is also called *'Dhana Muthi Anukula.'*

Due to the diversity of the terrain, some regions of the state have two agricultural seasons. In such fields, additional crops like gourds, melon and some lentils (usually nitrogen-fixing crops are preferred) are grown after harvesting paddy. Baisakha corresponds with a supplementary harvest season for such crops.

This month marks a seasonal shift. As the days turn warmer, people switch from relishing 'pitha' to gulping down 'Panaa.' Baisakha marks the beginning of a period of extreme heat. The cooling properties of Panaa and Pakhala cool down and hydrate the body. Hence, various regions of the state offer different varieties of 'Panaa' to the Gods on the first day of Baisakha. Subsequently, the Panaa offering is distributed to everyone as a reminder to drink enough fluids and stay hydrated during summer. While there are many kinds of Panna, only the Bela Panaa, Chattua Panaa, and Jhara Panaa are eligible for ritualistic offering on this occasion.

In some homes, the heirloom *'pakhala kansa,'* large bell metal bowls, are retrieved from a corner of the cupboard or a trunk and given a good scrub to make them gleam like gold. A portion of the utensil rack is cleared out, making space for the bowls which are a piece of our heritage.

The making of Pakhala is no less than an art, and most Odia folks agree that 'nafas' plays a role in it. *Nafas* is loosely described as that inexplicable quality in a person's hands that imparts their food with a distinct flavour. And it is not something that can be acquired with practise. A good Pakhala is always prepared by stirring the rice and water with hands, incorporating it with the right kind of Lactobacillus bacteria vital for the fermentation process that gives it that distinct tang.

With Pakhala taking centerstage, the menu switches to one that goes best with it. A popular variety of leafy greens like Khadaw, and vegetables like drumsticks, gourds, and cucumbers are added to the list of ingredients. The stash of *badi* and *sukhua* prepared last winter is put to good use. Dishes like raee, batibasa, bhaja, vegetables cooked along with the Pakhala (made with Usuna always) and various kinds of 'pagaw' dominate the menu. Various kinds of fish are also cooked depending on the availability.

Additionally, foods like watermelon, mangoes, litchi, kendu, chara, tender sugar palm fruits, and ripe tamarind pods are available around this time.

In the older days, this month was the firewood collection season because it was easy to find dry wood and twigs in the forests during this period. People used to gather and store firewood before the rains commenced. While LPG is now available in most homes, people in rural pockets still prefer woodfire for 'fuel-guzzling' activities like parboiling, cooking aged parboiled rice (a staple kind of rice consumed in Odisha), and even for preparing additional products like ghee and 'Dahi chenna.'

Apart from festivals like Pana Sankranti and Akshaya Tritiya, there are a couple of fairs that take place around this month. Notable among them is the annual fair of Maa Basuli at Bhograi near Balasore. Being a tantric goddess, she is offered fish during the 'Madhyana Alati' or mid-day rituals around the year. And the seula maccha or snakehead fish is considered to be dearest to her.

What's on the menu this month

PAKHALA

The term Pakhala, which means 'to wash,' is associated with the Jagannath Dham in multiple ways. Several unique varieties of Pakhala like Malliphulo pakhala, Tabha pakhala, Mitha pakhala, etc are part of the Mahaprasad offered to the deities throughout the year. Apart from the dish, which derives its name by virtue of being washed or soaked in water, one comes across terms like 'Mukha Pakhala' and 'Dho Pakhala' used in the temple jargon.

Mukha Pakhala refers to the ceremonial bathing carried out every morning. Since the idols are made of wood, the rituals are conducted with the reflection or 'pratibimba' of the Gods in the mirror.

Dho Pakhala is the cleaning of the Rosa ghara or temple kitchen after the last meal of the day has been prepared. It seems to be derived from the Sanskrit word 'dhoya-pakhala,' which means washing and cleaning.

The word 'Pakhala' appears to have originated from the Pali word 'pakhalita' or the Sanskrit word 'Prakshylan,' and, its antiquity seems to date back to the 5th century. However, the dish itself might have been prevalent among the agrarian class from an earlier period.

Her eyes were glued to the street. Once in a while she hurried back into the kitchen but abruptly returned the next moment. Her favourite grandchild was coming home after a long time and she couldn't have been happier. The morning had been spent announcing it to the neighbours and preparing a welcome meal for her. The Pakhala was ready as signalled by the beautifully ripe 'sweet sour' aroma that drafted from a corner of the kitchen where the '*Pakhala handi*' sat. The rice had been cooked last evening and had been left to ferment overnight. A little bit of the natural starch water and some *basi torani* has been added to the still-warm rice along with sufficient water to submerge the rice. Some *badi* had been roasted in the dying embers. A piece of 'sukhua' borrowed from a neighbour had been lightly charred in a pit in the backyard. She had been forced to give up meat and fish after being widowed at a relatively young age. But recently, she had improvised a small '*chulhi*' outside the house to indulge her grandchildren.

Suddenly, she remembered something and rushed into the backyard. A tender green mango was plucked from the lower branches of the mango tree that shaded her humble dwelling. The stem attached to it had been left intact on purpose. As she broke it off after immersing the mango in the Pakhala, an ethereal aroma drifted to her nostrils. The fragrant sap of the mango can cause blisters if it comes in direct contact with the skin but when it is diluted by the '*torani*,' it elevates the flavour by a few notches.

Mission accomplished, she returned to the door to check the streets. Grumbling about the long bus journey that would have tired her child, she paced the narrow space in front fussing over the meal menu and wondering if she had missed something. Even in old age, her memory had been as good as ever. It was the palpable excitement which temporarily hindered her ability to recall things. Finally, she remembered it and hurried to the small patch that she nurtured on a regular basis. The *Khada sagaw* looked good but most of it had been plucked just the day before. The *Leutia* was wilted. Hopeful of finding something, she ventured a little further and a smile lit up her eyes. The neighbour's pond had dried up under the relentless sun and the bottom of the exposed bed was covered with a green mat. The '*Pita sagaw*' had miraculously thrived under such adverse conditions. The flowers had not yet blossomed but tiny buds had started erupting at some of the nodes. It would be a tad more bitter than what she liked, but it was the best she could manage under the circumstances.

Meanwhile, in another 'Sasan' of the same village, a young girl came and sat on the *pidha* reserved for her. Being the eldest child born in a wealthy Brahmin family had its perks. Her mother would always have a little something extra for her meals. Today, it happened to be a small portion of the goat curry prepared the previous evening, with extra bits of the fat that laced the tender meat. Hidden away from the prying eyes of the other family members, it had remained suspended throughout the night in a '*sikka*,' swaying gently in the sea breeze that makes evenings bearable in the coastal districts of Odisha. A contraption designed to keep food safe from ants, cats and myriad other pests, it also provided natural air circulation that kept the food from being spoilt.

As the mother lovingly lowered the pot from the *sikka*, she peered into it. A whitish layer had transcended over the contents of the pot. It was the fat that had solidified due to the low temperature. She transferred it into a small bell metal bowl and placed it next to the Pakhala *kansa*.

A smaller steel bowl filled with water was kept by the side to clean the fingers before dipping them into the Pakhala Kansa after picking at the goat curry. This ensured that the torani did not get contaminated by the gamey smell of the goat curry. Irrespective of the lavish spread, drinking up the *torani* is considered to be the most sacred ritual associated with a Pakhala meal which cuts across class divides.

BELA PANAA
(Wood apple drink)

Panaa, a drink reserved for the Gods. Sharbat, a drink for mere mortals. As a child, I asked how a simple concoction of jaggery, pepper and water with a few bits of raw mango thrown into it, qualified as a drink for the Divine. Just the way Lord Rama accepted those half-eaten berries proffered by the Sabari, I was told. Intent precedes material value. Even though the definition of *panaa* varies as one traverses through the breadth of the state, it is the drink meant to appease the Gods. And sometimes, even the other creatures that inhabit his Universe.

The *Chaitra Panaa* for example, it a drink poured into a hole dug in an intersection of four roads. It is meant for the thirsty birds and animals. The *Adhara Panaa*, a stunningly tall pitcher filled with a heavenly drink is broken on the chariots of Lord Jagannath and his siblings, and the liquid is allowed to spill out. It is said to quench the thirst of the other worldly creatures that inhabit the Jagannath Dham.

Bela (Wood Apple) Panaa is one of the most popular coolers that is consumed throughout the summer months in Odisha. This amazing fruit is highly recommended for patients suffering from diabetes, high blood pressure and cholesterol, apart from benefiting those suffering from ailments of the stomach.

 **Preparation time: 15 minutes**

 **Ingredients:**

- 1 Ripened wood apple
- ½ cup curd/milk
- ½ cup chenna
- 1 small ripe banana
- 3 tbsp sugar or jaggery
- 1/4 tsp black pepper powder

🍽️ Preparation:

- Break the shell of the wood apple with a rolling pin and scoop out the flesh.

- Put it in a mixing bowl and add 2 cups of cold water. Mash it using your fingers to separate the fibre/seeds and extract the juice.

- Strain the juice using a sieve. Transfer the remaining pulp back to the mixing bowl, add 1 cup of cold water and extract any remaining juice.

- Strain the juice and throw away the pulp.

- Add the remaining ingredients and mix.

- Serve it as it is or cool it for a while before serving.

Note – In Western and Southern Odisha, some folks prepare the Bela Panaa on this day with only jaggery and black pepper.

CHATTUA PANAA
(Roasted Bengal gram drink)

Chattua refers to roasted Bengal gram flour. In large parts of Odisha, it is consumed as a quick and nutritious breakfast mixed with milk and sugar, or even water. But on the occasion of Panaa Sankranti, it morphs into a delicious concoction with the addition of numerous ingredients. The cooling nature of the 'Chattua' prevents the body form overheating while replenishing the energy levels.

 **Preparation time – 10 minutes**

 **Ingredients:**

- ½ cup chattua (roasted gram flour)
- 1 cup milk
- ½ cup chenna
- 1 small banana
- 1/2 of one apple
- A few green grapes
- 2-3 tsp powdered jaggery
- A pinch of cardamom
- A few slices of fresh coconut
- 1 tsp of freshly-grated coconut
- Water to adjust the consistency

Preparation:

- Chop the banana and apples into small pieces.
- Transfer all the ingredients (except fruits) into a large mixing bowl and mix it until the jaggery dissolves. Add the fruits.

- Check the consistency. While it is generally kept thick, you can add a little more water if you prefer a thinner consistency.
- Pour into a glass and serve immediately.

Note – Most of the Chattua that is commercially available these days is made from a mix of cereals, nuts and millets with added sugar. It is ideal for busy folks or students living in hostels. However, for making the Panaa offering, only pure Bengal gram flour is used traditionally.

JHILIRI PANAA/PALUA JHARA
(Arrowroot noodles drink)

Hardly any Odia festival goes by without a panaa or a pitha being offered to the Gods. If the heavier pithas are reserved for the colder months, the hotter months of the year witness a slew of Panaa offerings. While a Panaa is quite delicious by itself, it is the addition of ingredients like crushed peppercorns, cardamom, fennel, grated ginger, mishri, etc., to these drinks which helps soothe the stomach and keep digestive troubles at bay during the oppressive heat.

The 'Jhilri Panaa' is a refreshing drink that is prepared in some parts of the state. The addition of 'Palua jhara' which can be described as a kind of noodles made out of arrowroot paste, makes it different from the other kinds of 'panaa.'

 **Cooking time – 20 minutes**

 **Ingredients:**

- 4 tbsp Arrowroot chunks
- 1 cup fresh curd
- A few chunks of rock sugar (*mishri*) (as per taste)
- A pinch of cardamom powder (optional)
- Freshly grated coconut (optional; not used in the traditional recipe)

Preparation:

- Put the rock sugar in a bowl, add 2-3 cups of water and let it stand for 1-2 hours so that it can dissolve. (Break into smaller pieces before adding to water to speed up the process)
- Soak the arrowroot chunks in 2 cups of water for 30 minutes. Carefully drain off the water which contains the impurities and the astringency of the arrowroot.

- Mix and dilute the arrowroot with 3 cups of water. Transfer it to a thick-bottomed saucepan.

- Cook on low heat while stirring it continuously. It is ready when the colour changes from white to transparent and the texture of the arrowroot is thick and glossy.

- Remove it immediately from the flame and allow it to cool down a bit. Transfer into a steel strainer. Use a wide spoon to push out the noodles through the holes of the strainer into a bowl of cold water.

- Dilute the curd with the water in which the rock sugar had been dissolved. Carefully transfer the arrowroot noodles with the help of a perforated spoon and add to it. Sprinkle the cardamom powder and give it a gentle stir.

- Refreshing *Jhilri panaa* is ready to be served.

Note – Like most Odia recipes, one finds a few variations of the Jhiliri pana over regions. One of the most distinct variations is the jhara panaa made without cooking the arrowroot. A very thick paste is made by adding a little water to the arrowroot chunks and this paste is pushed through the sieve into the bowl containing the sweetened curd water. Mandia (finger millet) Jhara is prepared by the Aghria community of Sundargarh during the Shivratri festival.

ILLISI BIHANA SUKHUA BARA
(Preserved hilsa roe fritters)

Illishi (Hilsa) is considered to be the king among fishes. It is highly prized not just for its delectable taste but also for its status appeal as not everyone can afford it. The salted and dried roe of the fish is also a much-desired coastal delicacy which is rarely available these days as hilsa's availability itself has plunged. Much like the fish, it exhibits a certain waxy-oily quality that sets it to stand out.

Usually cooked into small discs much like the fresh roe, these baras can surely turn an everyday Pakhala into a special one.

 **Cooking time – 15 minutes**

 **Ingredients:**

- 50 gm Illisi Bihana sukhua
- 1 large onion
- 1-2 green chillis
- 2 pinch turmeric
- 2-3 tsp Mustard oil

Cooking:

- Soak the roe is warm water for 1-2 hours or until it is hydrated. Transfer it to a mixing bowl and mash it. Add onions, green chilli and turmeric and mix it well.

- The roe will have excess salt and it will get diluted during the soaking. Most of the time one does not need to add more salt to the preserved roe.

- Heat a griddle. Drizzle some oil. Put small portions of the mix and spread it to discs of about 5 mm thickness.

- Once it is cooked on the bottom, flip it over and cook on the other side as well.

- Serve hot with Pakhala.

PITA SAGAW BATIBASA
(Bitter greens cooked with mustard)

What's in a name? Actually, it is everything when it comes to this green which is aptly named 'Pita sagaw', meaning 'bitter greens.' The name is a dead giveaway for any buyer who might not be aware of its properties. Usually found growing wild at the bottom of dried-up ponds and water bodies during summer, the greens are extremely tender and have a pleasantly bitter flavour before the flowering starts. But as flowering sets in, the stems turn tough and fibrous, and the bitterness increases manifold. At this stage, one has to painstakingly pluck the leaves in order to use them.

 **Cooking time – 15 minutes**

 **Ingredients:**

- 1 cup cleaned and prepped Pita sagaw
- 1 small potato
- 2 green chillis
- 5-6 fat garlic cloves
- ½ tsp mustard seeds
- 2 pinch turmeric
- 2 tbsp mustard oil
- Salt as per taste

Preparation:

- Grind the pita sagaw, green chilli, mustard seeds and garlic cloves into a coarse paste.
- Cut the potato into thin long slices.
- Transfer to a mixing bowl. Mix all the ingredients along with 3-4 tbsp water.

Cooking:

- Transfer to a thick-bottomed wok and cook on the lowest flame setting for 10-12 minutes.

- Drizzle some mustard oil and serve it warm.

> *Note – This mix of ingredients can also be wrapped up in leaves and cooked over a low flame for a nice smoky touch.*

PITA SAGAW BARA

(Bitter greens and potato patties)

A recipe that is designed to make the best use of a limited quantity of bitter greens! With vegetables in short supply, potatoes are a rather integral part of summer meals. When the quantity of *pita sagaw* is not sufficient to feed the family, it is mixed with mashed potatoes and some minimal seasoning and turned into *baras*.

The is one dish that really highlights the amazing aroma of these greens even as it cuts down on the bitterness.

 **Cooking time – 20 minutes**

 **Ingredients:**

- 2 medium-sized boiled potatoes

- ½ cup pita sagaw

- 1 medium-sized onion (chopped into medium-sized pieces)

- 2 green chillis (minced)

- Salt to taste

- 4-5 tsp mustard oil

Preparation:

- Take the still-warm potatoes into a mixing bowl. Add the rest of the ingredients except for the oil. Drizzle about ½ tsp oil.

- Mash everything together.

Cooking:

- Heat a skillet. Drizzle a little oil over it.

- Shape the mixture into small discs and place on the pan. Cook on one side until brown.

- Flip it over, drizzle a little more oil and cook until brown.

- Serve hot/warm with meals.

BARADA SAGAW BHAJA

(Stir-fried tender bauhinia leaves)

Bauhinia Purpurea and Bauhinia Variegata, two cousins otherwise known (and sometimes confused) as Barada sagaw and Kuliari sagaw. These leaves need to be plucked off the tree at the right time, or else they turn hard and fibrous. Mostly foraged by the tribal communities, though some people might be lucky to have a tree in the backyard, these are almost like an annual luxury because of the small window within which they need to be harvested.

It is becoming increasingly rare to find such trees as forests are shrinking and the forest management programs do not focus on replenishing the lost vegetation with native plant species.

 **Cooking time – 15 minutes**

 **Ingredients:**

- 3-4 cups chopped Bauhinia leaves
- 1 medium-sized onion
- 2-3 garlic pods
- 6-7 phula badi
- 1 tsp mustard seeds
- 2 dry red chilli
- 3 tsp mustard oil
- ¼ tsp salt approx.

Preparation:

- Remove the stems from all the leaves. Wash it 2-3 times and drain all the water.
- Chop into small pieces. Also, chop the onion into medium-sized pieces.

Cooking:

- Heat 1 tsp oil to wok. Add the badi and fry it on a low flame until it turns light brown. Remove and keep aside.

- Add the remaining oil to the wok. Add the broken red chilli, mustard seeds, and slightly crushed garlic pods.

- Once the garlic starts to change colour, toss in the chopped onions.

- Sauté the onions until translucent. Add the chopped greens and sauté them on a medium-high flame until cooked. [Cover with a lid for 2 minutes and lower the flame if the greens seem to be taking time].

- Once the greens are done, lightly crush the *badi* and add to the wok. Mix it quickly.

- Remove from the flame and serve it immediately.

Note – Fried badi can also be added to leafy green like drumstick leaves, amaranthus greens and onion flower stalks. It adds a nice texture/crunch and flavour to the dish.

KHADA SAGAW BHAJA
(Stir-fried amaranth leaves)

Khada is a variety of *amaranth* that grows profusely and without much effort. The plants require minimal care and grow wild in mountainous areas where poor folks can forage some for their meals. Hence, it is said to be favoured by the lazy folks who seek subsistence on a bowl of 'khada sagaa-pakhala' and do not aspire for more. Such people are branded as 'Khadaa-khiaa,' in what can be termed as a beautiful example of one's eating habits influencing and enriching the vernacular.

Everything from the leaves to the tender stems to the mature stem (and even the roots) of this plant is edible. The plant is carefully chopped, segregated and prepped for use in different preparations. A mature plant in the kitchen garden ensures a good yield of leaves every few days as the new leaves grow back rather profusely after every plucking. In the olden days, almost every backyard had a few of these plants growing during the summer to guarantee an uninterrupted supply of greens. These local vegetables that we tend to overlook for being 'too common' hold the key to sustainability.

For pairing with Pakhala, the leaves are made into a simple stir fry with garlic and *badis* for that extra crunch. These plants grow wild but are also cultivated and sold in the markets.

 **Preparation time – 15 minutes**

 **Ingredients:**

- 4 cups of finely chopped khada sagaw
- 1/2 tsp pancha phutana
- 2-3 red chillis
- 1 small onion
- 6-7 fat garlic cloves (lightly crushed)

- 3 tsp mustard oil
- 1/6 tsp of salt (or) to taste
- 1/3 cup badi (fried and lightly crushed)

Cooking:

- Heat the oil in a wok.
- Add garlic, broken red chilli and pancha phutana. Allow the garlic to turn brown.
- Add the chopped onions and sauté until translucent.
- Add the chopped greens in small batches and stir on high flame for 1-2 minutes.
- Lower the flame, cover and cook for 1 minute on medium to high flame. Remove the cover and stir gently to prevent leaves from bunching/sticking together.
- Repeat the above step alternately until the sagaw is done and excess water evaporates. Add the salt and mix in. Switch off the flame and add the crushed badi.
- Serve hot with pakhala.

CHOTTA ALU ULI PIAJ BHAJA
(Crispy baby potatoes and shallots)

The locally harvested baby potatoes and shallots are an indispensable part of the summer menu. Known as 'uli piaj' in Western Odisha, shallots are served raw alongside Pakhala meals. Raw onions and shallots are known to regulate body heat and reduce the probability of heatstroke, making them a blessing in the hot climate of the state.

Often, these two ingredients are turned into a simple stir fry that goes well with Pakhala meals.

 **Cooking time – 12-15 minutes**

 **Ingredients:**

- 1 cup baby potatoes (cut into half)
- ½ cup shallots (peeled)
- 2 tsp mustard oil
- 2 dry red chillis
- 2 pinch mustard seeds
- 1/8 tsp turmeric
- Salt to taste

Cooking:

- Heat the oil in a wok.
- Add the mustard seeds and broken red chillis.
- Once the seeds start popping, add the potatoes and shallots. Sprinkle salt and turmeric.
- Mix and sauté for 2 minutes. Cover and cook until the potatoes are almost done.
- Cook uncovered until the potato skins crisp up a bit.
- Serve with Pakhala or rotis.

AMBULA PUDA

(Preserved green mangoes cooked with mustard paste)

Sun-dried green mangoes are known as Ambula in Odia. These were used as the primary souring agent in Odia cuisine before tomatoes took over. Usually, a good percentage of the mangoes fall off before reaching maturity, and only a small percentage ripen on the trees. This is a natural thinning process that works on the principle of 'survival of the fittest.' The Norwesters, locally known as *'kala baisakhi,'* also contribute to this process.

In rural and tribal areas, these fallen green mangoes are carefully sorted, sliced, cured with salt or sun-dried and preserved for use throughout the year. Excess produce is sold in the markets.

While its primary use is that of a souring agent, the ambula can be used as a Pagaw or a *raee*. Sour side dishes, when consumed in moderation, help to whet up an appetite and improve digestion. And both properties are much required during hot summer days.

 **Cooking time – 15 minutes**

 **Ingredients:**

- 4-5 pieces *Ambula* (Dried green mango slices)
- 1 tsp mustard seeds
- 5-6 garlic pods
- 2 green chilli
- 1 tsp mustard oil
- 1-2 tsp sugar
- ¼ tsp salt

🍽 **Preparation:**

- Soak the ambula for 3-4 hours in a cup of water. Grind mustard seeds and half of the garlic pods into a fine paste. Put long slits into the green chilli leaving it intact.

🍲 **Cooking:**

- Add all the ingredients except for sugar into a small wok. Add a cup of water to it.

- Put on the stove and bring to a boil on a low flame. Add the sugar and simmer for another 2-3 minutes.

- Cool it. Relish with rice or even with *Pakhala*.

CHAMPUTA
(Semi-ripe mango preserve)

Champuta is a sun-dried and preserved product, somewhat similar to the 'ambula.' Prepared from semi-ripe mangos that are more on the sweeter side, it has limited use as a souring agent. Some of the sweetened ones are tempting enough to be had as a quick nibble. But as the one responsible for emptying the stash at home, I can vouch that over-indulgence does lead to a bad stomach ache.

Wild mangoes with a thin stone are ideal for making *Champuta*. It is turned into a *pagaw* or a '*champuta puda*' on the lines of ambula puda during the monsoons, when excessively sour foods are not advisable.

 **Preparation time – 20 minutes**

 **Ingredients:**

- 2-3 nos half-ripened mangoes
- 1 tsp mustard oil
- 3-4 tsp jaggery
- ¼ tsp chilli powder
- ¼ tsp salt

Preparation:

- Wash the mangoes, dry them and peel the skin.
- Use a knife to shave off thick layers. Dry these layers under direct sun for a couple of days.
- Heat a wok and add a little water along with the jaggery. The jaggery will froth in some time.
- Around the same time, heat the oil until smoking point and then, allow it to cool down.

- Add the sun-dried mangoes to the jaggery once the froth starts to diminish. Mix well.

- Add the chilli powder, salt and oil at this stage. Mix it well and store it in a glass jar once cooled.

SUNSUNIA SAGAW
(Stir-fried summer greens)

A by-product of the paddy ecosystem, these ferns grow prolifically near slow-moving or almost stagnant water channels. Often mistaken as some kind of clover, these aquatic plants are a powerful herb and an accepted tribal remedy for ailments ranging from body aches to skin diseases, stomach-related disorders, migraines, hypertension, and even insomnia.

These soporific greens make a delightful pair with fermented 'Pakhala.' People in rural areas consume it in the evening to ensure a sound sleep during hot and sweltry nights. Given the bad press that Pakhala attracts for inducing drowsiness, the rest of us are usually warned to keep away from this combination.

 **Cooking time – 15 minutes**

 **Ingredients:**

- 1 cup sunsunia sagaw
- 1 small boiled potato
- 1 small onion (chopped into medium-sized pieces)
- 3-4 garlic cloves
- 2 dry red chilli
- 2 pinch mustard seeds
- 1 ½ tsp oil
- Salt to taste

Preparation:

Heat a wok. Add the oil and allow it to smoke.

- Add the broken red chilli, mustard seeds and crushed garlic cloves.

- Once the garlic starts to brown, add the chopped onions and fry them until they start to brown on the edges.

- Peel and dice the boiled potato. Add to the wok. Sauté for 2 minutes.

- Add the greens and turn up the flame. Sprinkle salt over the greens.

- Sauté and cook for 4-5 minutes on medium-high flame.

- Remove from the wok.

- Serve hot or warm with Pakhala.

Note – The potato has been used to bulk up the dish and one can choose to skip it. Foraged greens like this are always cooked with a vegetable or two to feed joint families. Depending on the season, various vegetables like eggplant, potato, tender pumpkin, onions, ridge gourd, flat beans, and even okra are used as the bulking agent.

SEULA MACHA AMBULA TARKARI
(Tangy snakehead fish curry)

Snakehead fish cooked with mustard paste and sun-dried green mangoes is a recipe meant for fish lovers. Lightly spiced and with a nice tang, this preparation allows the inherent taste of the fish to shine through. 'Seula' is considered to be a healthy option as compared to the farm-bred fishes like 'Rohi' and 'Bhakura' that flood the market. It is mostly caught in the wild from the muddy ponds, canals and even grassy areas near the canals and fields.

It is one of the few varieties of fish that can be consumed by someone who is unwell. It is used frequently in traditional medicine. Usually, people suffering from rheumatism or asthma are prescribed this fish by the local medicine men. The added advantage is that it has a single bone running through the body, and hence, suitable for people who find it difficult to separate the bones from the flesh.

⧖ **Preparation time – 30 minutes**

🥣 **Ingredients:**

- 500 gm snakehead fish (Seula Macha)
- 1 large potato
- 1 large tomato
- 1 small onion
- 2-3 green chillis
- 4-5 garlic cloves
- 1/4 tsp mustard seeds
- 3 tsp mustard oil
- 1 tsp turmeric powder
- Salt to taste

- Cilantro for garnishing
- 2-3 dried mango pieces

For the mustard paste:

- 2 tsp mustard seeds
- 1/2 tsp cumin seeds
- 5-6 garlic cloves
- 1-2 green chillis

🍽️ Preparation:

- Wash and clean the fish. Marinate for 10 minutes with salt and 1/2 tsp turmeric.
- Make a fine paste out of the mustard seeds, cumin seeds, green chillis and garlic cloves.
- Chop the onion into small pieces. Quarter the tomato.
- Peel and dice the potatoes.
- Soak the dried mangoes in 1/2 cup warm water.

🍲 Cooking:

- Heat 2 tsp oil in a wok. Add the fish and fry for 3-4 min on both sides on a medium flame.
- Remove and keep aside.
- Now throw in the potatoes and fry until light brown. Remove and keep aside.
- Add the remaining oil to the same wok. Add the mustard seeds and let them start popping. Then, add the slit green chilli and slightly crushed garlic cloves.
- Once the garlic turns light brown, add onion pieces. Fry to a translucent.
- Then, add the tomato pieces and sprinkle a little salt. Cover and cook until mushy.

- Add the mustard paste along with two cups of warm water. Slide in the fried fish and potatoes.

- Add a little turmeric and adjust the salt. Cover with a lid and let it simmer until the potatoes are done.

- Add the soaked mango pieces along with the water used for soaking. Simmer for 3-4 minutes.

- Remove from the flame and garnish with the chopped cilantro.

- Serve hot or warm with steamed rice.

Note - Fish curry offered to the Goddess is made without onion and garlic. Usually a paste of cumin, ginger and coriander seeds is used to flavour this curry. The preparation method remains the same as above.

JYESTA (MAY – JUNE)

This month, the scorching summer heat persists, while humidity levels rise steadily and days become increasingly oppressive. In the paddy fields, more ploughing and manuring activities take place. Dry sowing of paddy is carried out in a phased manner, depending on the forecast of the monsoon arrival. The rice seedlings need to be ready for transplantation when the rain arrives.

Cooling drinks, summer fruits, Pakhala and simple meals rule the menu this month. Regular vegetable supplies dry up, and there is increasing dependence on dried produce like *sukhua* (fried fish), *sula* (sun-dried tomatoes/eggplant), and varieties of badi. Most regions in the state have seasonal greens like the Khadaw, Poee, Leutia and Pita sagaw that thrive in the heat. Forest produce like ripe jackfruit and wild mangoes are available aplenty.

The most prominent festival celebrated throughout the state this month is the Sabitri brata. It draws inspiration from the tale of Savitri and Satyavan, mentioned in Mahabharata. On this day, married women observe a fast for their husbands. The fasting ladies worship Lakshmi Narayana with an offering of seasonal fruits like coconut, banana, mango, jackfruit, and local dates mentioned in the '*Katha.*' Additionally, fruits like *kendu*, tender sugar palm, cucumber, local berries, pineapple, and watermelon are also a part of the 'bhoga.' After the Puja and the recitation of the 'katha,' the women eat a single meal which consists of the fruits that were part of the offering.

Sitala Sasthi, or the divine marriage of Lord Shiva and his consort, Parvati, is celebrated in a grand manner in Western Odisha on the sixth day of the *Shukla Paksha* of this month. While a impressive two-days 'Jatra' organized in Sambalpur on this occasion, smaller processions are witnessed in most villages of the 'Garhjat Parts' of the state. This day marks the beginning of the monsoon season in Western Odisha. It is a local belief that the cooling effect of the first showers of rain on this day is symbolic of the heavenly union Shiva (who was burning from Sati's loss) and Parvati.

Deba Snana Purnima holds great significance for the followers of Lord Jagannath. This day commemorates the birth anniversary of the celestial siblings. On this occasion, the Holy Trinity receive a bath befitting their royal status. The masses of Odisha have long believed that it is a positive omen if it rains on this day. Taking into consideration the timing of Deba Snana Purnima and Sitala Sasthi, and the similar beliefs associated with these days, one can conclude that these are probable markers that monsoon is either on the way (indicated by pre-monsoon showers) or has arrived in the land. And there could scarcely be anything more welcome for folks who have solely relied on agriculture for centuries than the knowledge that rains are on the way. Years of keen observation of weather patterns intermingled with faith gave rise to numerous such sayings in most corners of the world. But they are dismissed as superstition in today's era, possibly because we have been taking most matters of faith at face value and not trying to uncover the layers of reasoning buried beneath them.

What's on the menu this month

NIYA SUKHUA TARKARI
(Smoked fish curry)

While I grew up relishing Pakhala with a little *Sukhua* on the side, I had scant knowledge of the universal nature of fish preservation until I heard a marine conservationist talking about it. Those words propelled me to understand the various methods of preservation and reasons behind it, and how preserved fish can be a sustainable source of protein for underprivileged communities. Aided by our own prejudices, *Sukhua* has morphed into a forbidden word in many Odia homes. Cooking it on the sly is out of the question, with the distinctive odour guaranteed to raise a stink with the neighbours. In fact, one's identity is intertwined with the kind of preserved fish one eats. Folks from the coastal areas are known to covet the '*Illishi sukhua.*' People from some of the western districts love their '*Niya sukhua.*' In my mother's home in Baripada, winters were the time to stock up on *Silamundi Sukhua* from their favourite vendor. Later, after my marriage, I discovered that my mother-in-law dotes on *Pita sukhua* and *Alana sukhua*. During the earlier days, Sukhua was yet another food resource to fall back on during lean times when fresh fish was not available readily.

Over the decades, preferences shifted towards the fresh fish easily available in the markets throughout the year, and the vendors selling 'Sukhua' gradually dwindled in numbers. And in the fast-paced life that we lead, most of us never questioned this abundance of fresh fish, nor did we weigh the merits of fish preservation. This attitude has piggybacked on rising affluence and led to the widespread ostracization of foods like 'Sukhua'.

This recipe uses preserved fish that has been procured from the paddy fields and smoked over wood fire for long periods to eliminate most of the moisture content..

 **'Preparation time – 15 minutes (plus 30 minutes soaking time)**

🥣 Ingredients:

- 1-2 small pieces of smoked fish
- ½ cup Baby potatoes
- 1/3 cup pearl onions/shallots
- 1 medium sized tomato (optional)
- 2 tsp mustard seeds
- 2 green chillis
- 3-5   garlic cloves
- 2 tsp mustard oil
- 2 pinch turmeric
- ¼ tsp salt approx.

🍽 Preparation:

- Soak the smoked fish in warm water for 1 hour. Discard this water before cooking.
- Wash and cut the baby potatoes in half. Peel and cut the pearl onions in half. Finely chop the tomato.
- Grind the mustard seeds with 1 green chilli and half of the garlic cloves into a fine paste.

🍲 Cooking:

- Heat the oil in a wok. Add the broken green chilli and crushed garlic cloves. Fry for 1 minute. Add the soaked fish pieces. Fry for 2-3 minutes and crush them lightly.
- Add the baby potatoes and pearl onions and fry for another 2 minutes. Add the tomatoes and cover with a lid till they start to turn mushy.
- Add the mustard paste with 1 - 1 1/2 cups water, salt and turmeric. Cover with a lid and allow to cook until most of the water is absorbed and potatoes are done. Remove from flame.
- Serve with 'pakhala.'

JHURI PURGA

(Freshwater fish roasted in Sal leaves)

Jhuri, or small fish, is a much sought-after delicacy in Odisha. These are primarily sourced from rivers and ponds, but rarely from the sea, as people prefer freshwater fishes which are labelled 'sweet'. However, saltwater fishes have always found acceptance in the coastal belt. Most folks swear by the distinctive smell of mud and strands of algae that seem to envelop the freshwater 'jhuri.' Its flesh seems to have imbibed a bit of its surroundings and this quality is evident even after cooking.

A big chunk of the attraction for 'jhuri' comes from the fact that is usually freshly caught and mostly likely sourced from a nearby water body. Earlier, most well-off families in rural areas had ponds in their own farms or backyards. People used to drag a piece of cloth like a dhoti or saree through the waters and land up with a handful of the small fish (and tiny shrimps), which added variety to their meals. Often, they are fried until crisp (sometimes with *pithau*) and enjoyed with a bowl of Pakhala.

But on leisurely days, a purga is prepared. Especially when fresh *siali* or *sal* leaves are available.

 **Preparation time – 40 minutes**

 **Ingredients:**

- 200 gm jhuri/small fish (freshwater preferably)
- 2 ½ tsp mustard garlic paste
- 4-5 minced garlic cloves
- 2-3 slit green chilli
- 1 finely chopped tomato (large)
- 2-3 tbsp chopped cilantro
- 1 ½ tbsp mustard oil

- ¼ tsp salt or to taste
- 1 tsp crushed Bamboo shoots (optional)
- Freshly plucked sal/siali/teak leaves

🍽 Preparation:

- Wash and prep the fish. Add all the ingredients in a bowl and mix gently using your fingers. Marinate for 15 minutes.
- Heat a pan. Put the leaf over it for 10-15 seconds to temper it a bit so that it can be easily folded.
- Wrap up the fish in 3-4 layers of leaves before placing it in the embers of a woodfire. Cover it with a layer on embers to ensure even cooking.
- Alternatively, it can also be cooked in a pan over a gas flame. Heat a wok on a medium flame and place the parcel. Cook for 15 minutes on one side and then flip over the packet and cook for 15 minutes on the other side as well.
- Remove from the wok/embers and open it carefully. Discard the leaves and scoop out the purga.
- Serve hot/warm with rice meals.

> *Note – If tender pumpkin leaves are available, then the fish is wrapped first in pumpkin leaves and then the siali or sal leaves are added as an outer layer. The edible pumpkin leaves add bulk and flavour to the purga.*

Odisha being a primarily agricultural state, demonstrates the Core-Fringe-Legume meal pattern that is the hallmark of established agrarian societies all over the world. Sidney Mintz's hypothesis about the categorization of the food under different heads prompts a broader conversation about how these eating habits might have developed as a result of the lifestyle and accumulated wisdom of the people.

In Odisha, these distinctions do not seem to be rigid at all times. During summers, the legumes and fringe segments certainly overlap (badi is derived from legumes but acts as a fringe, i.e., it helps the 'Pakhala' go down). Sometimes, the legumes are skipped. Instead, one finds fish, either fresh or preserved, take its place.

A similar overlap becomes evident during the paddy transplantation phase when rice is consumed with one single side dish prepared by cooking legumes, dried vegetables, and tubers together to minimize the cooking time.

In the tribal communities, the core and legume components are often cooked into a single semi-solid preparation. It is usually left to ferment overnight and is consumed in the morning with boiled leafy greens, chillis, or the local condiment, 'Pagaw.' This semi-solid diet gives them the ready energy required to trek through the hilly terrain or work in the fields. But since semi-solid food gets digested faster, it sometimes means supplementing meals with some fillers that restore energy levels. For example, foods like *Mandia Jau* or *Raav* are eaten for breakfast and meals, and *Mandia Pej* is taken in between to replenish the body.

KHADA TARKARI
(Lightly stewed Amaranthus stems)

If *Khada* leaves are a summer staple, the sweet and juicy stems are an occasional delight during the sweltering hot months. Apart from plucking the leaves regularly to encourage fresh growth, the lateral branches and the tip of the main branch are pruned periodically to make the plant bushy. These tender stems are added to the 'Tarkari' and 'bhaja.' The lower part of the main stem and the roots are harvested at the end of summer or during early monsoon. These tough bits are usually reserved for making the *Kanji*.

My favourite preparation with 'Khada' stems is light juicy 'tarkari' with a hint of mustard:

 **Preparation time – 30 minutes**

 **Ingredients:**

- 2 cups tender khada/amaranthus stems
- 1/2 cup pumpkin cubes
- 1/2 cup ridge gourd cubes
- 1/4 cup potato cubes
- 1 medium-sized onion (roughly chopped)
- 1-2 garlic flakes (slightly crushed)
- 1-2 dry red chillis
- 1/5 tsp turmeric
- 1 tsp mustard garlic paste
- 1/2 tsp *pancha phutana*
- 2-3 tsp oil
- salt to taste

🍽️ Preparation:

- The khada stems need to be soaked in water for half an hour and then washed 2-3 times with fresh water to dislodge any sand/mud sticking to them. Chop into 2-inch pieces and peel them.

🍲 Cooking:

- Heat oil in a wok. Add the broken chilli and pancha phutana. Once they start spluttering, add the chopped onion. Fry until they start turning red around the edges. Add the garlic and allow it to turn golden (but not brown).

- Add the khada and other veggies at this point. Fry on a medium flame for 3-5 minutes.

- Add about 1 1/2 cups water, salt, turmeric and mustard garlic paste. Cover and cook until all the vegetables are soft. If excess water remains, turn up the heat for 2-3 minutes.

- Remove from the wok and serve hot with white rice or Pakhala.

> *Note – If jackfruit seeds are available, cut them lengthwise and sauté a little before adding them along with the other vegetables to this preparation. It adds to the texture and the aroma.*

GOTA KALARA BHAJA
(Stuffed bitter gourd)

Bitter gourd is one of the vegetables that is plentily available during the summers in Odisha. A cultivar of small, light-green, and thin-skinned bitter gourd, called 'Thusi kalara,' is preferred by many people. It is less bitter than the larger dark-green ones and has a delicate aroma. The usual preparation involves cutting the bitter gourd into thin rounds, and pan frying them with salt and turmeric.

Occasionally, a stuffed version is also prepared. The thin-skinned 'Thusi Kalara' is best suited for this recipe. However, it can also be made with the larger ones by shaving off some of the outer skin.

⏳ **Cooking time Required: 20 min**

 **Ingredients:**

- 6 small bitter gourd
- 1 medium-sized onion
- 1 medium-sized tomato
- 4 tsp cooking oil
- 1/6 tsp turmeric
- ½ salt
- 1-2 dry red chillis
- 5 garlic pods
- 3 tsp mustard seeds
- 1 tsp cumin seeds

🍽 **Preparation:**

- Make a fine paste of the mustard, cumin, garlic and red chilli.
- Finely chop the onion. Chop the tomato into small pieces.

- Make slits along the length of the bitter gourd and put them in a pressure cooker. Add salt and turmeric along with 1 cup water. Cook on high flame for 4-5 minutes.

- Remove from flame and allow to cool down. Remove the seeds.

Cooking:

- Heat 1 tsp oil in a wok. Add the onion and stir fry until translucent. Add the chopped tomato and cook until it turns mushy.

- Add the mustard paste and fry all ingredients for another 3 minutes. Add a little amount of salt and mix well.

- Remove from fire and allow to cool down.

- Stuff the bitter gourds with the above-prepared paste.

- Heat oil in a wok. Add the bitter gourds and cook covered for 7-8 minutes or until done.

- Serve hot with rice meals.

LAU SANTULA
(Bottle gourd stew)

Summer meals are incomplete without a gourd or two making their presence felt in every Odia meal. Ridge gourd, snake gourd, bottle gourd, bitter gourd, ivy gourd at the start, and spine gourd towards the end of the season, all mark their attendance during meals in the form of a *bhaja, santula, batibasa, patua, tarkari* or a basic *pagaw*.

Among these gourds, the bottle gourd had remained the least conspicuous on the Odia menu before Baba Ramdev re-introduced it to the masses. Part of the bad press this vegetable had garnered earlier can be attributed to the 'Lakshmi Purana,' which forbids cooking this vegetable with any non-veg ingredient. As a result, many people had banished this vegetable from their kitchen and turned it into food for their cattle. Thankfully, this is no longer the case.

The mellow-flavoured bottle gourd is believed to have a wide range of health benefits ranging from curing heart diseases, lowering blood pressure, curing jaundice, treating gastrointestinal disorders, and improving liver function. With 96 per cent water and just 12 calories per 100 grams, it is quite beneficial if one is on a weight-loss diet. However, one must avoid the bitter ones as they contain cucurbitacins, a compound that can trigger a toxic reaction.

Lau Santula is one of the classic Odia recipes. It is highly recommended during a postpartum diet and even for elderly people.

 **Cooking time – 15 minutes**

 **Ingredients:**

- 4 cups peeled and diced bottle gourd
- 1 medium-sized onion,
- 3-4 garlic flakes

- 3 tsp chopped coriander leaves
- 2 dry red chillis
- 1/2 tsp pancha phutana (if not available use a mix of fennel+cumin+mustard)
- 1/3 tsp salt
- ¼ tsp Turmeric
- 2 tsp oil

Preparation:

- Boil the bottle gourd pieces in a pressure cooker with 1 cup water, salt and turmeric for 1-2 whistles. Remove from flame and allow steam to escape. Do not throw away the excess water.
- Chop the onion into small pieces. Crush the garlic flakes.

Cooking:

- Heat oil in a wok.
- Add the pancha-phutana and broken red chilli. Once the chilli changes colour, add the garlic and chopped onion. Fry until onions turn translucent.
- Add the boiled bottle gourd along with any excess water. Boil for 2 minutes.
- Add the chopped coriander leaves. Remove from flame.
- Serve hot with rotis.

LAU CHOPA PATUA
(A spicy bottle gourd peel preparation)

Most Indian cuisines have a long history of using the peels of various vegetables. Peeling vegetables before cooking them is a relatively new practice that gained popularity in recent decades with the advent of inorganic fertilizers and pesticides. Most Odia recipes are cooked with vegetables that retain their peels. Of course, in some cases when the peels are too tough and likely to act as an irritant, they are removed. But for certain vegetables, the taste and texture of the peel varies significantly from that of the flesh. In such cases, the edible peels are cooked separately as an entirely different dish. Vegetables like plantain, ridge gourd, and bottle gourd fall into this category.

 **Cooking time – 15 minutes**

 **Ingredients:**

- 1 cup bottle gourd peels
- 1 small onion
- 1 medium-sized potato
- 1 tsp mustard seeds
- 5-6 garlic cloves
- 2-3 green chillis
- 1 tbsp mustard oil
- 1/8 tsp turmeric
- 1/5 tsp salt (approx.)

Preparation:
- Soak the mustard seeds for 2-3 hours.

- Transfer the soaked mustard seeds, garlic cloves, one green chilli and a little amount of water to a chutney jar. Grind into a smooth paste.

- Wash the peels and add them to the same chutney jar. Grind into a coarse paste.

- Chop the onion into small pieces. The potato should be cut into thin long pieces.

Cooking:

- Heat the oil in a wok. Add the green chilli and chopped onion. Fry until just translucent.

- Add the potato and give it a quick stir before adding the bottle gourd peels paste along with half a cup of water. Sprinkle the salt and turmeric, give it a mix and close the lid.

- Let it cook on a low flame until the potatoes are cooked. If it feels too dry in between, add 2-3 tsp water.

- Serve it warm with rice meals.

Note – Patua is also paired with Mudhi in Baripada (Mayurbhanj).

The above recipe can also be used to cook plantain peels, ridge gourd peels and even the discarded stems of the cauliflower. But instead of grinding, the cauliflower stems are chopped into tiny pieces and cooked as above.

CHACHINDRA PURA DIA
(Stuffed snake gourd)

Abundance often leads to a snooty palate. Faced with a deluge of new ingredients in the early 90's, most people veered away from foods that did not fit a certain profile. Foods that were not good-looking enough, or lacked status reckoning were slowly edged out of the kitchen by the perennial capsicums, cauliflowers, cabbages and carrots. Even though they tasted like chalk during the off-season, these shiny new kitchen entrants scored over the flavoursome local vegetables.

To compensate for the absence of flavour, packaged curry masalas were brought into the picture. As a result of this shift, the indigenous spice mixes were largely forgotten, leading to a loss of both culinary diversity and the 'food wisdom' that accompanied them. While packaged curry powders are convenient, they can hardly compensate for the lack of flavour (and nutrients) in vegetables produced on a mass scale. Local and seasonal vegetables are the key to proper nutrition and they should form the major portion of one's diet.

Snake gourd is one of those vegetables that gets judged unfairly solely due to its 'uncommon' shape. Though it is more flavoursome than the ridge gourd, it hardly finds a mention in our menu. A simple mustard base preparation with a touch of coconut is the easiest way to highlight its inherent flavour profile.

But a stuffed preparation like this one is sure to make one a convert.

 **Cooking time – 30 minutes**

 **Ingredients:**

- 250 gm tender snake gourd
- 3 tsp oil
- a pinch of salt

For the stuffing:

- 2 medium-sized potatoes (boiled, peeled and lightly mashed)
- 1 large onion
- 1 cup grated coconut (chopped into medium pieces)
- 1 tsp grated ginger
- 1-2 green chillis (chopped into small pieces)
- 1/4 tsp cumin seeds
- 1/3 tsp red chilli powder
- 1/4 tsp coriander powder
- 2 pinch garam masala
- 2 pinch turmeric
- 2 tsp oil
- salt to taste

🍽 **Preparation:**

- Wash and peel the snake gourd. Chop into 3" long pieces. Hollow them out by removing the mushy insides.

🍲 **Cooking:**

- Heat 2 tsp oil in a wok. Add cumin seeds and chopped green chillis. Wait for them to start spluttering.
- Follow with the grated ginger and fry for 1 minute. Add the chopped onions and fry until red on the edges.
- Add all the powdered masalas and fry for 2 minutes. Finally, add the potatoes and stir fry for a couple of minutes until everything is nicely mixed.
- Add the grated coconut just before removing from the flame. Keep it aside until it is just warm to the touch.
- Stuff this into the hollow snake gourd.

- Heat a wok or skillet on a low flame. Add the remaining oil. Place the stuffed snake gourd pieces on the skillet and sprinkle a little salt over them. Cover with a lid. Remove the lid at regular intervals and turn them on their sides.

- Let it cook on a low flame until completely done. Remove from the skillet.

- Garnish with some more grated coconut and cilantro. Serve hot with white rice and dal.

BADI CHURA
(Fried and crushed lentil dumplings)

Badi is our ancestor's version of a 'ready to cook' food. In Odisha, most of the badi is made from black lentils which is said to build strength and keep *Vata* in check. Black lentils are said to be especially beneficial for women as it helps to regulate hormones and improve bone strength. This is one of the reasons why young girls are fed pitha during Rajaw, a festival that is symbolic of menstruation and fertility.

Badi is added to various preparations like leafy vegetables, mixed vegetable stews, and even stir-fried veggies to add texture while making it more nutritious at the same time. During summers, Pakhala becomes the mainstay of most meals and dals are no longer on the menu. A side dish like *Badi Chura* or *Badi Phula* becomes an important source of protein.

Even on the days when one is out of vegetables or it is simply too hot to sweat it out in the kitchen, a badi chura serves as a quick fix with a rice meal. Hence, one finds a packet or two of badi stashed in the travel bags of every Odia returning from a home trip.

 **Preparation time – 10 minutes**

 **Ingredients:**

- 1 cup biri badi
- 1/2 of a medium-sized onion
- 2-3 garlic cloves
- 2-3 green chillis
- A sprig of cilantro
- A dash of mustard oil
- Salt to taste
- More oil for frying the badis

- Heat a skillet. Drizzle oil over it and add the badis. Fry on low heat they turn golden with a few brown spots.

- Once done, remove and keep aside to cool down.

- Take the crisp badis and crush then lightly using a mortar and pestle. Keep aside.

- Chop the onions, garlic and green chillis into small pieces. Crush together. Finally, add the crushed badis to it. Sprinkle salt and mustard oil. Crush a little more as you mix everything together.

- Garnish with cilantro and serve immediately to prevent it from turning soggy.

MANDIA PEJ
(A fermented millet drink)

Mandia Pej is a probiotic powerhouse from the tribal-dominated areas of Odisha. This recipe is a natural cooler that incorporates traditional wisdom with a modern twist. Ragi (*mandiya* in Odia) is a millet or ancient grain, which is also a probiotic food. Probiotic foods are important for sustaining gut-friendly bacteria, so ragi in combination with another probiotic food like the *torani* (fermented rice water) is probably the best food/drink for the gut during summer.

The sourness of the torani, a hint of sweetness from the ragi, heat from the green chillis, and the aroma of the onions and coriander leaves topped with a sprinkling of black salt (kala namak), makes it a light and rejuvenating drink at any time of the day. But it is usually avoided at night. I love using curd in mine, but it is optional.

For an added rustic touch, smash the green chilli, onion and cilantro into the drink instead of adding it in the chopped form.

 **Fermentation time – 8-10 hours**

 **Ingredients:**

- 200 ml fermented rice water (torani)
- 2-3 tbsp ragi powder
- 2 tbsp curd
- 1 small onion (chopped/smashed)
- 1 green chilli (chopped/smashed)
- Black salt (my addition, optional)

¶ Procedure

- Dissolve the ragi powder with 1 ½ cup water. Cook it on a low flame for 7-8 minutes until it forms a thick slurry. Allow it to cool down.

- Mix with the fermented rice water and curd, and store in an earthen pot for a couple of hours for fermentation.

- Add the remaining ingredients and serve.

Note – Traditionally, this recipe is made by cooking the ragi in the excess water that is drained off after cooking parboiled rice (pej). The residual heat of the discarded pej is enough to cook the powdered millet. Afterwards, this liquid is diluted and stored in earthen pots and allowed to ferment over a few days. It is served in leaf bowls with a dash of chilli and onions. The shared recipe is an adapted version that can be readied within a day.

MANDIA JAU
(A lightly fermented millet and rice porridge)

This is another summer recipe that combines the goodness of rice with ragi. But unlike the previous recipe, a drink meant to be sipped throughout the sunny hours of the day, this is more of a filling breakfast porridge. It is cooked in the evening and allowed to ferment overnight.

Fermentation makes it easier for the body to digest the millet and also increases the bioavailability of the nutrients.

 **Cooking time – 40-50 minutes**

 **Ingredients:**

- 1 cup broken raw rice (Khudaw)
- ½ cup powdered ragi
- Salt to taste

Cooking:

- Bring 6-7 cups of water to a boil. Add the washed rice to it and allow it to cook until it is 70 per cent cooked.

- Dissolve the ragi powder in ½ cup water.

- Add it to the vessel in which the rice is being cooked. Keep stirring continuously else it will stick to the bottom and get burnt.

- After 6-7 minutes, both the rice and ragi would be cooked. Adjust the consistency as it will thicken considerably on cooling. The final dish should be somewhat runny and not solid.

- Serve it with curd and onions, or a dash of lemon juice and a little salt.

> *Note – This can also be prepared with normal rice but it will take a longer time.*

Most tribal communities use a mix of rice and millets in their meals. This eating habit has a lot to do with their cropping practice. Earlier, most of them used to practice 'jhum cultivation' in forests where the soil does not get replenished annually unlike the alluvial soils of the river plains. Since Paddy is a crop that depletes the soil, crop rotation is practiced, with legumes and millet sown to enrich the soil. The crops are then recycled into organic matter to fertilize the soil for growing paddy in the next cycle. Hence, their diet always constitutes a mix of rice and millets. Their meals include 'Suan bhata' or rice made from little millet, lentils and other vegetables. Finger millet replaces a portion of rice in various kinds of pitha. Gangei millets or Sorghum is popped and consumed instead of 'mudhi', or made into crisp 'muan.'

There are separate Nuakhai festivals that coincide with the harvest of the major millet crops. *Mandiarani* is observed for harvest of finger millet, *Kurumpandu* for little millets and so on…

PACHILA AMBA- KHUDAW KANJI

(Ripened wild mangoes cooked with broken rice)

During the last phase of summer, there is a glut of ripe wild mangoes. There are a lot of mangoes left, even after feasting on them throughout the day. And it totally makes sense to preserve this excess. With the sun cranking up its intensity, the weather is ideal for making mango leather. A visit to the villages during this time reveals sizable portions of mango leather (*'Amba sadha'*) drying on large mats woven from sugar palm leaves.

While making mango leather utilizes a sizeable proportion of the excess produce, there are still more mangoes left. To bring some variation to the palate, these are cooked into a thick creamy kanji with a little broken rice and topped off with a fragrant tempering made from pancha phutana and the preserved neem blossoms from *Chaitra*.

⧗ **Cooking time – 30 minutes**

🥣 **Ingredients:**

- 2 cups Mango pulp (from the sweet and sour 'desi' varieties)
- 2 cups water
- ¼ cup khudaw (broken rice)
- ¼ tsp salt
- 1/2 tsp pancha phutana
- 1 tbsp dried neem buds
- 2 -3 dry red chillis
- 1-2 tsp mustard oil

🍽 **Preparation:**

- Wash and soak the broken rice for 2-3 hours.

Cooking:

- Bring two cups of water to a boil in a deep vessel. Add the soaked broken rice along with some salt.

- Let it simmer on a low flame until the rice is completely cooked.

- Add the mango pulp and simmer it for a few minutes.

- Heat the oil in a small wok. Add the broken red chilli and pancha phutana. As the seeds start spluttering, add the dried neem buds. Sauté for a minute. Remove from the flame and pour it over the simmering kanji.

- Cover and switch off the flame.

- Serve it at room temperature.

SAJANA SAGAW BHAJA
(Stir-fried tender moringa leaves)

"All good things take time. As they should" - John Wooden

Food might have been the last thing on his mind when he penned these words. But then, words are forever open to interpretation. Some more than others. Hence, I took the liberty of quoting them to describe the joys of mindful cooking.

Drumstick leaves are probably one of the healthiest varieties of greens on the Odia menu. However, prepping the leaves is a task that takes up a lot of time and energy. From carefully inspecting under the leaves for insect eggs and caterpillars camouflaged in green, to removing the tiny leaves from the stalks, it is enough to wrest one's patience. But it is worth every bit of effort given the enormous health benefits. The West may have just woken up to the miracle of Moringa, but those tasty greens, called *Sajana Sagaw* in Odisha, have been a part of our meals for as long as anyone can remember.

This is a simple stir fry recipe prepared in most Odia homes.

Preparation time – 15 minutes

 **Ingredients:**

- 2-3 cups drumstick leaves
- 1 small onion
- 3-4 garlic cloves
- 1 red chilli
- 1 pinch mustard seeds
- ¼ tsp salt (or) to taste
- 2 tsp mustard oil
- 1/5 cup milk (optional but recommended)

🍽 Preparation:

- Remove the leaves from the stem, carefully inspecting them for any insects or insect eggs. The insects are usually tiny black ones while the eggs vary from pale green to white. Throw away such leaves.

- Wash the leaves carefully in warm water to which a little salt has been added. Transfer to a colander and allow the water to drain off.

🍲 Cooking:

- Heat the oil in a wok. Once it gets smoking, add broken chilli and mustard seeds.

- Add the crushed garlic flakes and sliced onions, and allow them to brown a bit before adding the leaves.

- Stir fry for a few minutes on medium to high until excess water evaporates. Most tender leaves get cooked by this time but if the leaves are somewhat mature, then cover with a lid for 1-2 minutes so that they can get cooked.

- Lower the flame and add about 1/5 cup milk. Cook for 2 minutes. This takes care of any bitterness and improves the flavour.

- Remove from wok and serve hot with white rice/rotis.

POEE CHENCHEDDA
(Fish head cooked with Malabar spinach and a medley of vegetables)

The rise of 'nose to tail' dining. Eating all parts of a slaughtered animal is gaining currency in the Western world, which has always placed a premium on select cuts. With 'sustainability' being the current buzzword, and an economic downturn looming on the horizon, the changed eating habits make perfect sense. In sharp contrast to the Western world, Odia cuisine has always treated every section/cut of the meat with respect. And this is especially true when it comes to fish. Everything from the head to the tail is considered edible and is prepped differently during the cooking process. This holds true even for seemingly unsavoury bits like gills, swim bladders and intestines.

But what might appear rather intriguing to the outsiders is the fascination of Odia people with the fish head. Most of them love it to the extent that they would probably rate it higher than the fleshy parts. Hence, they place a lot of stress on preserving every possible bit of the fish head. The fish head contains high levels of Vitamin A, Omega 3 fatty acids, iron, zinc and calcium and of course, those extra delicious fatty bits. No wonder that the head of the family, who is ideally the one making the highest contribution to the household kitty, stakes an undisputed claim to it.

But during the community feasts in the older days, there would have been too many claimants for this bounty. And any kind of refusal would have led to slighted egos and even fights. Probably, the cooks came up with this dish as a solution to appease everyone's egos and palates. Instead of dunking the fish heads into the gravy, they were cooked separately with an assortment of vegetables and leafy greens, thus adding a delectable new offering to the menu. While wedding menus have been drastically revamped in recent years, the *Maccha Munda Chenchedda* remains popular at smaller gatherings.

⧖ **Cooking time Required: 40 minutes**

🥣 **Ingredients:**

- ½ cup pumpkin cubes
- 2/3 cup pointed gourd
- ¼ cup brinjal cubes
- 100 gm Malabar spinach (*Poee*)
- 1 medium-sized potato
- 1/2 cup ridge gourd cubes
- 1 medium-sized tomato
- ½ inch ginger
- 8-9 pods garlic
- 1 medium onion
- 1 inch cinnamon stick
- 2 green cardamoms
- 1-2 cloves
- 1/3 tsp cumin seeds
- 2-3 red chilli
- 1/5 tsp turmeric
- 1 large fish head (Bhakura/Rohi)
- 4-5 tsp oil
- ½ tsp turmeric
- salt to taste

🍽 **Preparation:**

- Wash the vegetables and cut them into large-sized pieces. Keep aside

- Marinate the fish with salt and turmeric for about 5 minutes.

- Grind the onion, garlic, ginger, 1-2 red chillis, cardamon, cloves and cinnamon into a thick paste.

- Cut the tomato into small pieces.

Cooking:

- Heat oil in a large wok. Add the fish and fry until it turns reddish. Remove from wok and keep aside.

- Add the red chilli and cumin seeds. Allow to splutter and then add masala and the paste and cook until the raw smell goes away. Add the tomatoes and cook for 5 minutes.

- Add all the vegetables except the Malabar spinach leaves. Allow the vegetables to be half-cooked and then add the leaves. Cook for another 5 minutes and then add the crushed fish head. Cover with a lid and cook for 5-6 minutes till the excess water is absorbed.

- For folks who like the crispiness of the fish head, add the crushed pieces just before switching off the flame.

- Serve hot with rice.

> *Note – This was a regular dish during the marriage feasts especially in the summers when Malabar spinach is abundantly found.*

SUKHUA AMBULA PAGAW

(Smoked fish and dried green mango condiment)

Pagaw can be described as a legion of dishes that are rustled up on the go to tickle the palate. Probably created by women who were the last ones to eat, it made up for the lack of side dishes. It required minimal cooking, if any, and could be readied even as lunch was being served. A fiery green or red chilli, a souring agent most of the time, a little garlic or onion and perhaps, a few drops of mustard oil are the only seasonings required to put together a pagaw.

During summer, the slightly moist ambula pieces (from the freshly prepared lot) are often mashed together with sukhua and a little seasoning to create the most amazing 'pagaw' that one can pair with pakhala.

Here's how to make it:

 **Preparation time – 10 minutes**

 **Ingredients:**

- 2 pieces of sukhua
- A small piece of Ambula
- 2-3 shallots
- 1-2 green chilli
- 1-2 cloves garlic
- Salt as per taste

◉| Preparation:

- Lightly roast the dried fish on a low flame for a few seconds.
- Wash and soak it in water for 30 minutes. Discard this water.
- Take 3-4 tbsp water in a bowl. Add the ambula, soaked sukhua pieces and the remaining ingredients.
- Mash it together and serve.

> *Note – The thumb rule to be followed with any pagaw is that a little goes a long way.*

ASADHA (JUNE – JULY)

With the advent of rain, punctuated by thunderstorms, the weather shows signs of change. The days turn somewhat pleasant, but humidity levels are at their peak. Agricultural work commences in full swing, and the fields are turned into slush for the transplantation of paddy seedlings. The side walls or bunds for retaining water in the rice fields are inspected for damage and repaired as required. Traditionally, plants like *taro* and some kinds of millet are sown along with the paddy. Turmeric, sesame and groundnut crops are also planted this month.

Mushrooms like the Ruguda chatti (thunder mushrooms) and anthill mushrooms start showing up in the forests. Tribal women forage these mushrooms and sell them in the local markets as they fetch a lucrative sum. New leaves start sprouting and a wave of green washes over the lands browned by the harsh sun. Tender pumpkin, pumpkin shoots, moringa leaves, and somevarieties of bauhinia leaves add diversity to the menu. Pakhala gets phased out from the meals gradually.

Rajaw is the major agrarian festival that falls during this month. Largely restricted to the coastal districts during the earlier times, the celebrations have spilled over to almost every part of Odisha in recent years. Rajaw is a brief period of respite before the transplantation of paddy. Unlike most festivals, which are generally associated with deities, Rajaw is an out-and-out celebration involving feasting, playing, and singing. Swings crop up almost everywhere across the state and young girls and women can be observed swinging to the tune of folk songs. Thus, it is known as the 'swing' festival. The signature dish associated with this festival is '*Podaw pitha*,' a rice cake prepared by wrapping the dough in layers of leaves and cooking it for a long time over the embers. The menu also features Chunchipatra pitha, Kakara pitha, Chakuli, arissa, mutton curry, Dahi Bara, and other local delicacies. The '*Rajaw Panaw*,' a preparation that involves a betel leaf cone stuffed with a mixture of areca nut, slaked lime, catechu, and various aromatic spices, is very popular as it alludes to the older days when people used to bond over it. The digestive quality of the betel leaves helps to tide over the gormandizing that happens over the three days.

However, the most significant celebration during this month is *Ratha Jatra*, the Chariot festival of Lord Jagannath and his siblings. A sea of humanity descends on the small town of Puri for a glimpse of divinity when the Gods journey through the streets. As the temple restricts the entry of non-Hindus and the lower castes, Ratha Jatra, which finds a mention in the Puranas, was initiated to allow everyone an equal opportunity to get a view of the Celestial Trio.

What's on the menu this month

A cool breeze with a hint of rain. In short, what we Odia people called the 'Rajaw Pagaw.' It gives a much-needed reprieve and acts as a balm after being broiled, roasted, and steamed for three long summer months.

Rajaw festival is an annual event heralding the beginning of the paddy planting season for the agrarian communities of Odisha. It is also observed by some of the 'farming-centric' tribal communities in geographical proximity (primarily seen in case of the Santals and Kandhas). It is a classic example of a festival that came into being by the inevitable cultural osmosis that occurs when communities start depending on each other in multiple ways.

In the olden days, Rajaw involved an animal being sacrificed in the fields to appease the tribal deities to ensure a good harvest. The blood of the sacrificed animal was sprinkled over the soil to render it fertile. Over the centuries, the blood-soaked imagery gave rise to the notion of Mother Earth menstruating during those days. Hence, the word 'Rajaswala' or its more prevalent form 'Rajaw' came into being.

The meat of the sacrificed animal was considered a 'divine offering,' something to be distributed and eaten with reverence among the community members. With time, the custom of eating meat became an integral part of the festival even as the widespread practice of 'animal sacrifice' receded into the pages of history. But the custom still continues in some rural pockets.

Given the intensive involvement of the women folk in paddy transplantation, it is only fair that this festival provided them with a much-needed boost by setting them free from kitchen duties. All the heavy-duty tasks like chopping, digging and grinding are prohibited for three days. They resume only after the fourth day, *'Basumati snana,'* when the instruments are given a ceremonial bath, anointed with sandalwood and turmeric paste, and worshipped along with Mother Earth or '*Bhudevi.*' However, Rajaw is not a festival associated with temples. The only temple in Odisha where Rajaw is celebrated is the temple of Maa Bali Harachandi, where the goddess is worshipped as Kumari on the first day.

This festival is especially popular with young unmarried girls in the coastal regions of Odisha. They get up at the crack of dawn on the first day of Rajaw to take a bath with turmeric paste, wear new clothes and ornaments and adorn their feet with 'Alta.' As they are not supposed to walk barefoot during the three days, they wear special slippers made from the fibrous outer layers that make up the trunk of the plantain. Most of their time is spent on the huge swings that come up all over the villages and cities. Exposing the girls from a young age to the restrictions proscribed during menstruation and acquainting them with '*Shringaar*' is thought to prepare them for marriage, which took place at an early age in the olden days.

With the cultural fabric undergoing a huge transformation in the last century, Rajaw has evolved into yet another 'consumer-driven' occasion, that has almost severed its ties with its agricultural origins.

RAJAW PODAW PITHA

(A baked rice cake with a signature charred crust)

Since Rajaw is meant to be a period of leisure, most heavy tasks are prohibited during these days. People prepare several dishes during the previous day and only minimal cooking happens during the three days. The Rajaw *poda pitha* is one such pitha made to last through the entire period. Baked in the embers for a long time to reduce the moisture content and prevent spoilage, it develops a signature caramelization. It is always made in large quantities and distributed among neighbours. While podo pitha is made on other occasions, and even the ingredients vary from region to region, the Rajaw podo pitha carries a charm of its own.

⧗ **Cooking time: 2 hours**

🥣 **Ingredients:**

- 1 cup rice flour
- ½ cup thinly sliced coconut
- ½ cup grated coconut
- 3 ½ cup water
- 1/3 cup jaggery
- ¼ tsp freshly ground peppercorns
- 1 tsp freshly grated ginger
- ¼ tsp black cardamon powder
- 2 tsp ghee + a little more for greasing
- ½ tsp salt

🍽 Preparation:

- Boil 3 and 1/2 cups of water in a deep vessel. Add the salt, jaggery, cardamon powder, pepper powder, grated ginger, grated coconut and coconut slices.

- Lower the flame, add the rice flour in small batches and mix continuously so that no lumps are formed. Stir the mixture on a low flame for about 10 minutes until it takes on a pouring consistency. Add ghee at this stage and give it a good mix. Switch off the flame.

- Layer a thick-bottomed wok with banana leaves (or Sal leaves). Smear a little ghee and then pour the mixture over it. Shape it a little with your hands and cover it with another banana leaf. Finally, cover with a lid and cook on a low flame for 45-50 minutes.

- Carefully flip it over and cook on the other side for another 30 minutes. Remove from the wok and allow to cool down for 2-3 hours before cutting it into pieces.

- Serve with *ghanta* or *dalma*.

Note – Use a somewhat shallow vessel so that it becomes easier to flip over the pitha.

In the olden days, the pitha was cooked on embers and the smokiness of the dried cow dung cakes and dried coconut palm leaves imparted a unique aroma to it.

LAU PODO PITHA

(Baked bottle gourd and rice cake)

Back in the late 80's, my grandmother used to make the *Lau Podo pitha* in a round electric oven with a glass window on top. The insides of the contraption used to glow red when it was in use. And it was a real magnet for a curious kid like me. In an incident that is recalled every time the Lau Podo pitha is made at home, I ended up with a burn on my forearm trying to get it out of the hot oven.

This version of Podo Pitha is made from a thick batter rather than a dough. Hence, the texture varies greatly from the rajaw poda pitha. While it can be made without the bottle gourd, the addition of the latter gives it a spongy texture. I do prefer all sorts of savoury pithas over sweetened ones, yet this one has my heart. And a mark to prove it.

 **Preparation time – 1 ½ hour**

 **Ingredients:**

- 1 cup raw rice (*arua*)
- ½ cup parboiled rice (*usuna*) OR ½ cup black lentil (without skin)
- 2 ½ cup bottle gourd (peeled, deseeded and cut into small pieces)
- ¼ tsp salt
- 1 cup jaggery
- ½ tsp ghee

- Wash and soak both kinds of rice for 6-7 hours. Discard the water before using.

- Cook the bottle gourd pieces with ½ cup water for 1 whistle (on high flame) in a cooker. Keep aside until it is warm to the touch.

- Transfer the boiled bottle gourd pieces to a grinder jar. Add the soaked rice to the same jar and grind it into a smooth paste.

- Add the powdered jaggery and salt to the batter. Whisk the batter for 4-5 minutes to aerate it.

- Grease a baking tin with ghee. Pour the batter into a layer of 3-4 cm thickness.

- Preheat a convection oven for 10 minutes at 180 degrees. Place the baking dish in the oven and bake at 170 degrees for 40-45 minutes until a reddish crust is formed. [*One can make this pitha in a thick-bottomed iron wok on a gas flame*]

- Remove and keep aside until it cools down. Cut into pieces.

Note - It takes about 40-45 minutes to cook in a 7-inch baking tin having a height of about 2 inches. But the time taken will vary with the oven, the size of the dish and the thickness of the batter layer. Use the toothpick test to determine if your pitha is done.

*** Parboiled rice is a much cheaper option than black lentils and it makes the pitha lighter. So, for people who could not afford black lentils, it was the best substitute as it was readily available.*

**** Tarada (Sponge gourd) is another vegetable that is largely used for preparing pitha. One rarely finds it as a savoury dish on the menu except for a few instances when it is cooked with preserved fish.*

CHUNCHIPATRA PITHA

My first tryst with this pitha dates back to the school days. Our neighbours, who were originally from Cuttack, shared this gossamer like pitha along with other Rajaw delicacies every year. I was fascinated by this dish that literally melted in the mouth at the very first bite. Being an inquisitive kid, I gathered that it was dish that was primarily made in Karana households during Rajaw and employed a rather interesting technique. This just enough information for a ten-year-old to comprehend and retain. It would take a little more than a decade for me to fully appreciate the beauty of this pitha. A bunch of 'doob' grass tied at one end, dipped in a thin rice batter and used as brush to draw a cross on a skillet, this pitha is a rare example of culinary artistry. Such finesse is usually the hallmark of the upper echelons of society where food is no longer revolves around subsistence and has progressed towards being a vehicle of pleasure.

Sometime back in 2014, I was replicating it in my own kitchen under the guidance of my mother-in-law, using a recipe I had picked from a fellow blogger. While reminiscing about Rajaw, she narrated an episode from her childhood days. Her grandmother would draw the outline of a circle and then proceed to sprinkle just enough batter to fill it up. All this was done using one's fingers. The stuffing would be placed at the centre and the sides were folded over to a neat parcel. While my mother-in-law has given up this technique in favour of the 'cross and fold' method, she did retain the memory of cooking it alongside her grandmother.

It took a lot more digging over the years to understand more about this beautifully named pitha. And even then, I encountered two distinct yet plausible versions. The 'Chunchipatra', meaning 'needle-leaf', draws its name from a bunch of leaves (usually ones having nutraceutical properties) that were tied at one end and sliced into fine needle likeness using a cutting device called 'paniki'. This was employed as a brush to prepare the pitha mainly in the Karana households.

But in the Brahmin households, due to the restrictions imposed on the women, foraging such leaves was quite impossible. So, the sprinkling ('chinchiba' in Odia) method was employed to prepare this pitha. Over time, the caste distinctions broke down and these two recipes merged into one. Being the easier one among the two, the cross and fold method gained traction and today, almost everyone uses this method. But sadly, the leaves, or even the grass, have been replaced by a piece of clean muslin cloth.

⏳ Preparation Time – 30 mins

 Ingredients:

- 1 cup arwa rice (aromatic small grained preferably)
- 1 coconut
- sugar/jaggery to taste
- 1-2 green cardamoms
- 1-2 tsp ghee
- salt to taste

🍽 Preparation:

- Wash and soak the rice for 3-4 hours.
- Drain excess water. Grind it into a very fine paste. Add salt and more water to the batter. Make it quite runny in consistency. Keep aside for 1-2 hours.
- Grate the coconut and keep aside.

🍲 Cooking:

- Heat 1 tsp ghee in a wok. Add the coconut and fry till it starts turning light brown. Add sugar/jaggery at this point and cook for 3-4 mins on a low flame. Remove from flame and keep aside.

- Heat a skillet. Lightly grease with ghee. Use a paper towel to wipe off/remove the excess as it will not allow the batter to spread properly.

- Tie a bunch of doob grass at one end. Dip into the batter, remove and brush lightly over the skillet making a cross symbol with it. Keep the flame low. As it gets cooked, the ends will slightly lift up.

- Put the coconut stuffing in the centre and fold the ends over it to seal the pitha. Remove from skillet and keep aside.

- Sprinkle a little water over the skillet, wipe with a paper towel and proceed with another pitha. (After making 4-5 pitha, the batter gets slightly thicker. Add a few teaspoons of water to dilute it and adjust salt accordingly)

- Serve the pitha immediately.

MUTTON DALMA
(A hearty stew of goat meat, lentil and assorted vegetables)

<table>
<tr><td align="center">Dalma</td></tr>
<tr><td>

Dalma, a wholesome dish cooked with lentils and select vegetables, is prepared in most Odia homes on auspicious days and even for regular meals. A strong connection with the Mahaprasad prepared at Jagannath dham adds to its appeal. Generally, toor dal or roasted moong dal is preferred for making Dalma. The vegetables are limited to the indigenous variety. Usage of onion and garlic is not permitted. A generous amount of fresh coconut, and a fragrant tempering with ghee and cumin seeds completes this dish. Fried lentil sticks (called 'Nadi') are sometimes added to the preparation to enhance its texture.

However, these rules are largely fluid. The beauty of this dish, just like the Pakhala, lies in its adaptability. Both can be tweaked to suit different economic backgrounds. In rural areas, people prepare dalma with whatever vegetables they can afford. As they skip adding ghee, which is usually beyond their budget, the tempering of garlic and onion is employed to enhance the flavour. The evolution of the non-vegetarian variants seems to have occurred during a later period. It was likely driven by the necessity of feeding large families while ensuring equal distribution of nutrition.

</td></tr>
</table>

My father-in-law sometimes narrates the stories from his childhood days spent in a small village near Salepur. Large families, small patches of farmland, and many mouths to feed often forced the menfolk to migrate out of the state for work. In those days, the consumption of mutton was a rarity and it was restricted to two or three occasions in a year. But for families with limited income and many mouths to feed, it was not possible to buy meat in enough quantities to feed all family members. Perhaps, it was a case of necessity being the mother of invention when someone thought of adding a few pieces of mutton to the everyday Dalma. The flavour of the dal and vegetables was accentuated by the richness of the meat from the free-ranging goats. And, it ensured that no one was left out even as it kept the stringent budget in check. At times, jackfruit seeds were also added to this variation as a means of increasing the volume.

Looking beyond regional boundaries, and taking a comprehensive view of Indian cuisine, I am often surprised at the similarities that seem to pop up. Dhansak. Dalcha. Mutton Dalma. One can't help getting into comparisons about whether it was similar circumstances that led to the birth of these dishes. Paucity coupled with human ingenuity can throw up some amazing coincidences. And not to forget, amazing recipes too.

⧗ Preparation time – 40 minutes

Ingredients:

- 1 cup roasted moong dal
- ½ cup cubed green papaya
- ½ cup cubed pumpkin
- ½ cup eggplant
- ¼ cup taro
- ½ cup jackfruit seeds (optional)
- 1 medium-sized potato cubed
- 1 medium-sized tomato cubed
- ½ tsp cumin seeds
- 2/3 tsp jeera lanka gunda (roasted cumin-chilli powder)
- 2 green chillis

- 2 dry red chilli

- 1/3 tsp turmeric

- 1 bay leaf

- 1 ½ tsp oil

- salt to taste

For the mutton marinade:

- 200 gm mutton pieces (small size)

- 2 tsp oil

- 1 medium-sized onion

- 2 tsp coarse chopped ginger

- 2 tsp coarsely chopped garlic

- ½ inch cinnamon

- 5-6 peppercorns

- 1/6 tsp turmeric

- 1/6 tsp salt or to taste

Cooking:

- Marinate the mutton pieces with salt and turmeric. Keep aside for 30 minutes.

- Dry roast moong dal on low flame for 3-4 minutes

- Heat 2 tsp oil in a deep vessel. Add the peppercorns, cinnamon and green chilli. Once they start to release their fragrance, add the chopped onion and sauté until it turns brown.

- Add the chopped ginger and garlic and sauté for 2-3 minutes. Add mutton pieces.

- Mix and cook the meat on high flame for 2-3 minutes. Then lower the heat and cover the mutton. Keep checking at regular intervals until the mutton seems to be 80-90 per cent cooked. [Or has a bite left to it]

- Add 3-4 cups water along with salt and turmeric and bring to a boil. Now add all the vegetables along with the washed moong dal. Lower the flame to medium and let it cook until the dal and vegetables are just done. The mutton should be completely soft and falling off the bones by now. Add the slit green chillis.

- Prepare the tempering. Heat oil in a tadka pan. Add the bay leaf, cumin, mustard and broken red chillis. Once it starts spluttering, pour over the simmering Dalma. Simmer for 3-4 minutes. Add the roasted cumin-chilli powder and remove from the flame.

- Serve with rice/*chakuli*/roti.

KANDULA DALI
(Tangy pigeon peas stew)

Kandula is a local variety of pigeon peas that is cooked both in fresh and dried forms. The dried beans are roasted and then milled lightly before being sold in the local markets to be used as a 'dal.' Since it is minimally processed and retains the skin, it is more flavourful than the commercially processed toor dal. Even the whole beans are sold in the local market and these are cooked as a curry.

It is one of the major crops for some tribal communities and a ritual called '*Rago-n-aadur*' is observed towards the January-February period for eating the first kandula seeds of the season. It is an important part of a tribal dish called '*raav*.'

This recipe follows the Western Odisha version which is cooked with a good amount of tanginess and, of course, with the right touch of '*marcha*!'(chilli)

 **Cooking time – 30 minutes**

 **Ingredients:**

- 1 cup Kandula
- 2 ½ cup water
- 1 large country tomato (diced)
- 1 cup eggplant cubes (big cubes)
- 8-10 garlic cloves (lightly crushed)
- ½ tsp mustard seeds (Or pancha phutana if you prefer)
- 3-4 dry red chillis
- 1 ambula/1 tsp tamarind pulp
- 2 tsp mustard oil
- ½ tsp salt
- ¼ tsp turmeric

🍽️ Preparation:

- Dry roast the kandula on a low flame to release the nutty buttery notes. Once it cools down, crush it lightly in a grinder jar (use a *chakki* if you have one)

- Soak the dal for 2-3 hours. Discard this water before using.

- Soak the ambula or tamarind with a little water.

🍲 Cooking:

- Bring the water to a boil in a pressure cooker. Add the washed dal, turmeric, salt and vegetables.

- Cook on a medium flame for 3-4 whistles.

- Once the steam escapes, open the lid and mash the dal. Put it back on the flame, add the ambula or tamarind diluted in a little water and let it simmer.

- Heat a wok. Add the oil and let it smoke. Add broken red chilli, mustard seeds and garlic cloves.

- Once the garlic has browned, pour the simmering dal into the wok and simmer for 1-2 minutes.

- Serve it warm.

Note - I prefer adding 1/2 tsp sugar to balance the flavour of this dal.

SARU PATRA KHATTA

(A sweet-sour relish made from taro leaves)

'*Arbi*' or Colocasia is a vegetable that one will find in almost every single vegetable shop in Odisha throughout the year. While most districts of Odisha use *taro* profusely in everyday cooking, the usage or consumption of its leaves is restricted to a few pockets. However, these leaves are quite delicious when tender and are added to a wide range of preparations. The young leaves, which are still curled up or have just unfurled with the first kiss of monsoon, are the best pick for any given recipe. Finding the right kind of taro leaves that do not leave an itching sensation in the mouth is critical to cooking with this green leafy vegetable.

 **Cooking time – 15 minutes**

 **Ingredients:**

- 7-8 Taro leaves and tender stems
- 1 medium-sized onion
- ½ tsp pancha phutana
- 2 dry red chillis
- 1 tsp tamarind paste
- 2 tbsp powdered jaggery
- Pinch of turmeric
- 1/3 tsp salt (approx.)
- 2 tsp oil

Preparation:

- Roughly chop up the taro leaves and tender stems. Chop the onion into small pieces.
- Dissolve the tamarind paste in ¼ cup of water.

Cooking:

- Boil 4-5 cups of water. Add the chopped leaves to it and boil for 5 minutes. Drain off all the water and keep aside. Repeat if in doubt.

- Heat the oil in a wok. Add broken red chilli and pancha phutana. When the spluttering almost stops, add onion. Fry until translucent.

- Add the boiled leaves and sprinkle salt and turmeric over them. Stir fry for 4-5 minutes until they start to dissolve.

- Add tamarind paste and powdered jaggery. Cook for another 4-5 minutes or until it turns into a paste.

- Serve with rice meals.

The abundance of Taro in Odia cuisine is directly related to the crop being a part of the paddy ecosystem. In a relationship best described as an example of commensalism, the taro plant creates the ideal habitat for the cold-blooded frog which needs to switch between sun and shade to regulate its body temperature.

Frogs are known to be effective bio-control agents which feed on the organisms and insects that either compete with the rice plants for nutrients or cause damage to the plants themselves.

Hence, planting taro serves to create a healthy, self-sufficient ecosystem.

PURA DIA KAANKADA TARKARI
(Stuffed and curried teasel gourd)

The latecomer amongst the gourds, the spine gourd or teasel gourd makes its entry around the advent of monsoon. It has similar health benefits as the other gourds but in addition to those, it also has anti-pyretic and anti-inflammatory properties. The tender vegetable, sauteed with little oil and minimum spices, is beneficial for diabetics.

Two varieties are available in the local markets of Odisha. The bigger hybrid ones, which are almost as big as a kiwi, and the much smaller 'desi' ones. The latter one is undoubtedly more delicious. Most of the time, it is made into a simple stir fry or coated with rice flour and deep fried, but if you have the larger ones at hand, the stuffed version is highly recommended.

 **Preparation time – 35 minutes**

 **Ingredients:**

- 10 medium-sized spine gourd
- 1 medium-sized tomato
- 1 medium-sized onion
- 1/2-inch ginger
- 3-4 garlic cloves
- 1-inch cinnamon
- 1 dry red chilli
- 1/3 tsp garam masala
- salt to taste
- 1/5 tsp turmeric
- 4 tsp oil

For the stuffing:

- 1 small onion (finely chopped)
- 1 medium sized boiled potato (peeled and cut into small cubes)
- 1-2 garlic cloves (roughly crushed)
- 2 pinch coriander powder
- 2 pinch chilli powder
- 1 pinch garam masala
- 1-2 pinch salt
- 1 tsp oil

🍽 Preparation:

- Wash the spine gourd and peel the outer skin with a knife. Put a slit along the length.
- Transfer to a pressure cooker and add 1 cup water. Close the lid and cook on high for 1 whistle.
- Keep aside until steam escapes. Take each half-cooked spine gourd and scoop out the innards carefully.
- Make a paste out of the cinnamon, dry red chilli, onion, ginger and garlic cloves.

🍲 Cooking:

- For the stuffing - Heat 1 tsp oil in a wok. Add the chopped onions and fry until translucent.
- Add crushed garlic, boiled potato cubes, and the innards of the teasel gourd and fry for 3-4 minutes. Add all the powdered spices, and stir fry for 1-2 minutes. Season with salt and remove from the flame. After 2-3 minutes, stuff it into the spine gourds.
- Heat 1-2 tsp oil in a wok. Add the spine gourds and stir fry for 3-4 minutes on medium-high flame. Remove and keep aside.

For making the gravy:

- Heat 2 tsp oil in a wok. Add the onion and spices paste cloves. Fry for 4-5 minutes or until the raw smell goes away.

- Then add diced tomato, sprinkle all the powdered spices along with the salt and cover it. Cook until the gravy starts to leave oil.

- Add 1 cup water and bring it to a boil. Lower the flame and let it simmer for 4-5 minutes.

- Place the stuffed spine gourds in the gravy. Simmer for 5 minutes.

- Switch off the flame and garnish with chopped cilantro.

- Serve warm with rice or rotis.

Note – This recipe can also be prepared without doing the stuffing. Cut each spine gourd into half and fry it with a generous amount of oil before adding it to the gravy as described.

The teasel gourd is part of the list of indigenous vegetables that are added to the 'Mahaprasad.' While other spiny vegetables are not allowed as an offering, this vegetable was made legit during the period the wooden idols were hidden on a tiny island situated in the middle of Chilika Lake. Since this remote location had limited access to regular vegetables, the teasel gourd, a local vegetable available in abundance was added to the menu. A temple called 'Kankan Shikhara' stands on the island where the idols had been concealed from the Muslim invaders.

MADARANGA SAGAW RAEE
(Medicinal greens cooked with mustard paste)

Considered to be a weed that invades the paddy fields, the *Madaranga sagaw* (*Alternanthera sessilis*) is a medicinal plant that is equally prized for its culinary value. Its diverse phytochemical constituents like polyphenols and carotenoids in addition to nutritional components like iron, calcium, phosphorous, protein, and vitamins A, B, and C make it an indispensable health-promoting ingredient for the rural folks who do not have access to nutritional supplements.

Traditional medicine leverages these greens for several ailments like dysentery, asthma, and body pains. It also is referred to as an elixir for the eyes. Although it is perennial, it starts to grow in abundance almost everywhere during the monsoon or near the rice plants in the winter season.

 **Preparation time – 30 minutes**

 **Ingredients:**

- 200 gms of Madaranga Sagaw/Alternanthera sessilis
- 1 1/2 tsp mustard seeds
- 1/2 tsp cumin seeds
- 1 medium-sized potato
- 1 medium-sized tomato (country ones preferred)
- 1 small eggplant
- 1 small onion
- 5 garlic cloves
- 2 dried red chillis
- 2 tsp mustard oil
- Salt to taste
- A handful of badi/vadi

🍽️ Preparation:

- Keeping aside a pinch of the mustard seeds, grind the rest along with the cumin seeds, 1 dry red chilli and 3 garlic cloves into a smooth paste.

- Pluck the leaves from the stems and wash them 2-3 times in sufficient water. Drain the excess water.

- Finely chop into small bits. Chop the potato, eggplant, tomato and onion into small pieces.

🍲 Cooking:

- Heat a wok and throw in the badis. Fry them without oil for a few minutes before drizzling with a few drops of the mustard oil. Fry for another minute or two. Remove and keep aside.

- Add the remaining mustard oil to the same wok.

- Add the broken red chilli and a pinch of mustard seeds.

- Once it starts to splutter, crush and add the garlic cloves. After a minute, toss in the chopped onions as well.

- As the onions turn pink, add the chopped vegetables. Cover and cook until the tomato turns mushy.

- Dilute the mustard paste with ½ cup water and carefully decant it into the wok, taking care to leave behind the solid residue in the cup. Add the chopped greens and cover with a lid for 5 min.

- Add salt and simmer for 2-3 minutes. Add crushed badis just before removing the wok from the flame.

- Serve with Pakhala or hot rice.

MUGA SIJHA

(Sweetened moong beans)

A no-fuss recipe of boiled green moong sweetened with jaggery, and spiked with warming spices. Clean flavours and decidedly wholesome, it was probably conceived as a snack to satiate the afternoon hunger pangs and plug those nutritional gaps that are inevitable during hectic periods of transplantation. With the women out in the fields, regular cooking takes a backseat, and slow-cooked dishes like this supply the much-needed energy to get through the tough work.

Muga sijha is best enjoyed warm on a rainy evening.

Cooking time – 1 hour

 **Ingredients:**

- 1 cup whole green moong
- 3-4 tsp jaggery
- ½ inch ginger
- 1-2 bay leaf (Teja patra)
- 1/8 tsp salt
- A few spoons of grated coconut (optional but recommended)

Cooking:

- Dry roast the moong dal on a low flame until it turns fragrant.
- Once it has cooled down, wash and soak it for 3-4 hours.
- Discard the water and transfer it to a pressure cooker. Add just enough water to cover it and a little extra. Add the torn bay leaf and salt.

- Cook on a low flame for a couple of whistles. (Time will vary depending on the variety and age of the produce)
- The cooked moong should still be intact but soft.
- Mix the powdered jaggery and crushed ginger and mix it well.
- Serve with a garnish of freshly grated coconut.

SIMBA MANJI SULA TARKARI
(A monsoon preparation of preserved vegetables and seeds)

A dish cooked during the incessant rains when all vegetation seems to be turning into mush and paddy transplantation is in full swing. Ingredients carefully squirreled from the previous seasons are cooked into a warm and comforting dish that complements the hot parboiled rice and often does away with the necessity of preparing a *dal*.

Dried flat beans, sun-dried tomatoes, sun-dried eggplant/ripened eggplants, maybe a single taro bulb, and a dash of mustard paste are cooked together into a slightly watery preparation that is purely functional but does not fail to appeal to the tastebuds at the same time.

⏳ **Cooking time – 30-40 minutes**

🥣 **Ingredients:**

- 1 cup dried simba/flat beans
- ½ cup sun-dried tomato (sula)
- ½ cup sun-dried eggplant / (substitute with fresh but mature eggplant if not available)
- 2-3 dry red chillis
- 2-3 tsp mustard paste
- 4-5 garlic cloves
- ¼ tsp turmeric
- Salt to taste
- 2 tsp mustard oil

- Wash and soak the dried beans for a couple of hours. Drain the water and boil these beans until they soften.

- Wash and soak the dried vegetables

- Heat the oil in a wok. Add the broken chilli and crushed garlic.

- Sauté for 1-2 minutes before adding the rehydrated vegetables along with the beans. Add the mustard paste diluted in ½ cup water.

- Cover and cook on low flame until there is little water left and the flavours have come together.

- Serve this with rice or Pakhala.

SUKHILA MAACH PANAS MANJI TARKARI
(Smoked fish and jackfruit seeds curry)

The region of Bonaigarh and its surrounding villages has one of the most challenging terrains, with the Brahmani River branching into numerous rivulets and creating ravines prone to river erosion. These rivulets swell during the monsoon often marooning entire villages. Lack of connectivity compels the people have to survive on what they have preserved throughout the year and what grows in their backyard. Yams and their leaves, gourds and their leaves, jackfruit seeds, bamboo shoots, amaranth stems and seasonal greens are cooked in varying permutations and combinations during times of scarcity. Stocks of seeds, dried vegetables, smoked fish, and badi were essential to tide over this season during earlier times. Foraged foods were treated with the respect they demand, and rationed judiciously to last through the monsoon season.

Although the menu has changed with easier availability of vegetables and better connectivity in recent years, some of these frugal recipes are still revisited during the lean season.

 **Cooking time – 30-40 minutes**

Ingredients:

- 2 pieces of smoked fish
- 1/2 cup jackfruit seeds
- 10-12 shallots
- A few pieces of dried tomato (optional)
- 2-3 dry red chillis
- 2-3 tsp mustard paste
- 2-3 garlic cloves
- ¼ tsp turmeric

- Salt to taste

- 2 tsp mustard oil

Cooking:

- Roast the dried fish on an open flame for 1-2 minutes. Soak it for an hour.

- Rehydrate the dried tomatoes.

- Cut the jackfruit seeds along the length and divide each into four pieces.

- Heat the oil in a wok. Add the broken chilli and shallots.

- Sauté for 2-3 minutes before adding the fish. Slightly crush the fish. Add the jackfruit seeds and dried tomatoes. Sauté for 4-5mins.

- Add the mustard paste diluted with ¼ cup water. Add salt and turmeric

- Cover and cook until the liquid is absorbed. Check if the jackfruit seeds are done, else add a little water and cook a bit longer.

- Serve this with rice or Pakhala.

Note – Smoked fish can last up to two years if stored under dry conditions. Jackfruit seeds on the other hand can last up to 3 years if buried in dry sand contained in earthen pots as the tribals usually do.

BHABRA PITHA
(A thick pillowy rice cake)

A regular breakfast dish in parts of Western Odisha, it has a thick pancake-like appearance. Deceitfully similar to *Chittau pitha*, it varies in terms of the primary ingredient used. Unlike Chittau, it is prepared from parboiled rice, which makes it much lighter on the stomach. It goes well with most curries as the spongy texture is designed to soak up every bit of liquid. But the traditional way of consuming it is to dunk it in a bowl of warm milk or pair it with molasses.

It is usually prepared during monsoons and winters.

⏳ **Cooking time – 20 minutes**

 **Ingredients:**

- 1 cup parboiled rice
- Salt to taste
- Oil for cooking

 **Preparation:**

- Wash and soak the rice for 6-7 hours. Drain and transfer to the grinder jar.
- Grind into a smooth thick paste.
- Keep aside to allow the batter to ferment slightly. It takes 2-3 hours in hot weather and 5-6 hours in cold weather.

🍲 **Cooking:**

- Place a thick clay griddle on the flame. Smear a little oil on the bottom to season it and allow the griddle to heat up really well.

- Pour about 1/2 cup batter into the centre and spread a little to form a thick pancake. Cover with a lid. Take a wet cloth and put it around the rim of the lid. Let it cook for 2-3 minutes. Remove from the griddle.

- Serve with milk or any curry of choice.

> *Note – Unlike the Chittau batter, the Bhabra pitha batter is kept thick.*

SAJANA SAGAW MUGA

(Moringa leaves cooked with split moong)

For someone who was lured into eating Sajana Saag every other day with the promise of good eyesight and gorgeous hair, I find it hard to hold any grudges when it comes to grandmother's everyday potions. Although I detested most of them as a child, I have learned to acknowledge the hidden wisdom behind many of them.

According to Ayurvedic texts, Moringa leaves have the potential to cure almost 300 types of ailments. Perhaps that is why most Odia people used to have a little bit of these greens on the plate almost every other day during the summer and monsoon months when the leaves are at their lustrous best. Once the flowering sets in and the drumsticks start to emerge, the tree loses almost all its leaf cover as the nutrients are diverted to the growing fruits.

This frugal preparation of roasted moong dal and moringa leaves with a tempering of onions, garlic and red chilli happens to be my favourite as it is versatile enough to be paired both with hot rice and Pakhala. The addition of moong dal mitigates the slight bitterness of the greens.

⧗ **Preparation time – 25 minutes**

 **Ingredients:**

2   cups of drumstick leaves

- ½ cup diced pumpkin
- ½ cup diced eggplant
- A few cubes of raw banana
- 1 medium-sized onion (chopped into thin long slices)
- 5-6 garlic cloves (lightly crushed)
- ¼ cup lightly roasted moong dal/yellow lentil

- ½ tsp mustard seeds

- 1-2 dried red chillis

- 2 tsp oil

- 2 pinch turmeric

- Salt to taste

Preparation:

- Pluck the drumstick leaves from the stem while carefully checking for any insects/eggs. Wash thoroughly under running water. Keep aside for the water to drain

Cooking:

- Transfer the lentils along with pumpkin, eggplant, raw banana, salt and turmeric to a pressure cooker. Add 2/3 cup water and cook for 1 whistle on medium flame. Keep aside for steam to escape.

- Put the pressure cooker back on the flame. Add the drumstick leaves, mix gently and let it cook until the leaves are done.

- Heat the oil in a wok. Add the mustard seeds and broken red chillis followed by the crushed garlic and onions. Fry until the onion turns reddish.

- Pour the contents of the pressure cooker into the wok. Let it simmer for 3-4 minutes before switching off the flame.

- Serve hot with white rice and dal.

> *Note – One can prepare this recipe without adding the vegetables. But the vegetables help to add bulk when the leaves are in short supply.*

MACCHA BIHANA BARA
(Fish roe fritters)

Come monsoon and among the bounties that nature bestows upon us, is the little-discussed fish roe or *maccha manjee/maccha bihana*. While carrying eggs affects the taste and firmness of the fish adversely, the roe is a prized delicacy in itself. Some people prefer to avoid it. But with the wet months coinciding with the fish breeding season, even the most seasoned and eagle-eyed fish lovers, at times, cannot avoid buying a fish that carries roe.

Universally enjoyed in the form of fritters, it is occasionally dried/fermented with salt and preserved for later use. The Hilsa 'manjee sukhua' is one such legendary ingredient that is now sadly confined to family anecdotes.

The *Bihana bara* is the most common dish prepared with fish roe in Odia kitchens. It is a beginner-level recipe and can be attempted by almost anyone.

Cooking time – 10-15 minutes

Ingredients:

- 200 gm Fish eggs
- 1 finely chopped small onion
- ½ tsp chilli powder/1 tsp finely chopped green chilli
- ½ tsp coarsely crushed garlic
- 1/8 tsp turmeric
- 1 tsp besan (gram flour)
- 1 tsp rice flour
- 1/4 tsp salt (a little more or less as per preference)
- 2-3 tbsp oil for shallow frying

🍽️ Preparation

- Fish eggs are always enclosed in a sac (membrane). Wash the sac carefully before removing the outer layer.

- Mash the eggs and add all the remaining ingredients except for oil.

- Allow to marinate for 10 minutes.

🍲 Cooking:

- Heat a griddle and drizzle a little oil all over it. Take a spoonful of the above mixture and pour over the griddle. Repeat until most of the griddle is covered with small discs of the fish roe. Allowing some space between the discs makes it easy to flip them over for even cooking.

- Cook on both sides to a light brown colour.

- Remove and serve hot as a side dish with rice or even as a snack.

MACCHA BIHANA /MACCHA MANJEE PATUA

(Spicy fish roe preparation)

My family loves fish roe. For the first few times, every season, it is eaten straight from the frying pan. Then, it starts to become somewhat tedious. Hence, a little innovation goes a long way to ensure zero wastage. That's where the *Maccha Bihana Patua* recipe comes in. While patua is quite a versatile dish and can be prepared with a range of ingredients, it is identified by a pasty texture and a robust mustard flavour (due to the use of raw mustard paste and cold-pressed mustard oil).

Ironically, the Maccha bihana patua defies this rule. Instead of exhibiting a pasty texture, the finished dish has a texture that resembles scrambled eggs. After all, the primary ingredient is eggs. Hence, the thumb rule is not to overcook this dish.

 **Cooking time – 15 minutes**

 **Ingredients:**

- 1/2 cup fish roe (cleaned and mashed)
- 1 medium-sized potato
- 1 small onion
- 2-3 tsp mustard garlic paste
- 1/2 tsp red chilli powder
- 1/4 tsp turmeric
- 1/4 tsp salt (adjust as per taste)
- 2 tbsp mustard oil
- 1-2 slit green chillis
- 2-3 garlic cloves (sliced)
- A squeeze of lemon juice (optional)

☞ Cooking:

- Heat the oil. Add finely sliced onions and potatoes. Fry for 2-3 minutes or until potatoes are half cooked.

- Add the mustard paste followed by chilli powder, turmeric and 3-4 tbsp water. Stir for 2-3 min.

- Add the fish roe, mix and cook on a low flame. It needs regular stirring for 4-5 minutes to cook evenly. Finish with a squeeze of lemon juice and chopped cilantro. It goes best with plain dal and rice.

Note - One needs to be cautious while buying fish roe as they can lead to food poisoning. Never buy fish eggs unless you believe that it has been freshly removed from the fish. Instead, try to buy a fish that contains roe.

Also, use fresh roe instead of the frozen or preserved one for this recipe.

SHARBANA (JULY – AUGUST)

"Asadha Shrabana …Megha barase Ghana-Ghana." This line from an Odia poem taught in school, perfectly conjures the monsoon mood. Shrabana, is defined by heavy rain and a mist that rises from the ground due to the continuous downpour. The heady fragrance of ripe sugar palm permeates the air as the fruits ripen and fall to the ground in succession. The jackfruits left behind on the trees become overripe and start disintegrating. A musty smell hangs in the air as the rain progresses from sudden showers to a steady drizzle that continues for days at a stretch. It emanates from the pores of the wet earth, and the clothes that fail to dry completely. The dampness seems all pervasive and one instinctively turns to the kitchen for food and warmth to counter the gloom.

On the agricultural front, the transplantation work is almost complete by this month. Most paddy fields are now flooded. Grass and weeds start to crop up in the inundated fields, and they need to be cleared regularly. Additional ploughing in done to aerate the soil. Vegetables like flat beans and eggplants are sown in this month.

Due to excessive rainfall, the vegetation wilts, prompting people to dig into their cache of dried and preserved foodstuff. Along with ingredients like badi, sula, sukhua, saru, dried flat beans and jackfruit seeds, become the mainstay of the meals. Mushrooms are plentily available, and small fish (jhuri) and mud crabs caught from the flooded rice fields add diversity to the menu. Seasonal greens like *Chakunda saag* and *Kanjer saag* are foraged by tribal communities. Black lentil and horse gram are cooked on a regular basis with steaming hot rice meals.

One of the agrarian festivals celebrated this month is the *Chittau Amabasya.* 'Chittau pitha' is offered in the rice fields to appease the primitive forces that take the forms of insects, snails, snakes, etc. The paddy plants usually reach knee height around this time, and the farmers working in the fields sometimes suffer cuts to their feet from the snails hidden among them. This day holds great significance in Jagannath temple. The idols of Lord Jagannath, Balabhadra and Shubhadra are re-adorned with the Chitta, a head ornament studded with precious stones. In some Western districts, a 'Guhal puja' is performed on this day to worship the cows and bulls who contribute substantially to the agricultural process. The cattle are fed dried *mahua* flowers wrapped in Sal leaves and differentkinds of pitha. There is also a custom of leaving 'Chakuli pitha' outside the threshold. This is done to appease the witches who are rumoured to be active this month, especially on the new moon days (*Amabasya*). This superstition is linked to the increasing instances of fever and sickness during the monsoons, which were attributed to the evil forces in earlier times.

In recent years, the practice of Bol bam has become popular in Odisha. *Kaunriyas* carry water from a local water body and walk barefoot for miles to pour it on a holy *Shivling* on the Mondays of Shrabana. The colourful procession of men, and sometimes women, walking to the chants of Hari bol has become a common sight during this month. Due to this reason, the practice of giving up non-vegetarian food during Shrabana is catching on.

A significant festival observed by the Gauda (cattle-herders) community this month is Gamha Purnima, the birth anniversary of Lord Baladev or Balaram, the elder brother of Lord Jagannath/Shri Krishna. The word 'Gamha' is derived from 'Gau-Maa,' and hence, cattle are worshipped on this day. However, this practice has been on the decline due to the rise of mechanized farming, and the day is being celebrated as Raksha Bandhan. The *Kisan* community of Sundargarh plants the stems of the Kendu tree (*Diospyros Melanoxylon*) in their fields on this day. Since the timber this tree is quite resistant to fire, it is a belief that the stem will protect their crops from fire incidents. Not surprisingly, Kendu leaves also have antimicrobial properties and crushed leaves are applied to small cuts and bruises in rural areas. These little rituals, ingrained into the festivities, serve as a kind of code, reminding us of the valuable uses of the local flora.

What's on the menu this month

Ragini treaded with caution. Babu was home after many months. He did not like being disturbed by the humdrum noises that pervade the domestic quarters of lesser mortals. Even the garrulous children had fallen silent. Hence, she was extra careful not to make any sound as she went about her routine. The vessels had been washed, the floor swept clean and the vegetables prepped. As she carefully ground the spices, she wondered what Maa would make for lunch.

The kitchen was out of bounds for her. The only occasion on which she had been accorded a glimpse was when Maa had her time of the month and her mother-in-law had been away. It still remained a secret between the two of them. She smiled when she thought about the delicious food Maa sneaked out for her and her children. But she had never seen the family eating. Or Maa cooking for that matter. Their door would be closed before food was served.

As she picked up the basket of freshly plucked ash gourd leaves, Ragini wondered why Maa had asked her to leave them intact. She separated the older ones with hardened veins and any kind of discolouration. But she did not have the heart to throw them away. They would make a delicious *bhaja* with '*pithau*' after removing the veins and crushing the leaves. In her imagination, she was already pairing it with yesterday's leftover rice and the potatoes that had been cooked in the same pot along with the rice in order to conserve fuel. The rice and the boiled potatoes had been covered with water and left to ferment overnight in an earthen vessel. But she felt too shy to convey her thoughts to Maa.

The lady of the house stepped out of the kitchen to inspect the tender leaves that Ragini had segregated. Her eyes took in the neat pile of slightly discoloured leaves that the latter had kept aside. Maa read her mind. She gently asked Ragini to take some leaves for the children and ventured back into the kitchen with a small basket of tender ash gourd leaves that had been segregated.

Ragini was overjoyed. She gathered all the remaining leaves in the loose end of her saree and rushed home. As she announced the lunch menu to her children, her youngest child questioned her about what Maa was making with those leaves. Ragini did not have an answer.

Meanwhile, back in the confines of the cosy kitchen, Maa pulled out the veins from each leaf. She rubbed two leaves against each other to dislodge the tiny hairs from the surface before rolling each one into a long thin cylinder which was again rolled into a shape resembling a fiddlehead fern. This was carefully dipped into a thin aromatic paste of basmati rice, fresh coconut, cumin, red chilli and salt, and fried on a low flame until crisp.

On other days she would enclose a filling made with fresh small fish or shrimps sourced from the family pond and make a nice little packet out of the leaves before shallow frying them.

A couple of decades down the line, her daughter relived those memories as she shared these wonderful recipes from her mother's kitchen.

PANI KAKHARU PATRA PITHAU BHAJA
(Batter fried Ash Gourd leaves)

In the earlier days, the traditional processing of aromatic rice varieties resulted in a lot of broken rice as a by-product. Called '*Khudaw*' in Odia, it was utilized for preparing pitha, added to *Kanji*, turned into *Jau* or *Khiri*, added to leafy greens or simply turned into a '*pithau*' for crisping up pan-fried vegetables or small fish.

Most parts of the state make a *pithau* using broken rice, a little cumin and red chilli for heat. Occasionally, someone might add a garlic clove or two, maybe a small knob of ginger, depending on the primary ingredient used in the recipe. The coastal districts add fresh coconut to it, further enhancing the aroma and introducing a sweet note into the pithau.

Ash gourd leaves dipped into the seasoned rice batter and pan-fried to a crisp is one of the best ways to bring out the beauty of the unpretentious '*pithau bhaja.*'

 **Cooking time – 15 minutes**

 **Ingredients:**

- 10 Ash gourd leaves (Young ones)
- 3 tbsp aromatic rice
- 1 tbsp grated coconut
- A pinch of cumin
- 1 dry red chilli
- 2-3 tsp oil
- Salt to taste

🍽️ Preparation:

- Soak the rice for 1-2 hours and grind it into a smooth paste with coconut, cumin and red chilli. Adjust the consistency of the batter and add salt.

- Prep the ash gourd leaves by removing the veins, roll them between the palms and dip them into the batter.

- Heat a griddle and season with a little oil.

- Place the rolled ash gourd leaves on the pan. Drizzle a little oil. Cook on a low flame until crisp.

- Flip and cook on the other side.

- Serve immediately with meals or as a snack.

Pithau bhaja is a very versatile recipe that works across a multitude of Ingredients:

1. Almost all vegetables except watery gourds (teasel gourd is an exception)

2. Edible flowers like Pumpkin, Moringa, Agasti, Gilri phul, edible Bauhinia varieties and Tonkin jasmine

3. Bamboo shoots

4. Mushrooms

5. Small fish and tiny shrimps (usually caught together from small ponds)

6. Edible greens like onion and garlic chives, onion flower stalks, bitter gourd leaves and Malabar spinach leaves

PANI KAKHARU PATRA PURA BHAJA
(Stuffed ash gourd leaves)

Tender ash gourd leaves offer an excellent canvas to showcase one's culinary prowess. They are often cooked by themselves or as a 'mixed greens' dish with other leaves foraged from the backyard. Ladies in the rural areas would sometimes wrap up little parcels of food with it and surrender it to the embers for that added charred effect.

But on rare occasions, these leaves are turned into edible little pockets bursting with flavour.

 **Cooking time – 15 minutes**

Ingredients:

- 10 Ash gourd leaves (Young ones)
- 1 cup shrimp
- 1 tbsp chopped onions
- 3-4 garlic cloves
- 2-3 tsp freshly grated coconut
- 1 green chilli (chopped)
- 3-4 tsp oil
- 2 pinch turmeric
- Salt to taste

Cooking:

- Wash and marinate the shrimp with salt and turmeric for 15 minutes. Heat a griddle. Drizzle a little oil.
- Add the marinated shrimp. Sauté for 3-4 on medium flame.
- Remove from the griddle and allow it to cool down.

- Crush the shrimp with the onion, garlic, coconut and chilli into a coarse paste. Season with a little salt.

- Stuff each prepped ash gourd leaf with 1 tbsp of shrimp paste. Fold it into a parcel and place it on the griddle. Cook on a low flame with a little oil.

- Flip and cook on the other side.

- Remove from the pan and serve immediately with meals.

Note – Tweak the above recipe by dipping the parcel in pithau before cooking it in the pan. It adds extra crunch to the dish.

CHITTAU PITHA

(A pillowy coconut and rice cake)

A beautifully pock-marked and porous preparation, Chittau is one of the pithas cooked regularly in Odia homes. Made with raw rice and a generous amount of coconut, it has an inherent sweetness that goes well with warm milk. It is prepared for breakfast, and sometimes, even for dinner in the Coastal districts of Odisha

It is one of the dishes offered to Lord Jagannath.

Ingredients:

- 2 cups Raw rice/ *arua chaula*
- 1 medium-sized coconut (mature ones preferred)
- Salt to taste
- ½ tsp sugar (optional)
- Oil for cooking

Preparation:

- Wash and soak the rice for 4-5 hours. Drain and transfer to the grinder jar.
- Break the coconut and cut into small pieces. Add the coconut pieces to the same jar along with a little water. Grind into a smooth paste.
- Transfer this batter to a mixing bowl and add about ½ tsp salt and sugar. Dilute the batter until it acquires a thin consistency.
- Keep aside to allow the batter to ferment slightly. It takes 2-3 hours in hot weather and 5-6 hours in cold weather.

🍳 Cooking:

- Place a thick clay griddle on the flame. Smear a little ghee on the bottom to season it and allow it to heat up really well.

- Pour about ¼ cup batter into the centre. Cover with a lid. Take a wet cloth and put it around the rim of the lid. Let it cook for 2-3 minutes.

- Remove from the griddle.

Note: Chittau pitha is cooked on one side only and remains uncooked on the other side. Its distinguishing feature is the presence of tiny holes all over its surface which can be achieved by heating the wok really well before adding the batter and by creating steam (wet cloth around the rim) during the cooking process. While it is traditionally prepared on a clay griddle, one can use an iron one too.

Variations of the chittau across Odisha:

**Biri Chittau – In Northern parts of Odisha, a little black lentil is added to the recipe along with the rice and coconut.*

**Dahi Chittau – Fresh curd is used instead of coconut*

Mature coconuts with a higher oil content are ideal for making the chittau pitha. Interestingly, coconut trees are categorized into two groups, one for culinary usage and the other for oil extraction primarily. The latter practice is mostly is vogue in some of the Brahmin 'sasans' which have an abundance of coconut trees.

The mature oil-rich coconut is grated, mixed with hot water and extracted. The extracted liquid is cooked in huge open vessels until all the moisture evaporates. It is called 'randha nadiya tela' or cooked coconut oil as opposed to the cold pressed one made in Kerala. It is used both for cooking and external application.

BIRI DALI
(Black lentil dal)

A few decades ago, black lentil dal was prepared in most Western Odisha homes every week during the monsoons and even during winters. I have wonderful memories of coming back from school and sitting down to a meal of piping hot rice and 'biri dali.' But it never came up in the conversations I had while writing this book. Except for a mention that it was served to the farm hands on rainy days. The reason for this is probably the fact that most Odia folks tend to treat dal as the proverbial 'poor relative.' As long as it is around, nobody notices. But the moment it disappears from the plate, egos are bruised. The Dalma is the only exception as it steals the spotlight every time it is on the menu.

Just like vegetables and fruits, the consumption of lentils also follows a seasonal pattern. The thumb rule is that the best time to consume them is in the months that follow the harvest. But there are exceptions to this rule. This recipe is a rather simple preparation without any culinary history. It probably originated from a farmer's kitchen in the monsoon when the continued downpour brought down the temperatures and people craved for comfort food. Thick, slightly sticky and with an inherently deep earthy flavour, the *biri dali* eliminates the need for serving a side-dish with the meal. As I delve deeper into the stories that revolve around our traditional foods, I realize that not all foods need to have a fabled history and that some popular stories may just as well be stories meant to regale a gathering.

⏳ **Cooking time – 30 minutes**

🥣 **Ingredients:**

- 1 cup split black lentil (with skin)
- 7-8 garlic cloves

- 1 medium-sized onion

- 1 tsp pancha phutana

- 2-3 dry red chilli

- ¼ tsp turmeric

- 1/3 tsp salt or as per taste

- 2 tsp mustard oil

🍽 Preparation:

- Dry roast the lentils for 3-4 minutes on a low flame.

- Wash and soak the lentils for 4 hours.

🥘 Cooking:

- Drain the water and transfer it to a pressure cooker. Add 2 ½ cup water, salt and turmeric.

- Cook on a medium flame until 2-3 whistles. [*We need to cook it 50 per cent in the cooker*]

- Open the lid and let it simmer on a low flame until the lentils are soft.

- Heat the oil in a wok. Once it starts to smoke, add the broken red chilli, pancha phutana and crushed garlic. Allow garlic to turn brown before adding the roughly chopped onions.

- Sauté until it turns light pink. Pour the simmering dal into the wok and simmer until it reaches a creamy consistency.

- Switch off the flame and serve warm.

---

*Note – *The newly harvested dal is relatively sticky and has a better fragrance.*

*** Roasting makes the lentil easier to digest.*

CHINABADAM JUKHA
(Congee with peanut milk)

Congee, otherwise known as '*Jukha*' in Odia, used to be my grandma's go-to food on a cold gloomy day. She knew the importance conserving the body's warmth when the mercury dipped. A diet comprising rice gruel served with roasted or stir-fried potatoes minimized the cooking and cleaning chores. It also provided the ladies with much-needed respite during the olden days when there was no running water. Utensils had to be washed near the well or a nearby water body. Those with the means, engaged labour to carry water from a water body and store it in huge vessels.

Lifestyles have changed drastically but the cold weather still affects one's body, especially those with a 'vata' constitution. Hence, these traditional recipes still remain relevant in today's world. 'Jukha' is often labelled as the 'poor man's food' because it can make a little rice go a long way by retaining the starchy part. The excess water containing starch, is usually discarded while cooking rice using the regular method. The broken grains ('Khudaw') and rice bran ('Kunda') accumulated during the traditional milling of rice make a richer and more nutritious congee. The right way of cooking 'jukha' is simmering the rice with an excess amount of water (1:8-1:10 ratio) on a slow fire until the grains start to disintegrate on their own. At this stage, a little milk/ghee and sugar/salt are stirred into it depending on one's preference.

Although similar to the rice gruel or congee consumed in most parts of Asia, it does not have any herbs, vegetables or meat added to it. Rather, it is served with a simple side of fried or boiled potatoes and some charred vegetables.

A rather interesting variant of the 'Jukha' is prepared in the Bonaigarh region. Made with parboiled rice and peanut milk, it needs just a little something on the side. The sweetness of the freshly harvested peanuts lends it an almost milky taste. Salty and nutty with an underlying earthiness, it is quite a mouthful. And not to forget, filling to the core.

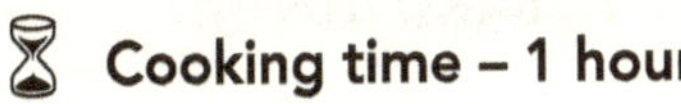 Cooking time – 1 hour

Ingredients:

- 1 cup parboiled rice (broken grains preferred)
- 1 cup raw peanuts
- Salt to taste

Preparation:

- Wash and soak the peanuts for 1-2 hours. Grind it in a smooth paste, dilute it and extract the peanut milk.

Cooking:

- Wash and soak the rice for 2-3 hours.
- Heat 6-7 cups of water in a heavy-bottomed vessel. Add the soaked rice and give it a stir.
- Let it cook on a medium flame, with some stirring at regular intervals, until the grains start to disintegrate and the liquid starts to turn thick.
- Now, add the peanut milk and salt. Simmer it for 8-10 minutes until the raw smell of peanut milk changes.
- Serve warm with a side of mashed potato/stir-fried veggies.

JANTA RUTI

(A native bread made from pre-cooked dough)

'*Janta Ruti*' roughly translates into rotis prepared from a '*jantuni*' aka 'cooked dough.' Unlike the regular version, these rotis are prepared by first cooking the wheat flour and then kneading and preparing rotis from it. There are two versions made in most Odia homes, a sweeter one with fennel and a little *khand*/sugar, and a savoury one with carom (*ajwain*) seeds. The preparation process and the rest of the ingredients remain the same. Some people also add a little milk while preparing the sweeter version.

Sometimes, the dough is also deep-fried instead of being cooked on a tawa or griddle. These *pooris*, also called '*khali poori*,' are extremely delicious but soak up a lot of oil. Hence, they are usually eaten during fasts.

 **Cooking time – 30 minutes**

 **Ingredients:**

- 1 cup whole wheat flour
- 1 ½ cups water (a little more or less might be required as different wheat varieties absorb different quantities)
- 3 tsp sugar
- 2-3 tsp ghee
- 2-3 pinch salt
- Extra flour for dusting

Preparation:

- Boil the water in a wok. Add the sugar and 1/2 tsp ghee to it.
- Dissolve 2 tsp of flour in 2 tbsp of water. Reduce the flame and add this to the boiling water.

- Then, slowly add the remaining flour while stirring continuously. Cook for 4-5 minutes on a very low flame until the mass feels somewhat tight to move around. Switch off the flame and allow it to cool down until it is just warm to the touch.

- Transfer the mass to a working surface. Dust the surface with flour and drizzle 1 tsp ghee over the dough. Knead the dough until it forms a smooth mass.

- Pinch small portions from the dough. Shape them into smooth balls just like one does while making roti and flatten them slightly.

- Dust the working surface with more flour and roll out the balls into small circles or rotis.

- Heat a griddle and place the roti over it. Cook on medium flame until you can see small bubbles coming up on the surface of the roti. Flip it over and cook on the other side. The roti will swell up. Cook for another minute before removing it and keeping it aside.

- *Optional - Smear a little ghee on the ruti after removing it from the griddle.*

- Repeat for the remaining rotis.

- Serve with boiled veggies/dalma*santula* (or any other curry of choice).

Note – Janta Ruti is also called Khali Ruti (in Puri).

Sometime back in 2013, when I was experimenting with meal options for my toddler, I discovered the *'Janta ruti.'* It was tasty, easy enough to chew, and light on the stomach too. As an added bonus, it made a perfect pair with the boiled veggies (read *'Santula'* minus the *'chunka'* or tempering). On some level, it provided the same comfort that I had come to associate with a bowl of Jukha. It became a part of our menu and stayed that way until I realized I had been overlooking one of its most salient features.

While reading up on research papers about gluten and ways to minimize the formation of this unavoidable protein that has been haunting quite a few people, I realized that taking the sourdough route or switching to 'Gluten free' flour isn't an economically viable option for everyone. Nor do people have the resources to switch to home-milled flour. Increasing cases of gluten intolerance are coming to the fore because of changes in the way wheat is processed. Earlier, wheat was harvested, shade-dried, washed down, and sun-dried before making it to the local chakki, where it was ground and distributed. However, increased demand has led to manufacturers bypassing all the steps between threshing and processing. Most of the packaged wheat is not properly shade-dried and sun-dried – the two processes that break down gluten (or rather glutenin as gluten comes into the picture only after the flour is hydrated) into smaller particles.

Preferences also play a role here. Demand for white-looking bread or 'roti' has led to the market being flooded with certain varieties like durum which have higher gluten content in comparison to varieties like *'Emmer'* or *'Kaphali'* which have lower gluten but are much darker in colour. Despite this selective breeding, the gluten content has remained constant over the last 120 years, although the composition of the gluten has changed slightly. While the proportion of Gliadin fell by around 18 per cent, the proportion of

Glutenin rose by around 25 per cent. And this is one of the major triggers.

Brushing aside the external factors, the formation of gluten has a lot to do with how the dough is manipulated. Everything from the amount and temperature of water added to the dough, to the kneading technique and duration of kneading to the usage of shortening agents (term used for fats that coat the gluten components and prevent them from forming lengthy chains resulting in a flaky crumbly texture) plays a definite role.

This is why the Janta Ruti scores extra points. Temperature, hydration, and fat. The boiling water denatures the wheat proteins, limiting the formation of gluten. This makes the dough soft but not stretchy. Second, the hot water gelatinizes the starch allowing it to absorb more water. This makes the dough smooth and supple and a lot easier to work with. As a bonus, it stays soft long after it has cooled down. The fat, although in a limited amount, prevents the linkage of gluten strands and ensures that the dough doesn't turn sticky. Hence, one ends up with a dough that is easy to work with and the end product stays soft and fresh for a longer duration. As a bonus, it is much easier on the digestive system and the jaws.

RUKTA/RUGDA CHATTU TARKARI
(Spicy thunder mushroom curry)

Rukta Chattu or Ruguda Chattu are often labelled thunder mushrooms as they occur only during early monsoon when such weather phenomenon is common. These mushrooms develop underground and the only giveaway is that the soil above it is slightly raised or has a small crack. They occur near the Sal trees, and are often hidden from sight by the fallen Sal leaves scattered around. It takes the experienced eyes of tribal women, who are natural foragers, to make out their presence as one needs to know where to look for them.

Their meaty flavour is greatly sought after by everyone in Western Odisha, where it grows in abundance. However, these mushrooms are also found in Koraput (locally called 'Boda') and the neighbouring states of Chhattisgarh and Jharkhand.

⏳ **Cooking time – 30 minutes**

 **Ingredients:**

- 250 gm *rukta chattu*/thunder mushrooms
- 1 medium-sized potato (cut into small cubes, optional)
- 1 large onion
- 12 garlic cloves
- 1-inch ginger
- 2 pinch garam masala
- 2-3 dry red chilli
- 1/3 tsp cumin seeds
- 2/3 tsp turmeric
- 3 tsp mustard oil
- Salt to taste

🍽 Preparation:

- Thunder mushrooms are usually coated with a thin layer of mud. Soak the mushrooms in water for an hour. Rub them on a rough surface to dislodge the dirt.

- Wash these mushrooms a couple of times and then soak in turmeric water for 30 minutes. Cut each one into two halves. If the inside is blackened or grey, discard it. Use only the white ones.

- Grind the ginger, garlic, chilli and cumin into a semi-fine paste.

🍳 Cooking:

- Heat a wok and add 1 tsp oil. Add the mushrooms and sauté for 2-3 minutes on a high flame. Remove and keep aside.

- Add the remaining oil to the wok. Once it is hot, add the onions and sauté until light brown.

- Add the masala paste and cook until the raw smell goes off.

- Now, add the mushrooms and potatoes. Add salt and ¼ tsp turmeric.

- Mix and cover with a lid. Lower the flame and cook for 2-3 minutes.

- Open the lid, sauté a bit and then cover again. Repeat until the potatoes are almost cooked.

- Add 1 cup water and garam masala. Let it simmer for a while.

- Serve hot with rice or roti.

THETHRI

(A crunchy stick-like snack)

No cuisine is complete without these little fillers or 'snacks' as we call them. They serve to manage those hunger pangs between meals and, also add diversity to the everyday diet. Odia cuisine is replete with healthy 'ready to eat' snacks like different kinds of Muan, roasted/boiled lentils, and laddus prepared with groundnuts or sesame. But some lesser-known treats also deserve a mention.

A crispy stick-like snack, *Thethri* is made in some parts of in the Sundargarh-Sambalpur region. It probably owes its origin to the Aghria community – a group of settlers who migrated from North India and settled in parts of Odisha, Jharkhand, and Chhattisgarh. While rice flour is the primary ingredient used in this recipe, I came across two variations during the research. While one uses black lentil (*Biri*) paste, the other makes use of *semolina* (Suji). The latter could be a more recent adaptation, given that semolina has become a common substitute for rice and wheat in quite a few varieties of pitha. Since semolina is easier to work with, this practise has gained popularity in the last two decades.

Here's a recipe that keeps the kids happy on any given day.

 **Preparation time – 1 hour**

 **Ingredients:**

- 1 inch Ginger
- 10-12 cloves of Garlic
- 2-3 dry red chilli/Green Chilli
- 1 tsp jeera
- 2 cups semolina

- 1 cup rice flour/*Chaula gunda* [*Always keep extra handy as it will be required*]

- ½ tsp carom seeds

- 1 tsp salt (approx.)

- Oil for deep frying

🍽 Preparation

- Grind the ginger, garlic, cumin and chillis into a fine paste.

🍳 Cooking:

- Bring about 6 cups of water to boil. Add salt and the ground masala paste to it.

- Once it has boiled for 2-3 minutes and the raw smell goes away, add the semolina and let the semolina cook by stirring continuously until it resembles a thick slurry.

- Now, add the rice flour while mixing continuously and cook for a few minutes until it becomes tough to move around with a spatula. Remove from the flame and let it cool down a little bit.

- Dust a working surface with more rice flour. Spread the dough over it and sprinkle carom seeds. Mix and knead the dough thoroughly until it forms a nice tight ball. [It should be similar to a *nimki/namak para* dough]

- Pinch out small portions from it. Dust your palms with more rice flour and roll it between your palms into 2-3-inch-long thin cylindrical shapes.

- Heat oil in a wok. Deep fry on medium flame to cook and crisp the thethri.

- Serve as a snack.

KANJER SAAG
(Stir-fried monsoon greens)

One of the rare monsoon greens, it is foraged from sandy soils in the forest areas. Although considered as heavy to digest, it is recommended for rheumatism by traditional medicine practitioners. Over-exploitation and unscientific methods of foraging this plant have resulted in this plant being categorized as 'endangered.'

It is also called Leper saag or *mahisaa* saag in some parts of Odisha.

Ingredients:

- 3 cup chopped greens
- 1 large onion
- 4-5 garlic cloves
- 2-3 dry red chilli
- ½ tsp mustard seeds
- 2 tsp mustard oil
- Salt to taste
- Fried and crushed urad dal badi (optional but recommended)

Preparation:

- Wash the saag a couple of times by soaking in water to dislodge the dirt. Most greens have a lot of sand, mud and sometimes, even insects during the rains. So, they need to be washed thoroughly.

- Keep the washed greens in a colander to drain excess water.

- Cut into 1 cm sized pieces.

Cooking:

- Heat a wok and add a little water. Add the greens along with salt and cover it until it's 50-60 per cent cooked. Remove a keep aside.

- Heat the oil in the wok. Add mustard seeds, broken red chilli and lightly crushed garlic cloves. Once the garlic starts to brown, add the chopped onions. Fry until it turns brown.

- Add the boiled green and mix everything together. Adjust the salt.

- Cover for a few more minutes to cook the greens. Remove the lid and sauté for some time until all the excess water evaporates and the greens are done.

- Add some fried and crushed badi just before removing it from the wok.

- Serve immediately.

CHAKUNDA SAAG

(Stir-fried monsoon greens)

One of the greens available during the monsoons, it grows aplenty in the wild. Rich in calcium, magnesium, and vitamin C, it is one superfood that is available for free and can address the problem of malnutrition in areas where such greens grow abundantly. Unfortunately, the traditional knowledge and awareness of such ingredients is diminishing at an alarming rate as people's preferences shift more and more towards cultivated greens and vegetables.

 **Cooking time – 15-20 minutes**

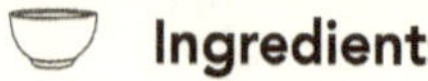 **Ingredients:**

- 3 cups of tender Cassia Tora leaves
- 2 tbsp finely chopped garlic
- 2-3 dry red chillis
- ½ tsp mustard seeds
- 2 tsp oil
- Salt to taste

Preparation:

- Remove all the stems from the greens as they don't get cooked easily. Wash a couple of times in water and keep aside for excess water to drain off.
- Chop the greens into small pieces.

Cooking:

- Heat oil in a wok. Add the mustard seeds, broken red chilli and chopped garlic.

- Once the garlic starts to brown, add the greens and mix. Sauté on high for 2-3 minutes.

- Cover with a lid for 3-4 minutes and then, cook on an open flame until the greens are done.

- Serve hot or warm with rice meals.

PALA CHATTU BARA

(Pan-fried paddy mushroom patties)

Paddy mushrooms used to be available abundantly in rural areas a few decades back when people used to grow traditional rice varieties. The straw from the harvest used to be gathered and stored to feed the cows and bullocks. These mushrooms grew on the rotting straw during the monsoons. With hybrid paddy and mechanized farming taking over, the supply of these mushrooms has dwindled, but they are still available in some rural pockets. However, cultivated paddy mushrooms are also available in Odisha.

These have a unique flavour and excellent texture.

 **Preparation time – 30 minutes**

 **Ingredients:**

- 250 gm paddy mushrooms
- 1 large boiled potato
- 1 large onion
- 3-4 green chillis
- 5-6 garlic flakes
- ½ inch ginger
- 3 tbs chopped coriander leaves
- 1 tsp roasted jeera-lanka gunda
- ¼ tsp garam masala
- 2 tsp turmeric powder
- ¼ tsp salt or to taste
- 4-5 tbsp oil

🍽 Preparation:

- Take water in a large vessel. Dissolve 1 1/2 tsp turmeric in it. Add the mushrooms and allow to soak for 30 minutes.

- Drain off the water and chop into small pieces. Repeat twice to dislodge any sand or dirt sticking to the mushrooms. Do not throw away the stem as it is also edible.

- Chop the onion into small pieces. Crush the garlic and ginger into a coarse paste.

🥘 Cooking:

- Heat 1 tbsp of oil in a wok/frying pan. Add the chopped mushroom along with 2 pinches of turmeric and a little salt, and stir fry on high flame until excess water evaporates. Remove and keep aside.

- Add another tbsp oil to the wok. Add the onions and fry it until it turns translucent. Add the ginger garlic paste and fry until the raw smell goes off. Add the roughly mashed potato along with all remaining spices and salt. Cook for 2-3 minutes and add the mushrooms. Mix everything and remove from the flame.

- Once it cools down, pinch some of the mixture and shape it into circles of about ½ inch thickness.

- Heat a frying pan. Drizzle generously with oil. Place the circles over the pan and cook both sides to a light brown/deep brown colour as per preference. Each side takes about 6-7 minutes on a low flame

- Serve it with meals or as a snack.

PANASA BARA
(Deep-fried tender jackfruit patties)

While Sabitri Brata in Jyesta marks the beginning of the ripe jackfruit season, the fortnight leading up to Rajaw is a period of accelerated ripening of this fruit. As the heat and humidity levels peak during this interval, all kinds of summer fruits inundate the local markets. This glut synchronizes perfectly with the temporary pause in cooking during Rajaw. Along with the various kinds of pitha, ripe fruits form a good proportion of the Rajaw menu.

However, some late-ripening jackfruit varieties mature in the middle of the rains. Since the body no longer craves these summer fruits in their original state, they are turned into recipes more adapted to the monsoon palate.

A plateful of comforting fritters, for example, is a good start.

 **Cooking time – 15 minutes**

 **Ingredients:**

- 12 ripe jackfruit pieces (de-seeded)
- 1/3 cup raw rice
- 1 tsp jaggery (or) 2 tsp sugar
- Oil for deep frying
- 1-2 pinch salt

 **Preparation:**

- Take the jackfruit pieces, rice, jaggery and 1-2 teaspoons of water in a small chutney jar. Grind into a smooth paste. Let it stand for 10-15 minutes.

🥘 **Cooking:**

- Heat sufficient oil in a wok for deep frying the fritters.

- Drop a few teaspoons of the batter at a time. Fry evenly on all sides to a rich brown shade. Remove and keep aside.

- Repeat the process with the remaining batter.

- Let it cool down completely before enjoying the fritters. Keep away some of them in an airtight container as they taste even better on the next day.

Note – I have used Khajaw panasa (the crunchy variety) to make this bara.

There are two varieties of jackfruit popularly found in Odisha, the *Rasua* (juicy) one and the *Khaja* (crunchy) one. The Khaja variety is usually eaten as it is, while the Rasua variety is most suitable for making bara, poda pitha, etc.

The jackfruit pods are deseeded and mashed with some water in a vessel to free the juices from the fibres. Once the mixture starts to liquefy, a clean stick (usually a *dantakathi*) is inserted and swirled around the liquid to catch the fibres. It is a time taking process but cleans up the juice quite effectively, which is then boiled and used for making all kinds of recipes.

A similar process is used to clean up the stray fibres in mango pulp before preparing the 'Aam Sadha' or mango leather and even the *Pachila Aam Kanji.*

JUKJUKIA SAJANA SAAG
(Mushy moringa leaves preparation)

The tender green leaves of the *Sajana* (Moringa, the 'superfood' as it is called these days) are a lifeline during the rainy days when foraging for greens is almost impossible. Conveniently located in the backyard, it offers an abundant supply of greens during the monsoon. I often think of it in terms of being the monsoon equivalent of the 'Khada sagaw.' And quite coincidently, both turn inedible almost as soon as their season ends. While the khada leaves wilt off in the rains, the Sajana leaves harbour thousands of eggs and larvae at the end of the monsoon. Hence the tree is ritualistically chopped off after the rains. The new shoots emerge during spring and become a source of food during summer and monsoons.

A somewhat 'hot' and mushy preparation of the greens makes for a great lunch with some piping hot rice and a luscious black lentil dal.

 Cooking time – 20 minutes

Ingredients:

- 3 cups of cleaned and prepped sajana saag
- 1 cup tender ridge gourd OR sponge gourd (chopped into small pieces)
- 1 small onion
- ¼ tsp mustard seeds
- 2 tsp oil
- Salt to taste

For the paste:

- 2 tsp aromatic rice
- 4-5 garlic cloves
- ¼ tsp cumin
- ¼ tsp mustard seeds
- 1-2 dry red chillis

🍽 Preparation:

- Soak all rice, cumin, mustard and dry red chilli for 1 hour. Add the garlic and grind into a smooth paste.
- Chop the onion into thin long strips.

🍲 Cooking:

- Heat the oil in a wok. Add the onion and fry them until they turn reddish.
- Add the greens along with the chopped ridge gourd. Stir on high for 2 minutes and cover it with a lid.
- Once the greens are half done, add the prepared paste along with 3-4 tbsp water. Add the salt.
- Cover and cook until done.
- Serve hot.

CHARU PANI

(A tangy soup made with dried green mangoes)

The Odia counterpart of the *rasam*, Charu, is meant to be slurped during wet monsoon and cold winter days. A staple in the Southern districts of the state, it is a lot like the '*Phala*' kanji, minus the vegetables and the hint of sweetness. Meant to revive the appetite after a bout of seasonal flu or even soothe a troublesome tummy, the *Charu* works like a charm to perk up the mood during those long dull spells of rain.

⏳ **Preparation time – 15 minutes**

 **Ingredients:**

- 5-6 pieces of dried mango
- 4-5 garlic cloves (crushed)
- 1 inch ginger (crushed)
- ½ tsp pancha phutana
- 2-3 dry red chilli
- 2 sprig curry leaves
- 2 pinch turmeric
- ½ coarsely crushed mustard seeds
- 1 pinch asafoetida
- 1-2 tsp mustard oil
- Salt to taste

🍽 **Preparation:**

- Wash and soak the dried green mango in water for 1-2 hours.

🍳 Cooking:

- Take 1.5 litre of water in a saucepan. Add the soaked green mango along with salt and turmeric. Bring it to a full boil.

- Add the ginger and crushed mustard seeds. Boil for another 2-3 minutes.

- Heat the oil in a wok. Add the broken red chilli and pancha phutana.

- Once it starts spluttering, add the asafoetida, garlic and curry leaves. Sauté for a minute before adding the contents of the saucepan to the wok. Cover immediately. Switch off the flame

- Serve as a side with rice or sip it as a warming brew.

Note - This recipe is also made with ripe tamarind pods.

During late monsoons when vegetable supplies are low, a version of Kanji called 'Bhuda Kanji' (a colloquial form of Bhadraba) is prepared from taro stems, amaranthus stems, the sun-dried eggplants or ripened eggplants, and taro. But even these ingredients are scarce. Hence, some people in the Western parts prefer to prepare charu at times. Unlike other seasons when some of the kanji is kept aside and consumed on the next day, the Bhuda Kanji and Charu pani are always consumed warm and fresh.

CHAULA BHAJA/HUDUMA
(Spicy toasted rice snack)

One of the earliest memories from my childhood is of being huddled around the 'chulhi' or coal-fired stove in our kitchen on cold rainy days. The incessant rains brought about cravings for food and warmth, driving the kids into the kitchen. With very limited 'store-bought' snack options, we were often handed a warm bowl of 'kanji' or a few pieces of *bhaja* straight off the griddle around noon. Late afternoons or evenings meant home-made snacks like *muga sijha*, *mudhi bhaja*, *chuda bhaja*, roasted corn on the cob, and on those rare occasions, a spicy *'Chaula bhaja.'* The lack of fast-food options seems like a blessing when I contemplate the unprocessed food on our plates during those days.

As a kid, the process of making 'Chaula bhaja' was something that mesmerized me. I would watch with fascination as my grandmother anointed the soaked grains of parboiled rice with salt, turmeric, and a little red chilli powder. A big black iron wok would be brought out and heated to a high temperature. Then, the rice would be added in small batches, and within a few moments, it would start popping with those crackling noises that reminded me of firecrackers going off. More than the crunch of *Huduma*, the process etched itself into my memory.

 **Preparation time – 20 minutes**

 **Ingredients:**

- 1 cup parboiled rice
- ¼ tsp turmeric
- ¼ tsp chilli powder
- ¼ tsp salt
- ½ tsp oil

🍽️ Preparation:

- Wash and soak the rice for 30 minutes.

- Drain off all the water, spread it out on a clean kitchen towel and allow it to dry for an hour under the fan.

- Transfer to a plate and add the remaining ingredients. Mix it nicely and let it stand for 30 minutes.

🍲 Cooking:

- Heat a thick-bottomed wok until it is quite hot.

- Add half of the rice in the first lot and keep stirring it continuously.

- It will start puffing up within a minute or two. Keep stirring continuously for the next 2-3 minutes and lower the flame if the wok is becoming too hot, else the rice will burn.

- Remove to a plate.

- Serve warm with tea or even by itself.

Note – Chaula bhaja is sometimes jazzed up a bit by adding a few fried curry leaves, thin toasted slices of coconut and even a handful of roasted peanuts.

Khuda bhaja is also prepared using the above method. It puffs up quite nicely due to the small size and actually tastes better because of the bran that imparts it a nutty flavour.

BHADRABA (AUGUST – SEPTEMBER)

The rains show signs of slowing down. The early varieties of paddy start to ripen in the fields. They need to be monitored regularly for signs of infestation. Routine clearing of grass and weeds is carried out without fail. The bunds are broken at some points to allow the accumulated water to flow out. The soil needs to be dry before the paddy can be harvested. Crops like black lentils, moong, horse gram, and chillis are sown around this time.

Late varieties of mushrooms, and tender bamboo shoots make their entry. A kind of mushroom called *Bihiden Chattu* grows around this time. It is named after the cycle of additional ploughing or '*Bihiden*,' carried out between August-September, to aerate the soil for the late varieties of paddy. Associating the flora of a given month with the agricultural cycle served the dual purpose of a log and a handy reminder for our ancestors, who often lacked access to writing tools.

Sour fruits like lemon, lime, starfruit and tender hog plums begin to tickle the palate. Vegetation turns lush and rivers start overflowing with fish. The fish trapped in the flooded fields are caught during the breaching of the bunds. In the Western parts, some of these fishes are smoked and preserved for use in the later months. Locally known as *Niya Sukhua*, they are cooked with bamboo shoots, jackfruit seeds, shallots, baby potatoes, country tomatoes, leafy greens and even by themselves.

However, this month is considered to be a lean period for some regions as the major food reserves [carbs that make up the largest portion of the meals] get over by this time and the harvest has not yet started. So, in the past, this used to be the time when entire communities would scour the forests in search of wild yam and tubers. Many varieties of yams like '*Jhar kanda*', '*pitalu kanda*', '*kantalu kanda*', '*Mandei kanda*', and '*Surkia kanda*' used to be available in the forests of Bonaigarh some decades back.

The first of the harvest festivals, *Nuakhai*, is celebrated in Western Odisha. A few sheaths of the early varieties of paddy are procured before they have fully ripened, and the grains used to prepare an offering for the local deity. The rice is dried and threshed. Some of it is turned into rice flakes and mixed with panchamrita (ghee, milk, curd, honey, sugar) while the remaining portion is cooked into a kheer. Another preparation made from this rice is Arissa pitha. Both are offered to *Maa Samalei*, and the village goddesses before being distributed among the family members. This kind of premature or symbolic harvesting is done with an objective to ensure that the birds or rodents do not eat the paddy before it is offered to the Goddess.

Nuakhai is akin to a mid-term respite before the actual harvesting takes place. It is a period of feasting and rejoicing meant to lift flagging spirits and renew the enthusiasm required to trudge through the physically demanding harvest period. Some of the dishes cooked for Nuakhai are *Ambil, makhan saag, karadi, tiasi chana, kakara, arisa, Khiri* and *mug bara*. With farming becoming increasingly mechanized, the harvesting process has become less laborious. But the old traditions have lived on. It is interesting to note that while 'Gundikhai' focuses on the role played by forests, 'Nuakhai' is focussed on the role of agriculture in our life. Celebrating both these occasions underlines the need to maintain a fine balance between them.

Karma Puja is celebrated by the tribal population of Sundargarh, Sambalpur, Bolangir, Keonjhar and Mayurbhanj. A branch of the auspicious Karam tree (*Nauclea parvifolia*) is brought from the forest, and planted in the fields. Highly regarded for its medical properties, it is believed to be the original *Kadamba* associated with Lord Krishna, and the general folklore woven around it also points to the same theory. The trees are worshipped with seven kinds of grains. They are paddy, wheat, black lentil, green gram, horse gram, mustard and flax seeds. This points towards the crops being cultivated in the region for a long time. Pura Uans is another little-known festival observed in Western Odisha during Bhadraba. It marks the completion of a phase of weeding. It is a day when the farmers worship their cattle and feed then various kinds of pitha and 'mudhi ladu.' Young boys pull wooden or clay toys like bulls, elephants and horses through the village streets, while the little girls play with clay utensils called 'kudhi-kanchi.' This kind of role-playing helps them to become aware of expectations at a later stage of life.

From this month onwards, a series of observances, called 'osa', dot the calendar. These 'rites of protection' are observed for the well-being of the offspring and the family members. The coastal areas celebrate *Sathi Osa* and *Budhei Osa* for the long life of the offspring during this month. The most interesting aspect of an 'osa' is that it is generally a community affair, which requires the ladies to come together. These occasions offer them an opportunity for female bonding as they move in groups foraging wild plants, flowers and fruits required for the rituals. It also gives them an occasion to do '*shringaar*,' wear '*alta*', put on flowers and various ornaments which boost their self-esteem and ultimately benefits their emotional well-being.

Other prominent festivals celebrated during this month are *Janmashtami* and *Ganesh Chaturthi*. An offering of black sesame seeds laddu is prepared on both these occasions as the timing coincides with the harvest from the secondary sesame growing season.

Bhagabata Janma, a day when people commence a fresh recitation of the Odia version of 'Bhagwad Gita', also falls during this month. It is observed on the full moon day.

What's on the menu this month

KARADI MACCHA CHUDCHUDA
(Bamboo shoot and fish cooked in mustard paste)

Fresh bamboo shoots available in the rainy season are often cooked with 'bila maccha' or paddy fish. Fish get trapped in the *'bila'* or farmland inundated by the swelling waters of the flooded rivers. The flavours of the wild fish and the unmistakable tartness of the bamboo combine with the pungent mustard, garlic, and chilli paste to create the most unforgettable sensory experience.

 **Cooking time – 15 minutes**

Ingredients:

- ½ cup fresh bamboo shoots/*Karadi*
- 1 large piece of fish belly (Rohu/Catla)
- 1 ¼ tsp mustard seeds
- 2-3 flakes of garlic
- 1-2 green chillis
- 4 tsp mustard oil
- ¼ tsp salt
- 2-3 pinch turmeric

Preparation:

- Grind the mustard seeds (keeping aside a few for tempering) along with the garlic pods into a fine paste.
- Marinate the fish with salt and turmeric for 10 minutes.

- Heat a pan and drizzle with oil. Fry the fish on both sides until it turns slightly brownish. Keep it aside.

- Heat a wok. Pour 2 tsp oil into it. Add the remaining mustard seeds and slit green chillis. Once the seeds start spluttering, add the fried fish and crush it slightly. Fry it for 2-3 minutes.

- Dissolve the mustard-garlic paste in a cup of water. Let it stand for 2-3 minutes before pouring the top layer carefully into the wok. The sediments are left behind in the cup and are discarded.

- Bring the contents of the wok to a boil and add the bamboo shoots along with a pinch of turmeric and salt.

- Allow to cook on low flame for about 10-12 minutes or until the bamboo shoots turn tender and all the water is absorbed. Serve hot/warm with rice.

> *Note – One can also substitute the fresh fish with smoked fish in this recipe.*

A bamboo basket filled with white cone-like objects basket lay in the courtyard (*agana*). The women were engrossed in chopping the freshly dug bamboo shoots. Only the tender top portion of each cone (*kenda*) was being sliced and turned into thin long pieces that were tossed into another basket kept nearby. The hardened ends of each cone were carelessly tossed into a smaller basket. This routine continued for the next few days. It was a ritual they followed every monsoon when the bamboo thickets sprouted new shoots. The women, expert foragers, could spot a fresh shoot before it emerged from the soil. These shoots yielded the most tender *karadi,* an ingredient used in Western Odisha kitchens throughout the year.

The sliced bamboo shoots collected in the large baskets were squeezed out, and spread on a mat to dry for a day or two. This period is usually earmarked as the best time to prepare dishes like *karadi pithau bhaja* and *karadi raee*, before the fermentation sets in and a sour note develops.

After the surface moisture evaporated, the shoots were carefully packed into earthen pots, and they would stay good for the next 2-3 years at the least. Sometimes, these shoots tend to darken due to oxidation, and hence, people mix a little turmeric with the freshly chopped bamboo shoots. The segregated ends were collected over a few days, crushed into fine pieces, squeezed out completely, and stored separately in earthen pots. This process yields *Hendua, which* is initially moist but dries out over time. *It is* more intense in flavour than Karadi.

As I sniffed the slightly squishy sugar palm fruit I held in my hands, I realized my childhood memories were replete with myriad scents. Toddy palm carried the smell of the monsoons. Not the much romanticized 'petrichor' kind but one that develops as the rains progress from sudden showers to a steady drizzle and continues for days. The wetness of the grass, the musty odour of clothes that had no chance to dry completely, and the dampness of the walls and floors that would send me scurrying to the kitchen for warmth. And of course, the nibbles that came with the turf.

On one of those rainy days, a large can would arrive from Jangra. I clearly remember being fascinated by the sticky saffron-coloured contents. But it was the smell that stayed with me to date. The golden-orange pulp of the sugar palm would fill the home with an ethereal fragrance.

Every time the familiar scent reaches my nostrils, I am transported to a different realm. Jangra. The land of my forefathers. The ancestral home that was built by my grandfather's great-grandfather. The numerous rooms, courtyards, and doorways put together in a complex interconnected maze that often caused an 8-year-old to lose her way. Yet, my curiosity got the better of me and I would sneak around exploring the fascinating labyrinth that stood almost at the edge of the river cliff. Most of it has been lost to the murky black waters of the mighty Brahmani River.

As the cousins and other ladies clambered down the treacherous slope with practised ease, I would find myself sitting near the edge and counting the sugar palm trees growing near the river. They looked like sentinels, standing tall and formidable. Years later, I realized they were real sentinels, acting as windbreakers and slowing down soil erosion. They stood where they did for a good reason. Another reason they were planted a little away from the inhabited village was the propensity of the fruits to fall in quick succession once they ripened, raising the probability of bodily harm.

TALA KAKARA

(Sugar palm and rice cakes)

A few months ago, I had corrected someone for mentioning that pithas are festival recipes. I would rather use the word 'festive,' I had responded. While it is undebatable that certain *pithas* have exclusively been prepared on festivals, categorizing them solely as 'offerings for the Gods', is incorrect. They have always been a part of our celebratory menu. Before the fast-food culture changed the way we eat, making a pitha at home our way of expressing happiness. The wide range of *pithas* prepared during Rajaw and *Pus Puni* celebrations is nothing less than an exuberant display of joy.

I grew up seeing my grandmother take out her brass utensils to make the *Kakara* or *Suanli* every time she was in a good mood. For her, watching the golden-hued Kakara bobbing gently in hot oil was perhaps the moment to bask in some of that happiness.

 **Cooking time – 45 minutes**

 **Ingredients:**

- 1 cup rice flour
- 1 cup sugar palm pulp
- 1/2 cup jaggery
- 1 tsp fennel seeds
- 1/2 tsp salt
- Oil for deep frying (cold-pressed mustard oil gives it an authentic taste)
- 1 tsp of ghee (optional)

Note: The freshly extracted sugar palm juice needs to be strained, boiled for 10-15 minutes and allowed to cool down in order to reduce the bitterness before using it in any kind of recipe. The consistency of this liquid will also vary with the amount of water used during the extraction. I boiled and stored a big batch of the sugar palm extract which I have used in this recipe. If making it with freshly extracted juice, you will need to add a little more water, boil it for 15 minutes and let it come down to room temperature before proceeding with this recipe.

Preparation:

- Take the sugar palm juice in a thick-bottomed pan or wok. Bring it to a boil on a low flame. Add the jaggery, fennel, and salt to the boiling juice. Once the jaggery melts, sift in the rice flour and keep stirring continuously to avoid the formation of lumps. Keep the flame low all the time.

- Remove from fire once the liquid is completely absorbed and the mixture resembles a loose dough. Do not overcook.

- Allow to cool down a bit. Add a few drops of ghee. Knead the mixture into a smooth dough. The kneading should be done when the dough is still hot (should have a tolerable temperature as one needs to work with hands).

- Divide the warm dough into small balls (given quantity makes about 10 of them). Flatten them into small discs but do not make them very thin.

Cooking:

- Heat a wok. Add sufficient oil for frying. When the oil is sufficiently hot but not smoking, add the flattened balls. Reduce the flame a bit and fry them until they are golden brown in colour.

- Remove from the hot oil using a slotted spoon and allow them to cool down. Serve at room temperature. Tastes best the next day.

TALA BARA
(Sugar palm fritters)

How does one even separate the word 'deep-fried' from the 'monsoon?' These little delights that perk up the dull, dreary monsoon evenings basically deliver a little dopamine punch that keeps us going through a period of less than ambient amounts of sunlight. With natural sunlight being the best mood enhancer, the lack of it brings about a feeling of deprivation (thanks to the lower serotonin levels). And fried snacks have always been the easiest way to plug that gap.

Odia cuisine is no novice to this kind of culinary sorcery. It channelizes seasonal ingredients like ripe jackfruit and sugar palm into a wide range of fried snacks that compensate for the lack of sunshine. The sugar and fats do a little happy dance on the nerve receptors on the tongue, which in turn trigger the brain to release the much-needed 'dopamine.' And one instantly feels their spirits lifting.

⌛ **Cooking time – 15 minutes**

🥣 **Ingredients:**

- 1 cup sugar palm juice (extracted and processed as described in the previous recipe)
- 1 cup rice powder flour
- 2 tsp semolina (optional)
- 3-4 tsp sugar
- oil for deep frying
- 1-2 pinch salt

🍽 **Preparation:**

- Take all the ingredients in a mixing bowl. Mix together to get a thick batter with a dropping consistency. Let it stand for 10-15 minutes.

Cooking:

- Heat sufficient oil in a wok for deep frying the fritters.

- Drop a few teaspoons of the batter at a time. Reduce the flame to low. Fry evenly on all sides to a rich brown shade. Remove and keep aside.

- Repeat the process with the remaining batter.

- Let it cool down completely before enjoying the fritters. Keep away some of them in an airtight container as they taste even better the next day. Stays good for 3-4 days.

TALA ENDURI PITHA

(Steamed sugar palm and rice cakes)

Rice and sugar palm pulp steamed in fresh Sal leaves. The divine fragrance of the green leaves betrothed to the equally aromatic palm. A marriage of 'ta-law' and 'sa-law' is not just a culinary celebration but an affirmation of the anti-bacterial properties of the latter, invoked to prolong the shelf life of a fast fermenting/spoiling fruit.

Surprising? Hardly, given that both trees are endemic to Western Odisha.

Preparation time – 30 minutes

  **Ingredients:**

- 1 cups sugar palm pulp (thickened)
- 1 cups rice flour
- 2-3 tsp Sugar
- ½ tsp salt
- Fresh Sal leaves
- 1 tsp oil (optional)

Preparation:

- Take the sugar palm pulp in a mixing bowl and add the rice flour in batches. Keep mixing in between until the consistency is similar to that of cake batter.
- Add the salt and sugar. Whip the batter for 2-3 minutes.
- Heat water in a steamer/pressure cooker. Bring to a boil.

- Wash the Sal leaves and wipe them dry. Rub a little oil over each leaf. Take a blob of the batter and spread it on the leaf. Fold the leaf carefully and place it on the steamer stand. If using a pressure cooker, please remember to remove the weight.

- Repeat the process for the remaining batter/leaves. The folder leaves can be stacked one over the other. Close the lid and steam for 10-15 minutes. Remove from the stove.

- Allow to cool down until it is just warm to touch.

- Remove the leaf and serve.

GAHAMA KHIRI
(Wheat pudding)

Some recipes are nothing short of intriguing. The influences behind it seem elusive to the point where it almost seems like a glitch in the matrix. My grandmother making the 'Atta Bhaja' for example, is something that I haven't been able to fathom. I recall her slow-roasting wheat flour with a copious amount of cow ghee on a low flame until it turned brown and fragrant. She finally added sugar to it and allowed it to melt in the residual heat. It was called 'atta bhaja' at home but many years later, I realized that she had been making a version of the *Panjiri*. Was it something my grandfather had picked by during his travels? I entertained this possibility for a while before I stumbled upon more evidence of it being a ubiquitous preparation in rural pockets near Puri. With wheat being used generously in the dishes that make up the *Chappan Bhog*, it seems likely that the usage of wheat in this part of the state spread from the Jagannath temple which enjoyed immense patronage.

Very little wheat is grown in Odisha and the crop is something of a late entrant. However, some dishes like the 'Atta Bhaja' have ingrained themselves into the vast Odia cuisine. It would have been less of a surprise had our village been on the pilgrim or trade route. But when one stumbles upon a dish like this in a quaint little village on the banks of the Brahmani River, one is possibly missing a piece of the puzzle. How does one even keep track of all the influences that have swept through a region? Or even trace it back to a specific one? Maybe it was something brought in by a group of settlers, or the Garhjat rulers with their Rajput origins. It might even have been the ingenuity of the women combined with some sheer coincidence.

The whole wheat kheer is another intriguing recipe which seemed to have popped up in different parts of the state. It is prepared by a sub-caste of Brahmins in the coastal region during Janmashtami (my source for this recipe). However, it is also made in Nayagarh and parts of Western Odisha without any evident link to any specific caste or community.

⏳ **Cooking time – 45 minutes**

🥣 **Ingredients:**

- ½ cup Whole wheat
- 1 litre milk
- ½ cup jaggery
- 2-3 tsp ghee
- ½ cup dry fruits (cashews, raisins, *charoli*)

🍽 **Preparation:**

- Wash and dry the wheat for 30 minutes. Pulse it in a mixer jar for a few seconds to a coarse texture. Sieve the mixture to remove any finely powdered particles.

🍲 **Cooking:**

- Heat the ghee in a heavy-bottomed wok. Add the dry fruits and fry for 30 seconds. Remove and keep aside.
- Add the coarsely powdered wheat and roast it for 4-5 minutes.
- Transfer to a pressure cooker. Add 1-2 cups of water and cook for 2 whistles on medium flame.
- Transfer it back to the wok and add 1 litre of milk. Add the dry fruits.
- Let it cook on a low flame for 20-25 minutes until it thickens sufficiently. Keep stirring in between to prevent the bottom from catching.
- Stir in the jaggery just before switching off the flame.
- Serve warm.

In Ayurveda, the term kanji is broadly used to describe a liquid created by cooking something sour with water or allowing it to ferment after cooking. Usually, rice or broken rice is one of the constituents of a kanji. Charaksanhita refers to Kanji as an 'amla' or sour food which is not necessarily cooked. It even lists a recipe for powdered rice and radish kanji that is not cooked but left to ferment. Despite its extensive usage in Ayurveda, the word is repeatedly found in Southern literature, where it refers to the either starchy water or the gruel obtained by boiling rice or other grains (for example, barley as per some of the older texts). Kanji refers to starch in other parts too which indicates that the word originated as a part of an ancient language spoken by a community that was extremely influential or very well-travelled.

Digging into the culinary history of the various Indian cuisines, 'kanji' comes across as a very pan–Indian dish. From the fermented carrot kanji in the North to the myriad varieties of kanji made in Odisha and the various South Indian versions, one stumbles upon an entire genre of 'namesake' liquid-y dishes across the sub-continent that are possibly a part of a broader matrix. For the sake of a providing a definition, we may choose to sum it up as "An easy to digest liquid preparation that hydrates the body, improves digestion, re-energizes and also soothes the soul at the same time."

Ambil. A liquid preparation that is predominantly sour either due to fermentation or by the use of a souring agent. It derives its name from the Sanskrit word 'Amla.' The usage of this term is not as common as 'kanji.' Apart from some of the Western parts of Odisha, the term ambil is used in Maharashtra where it refers to a fermented millet drink. It serves the same purpose as the 'kanji.'

Some regions in Odisha have a dish called 'Maccha ambil,' which is a typical sweet sour fish curry. However, it is not to be confused with the above dishes.

A Comparison of Kanji, Ambil and Letha (within Odisha)

Within the state, words like kanji, ambil and letha to a smaller extent, are sometimes used interchangeably. While they do refer to somewhat similar dishes, the terms hold significance within various communities and geographies. I have tried to explain the similarities and differences between these dishes but there might be more versions outside the ambit of this book.

	Kanji	Ambil/Ambila	Letha
Consistency	Thin	Considerably thicker	More like a slurry (the term 'letha' refers to viscosity)
Primary Ingredients	Seasonal Vegetables like radish, eggplant, amaranth stems, raw papaya, ripe pumpkin, taro, okra, taro stems.	Vegetables, Horsegram or Kulith (western Odisha variant).	Coarsely ground rice and vegetables. Pulses like *dhob chana*, and *kala chana* are also added.
Souring Agent Used	Green mango, dried green mango, ripe wild mangoes, tamarind, curd, tamarind, fermented rice water (torani), Khatta palanga leaves, Bamboo shoots, country tomato, *mahi/ buttermilk*.	Curd, tamarind, dried green mango, bamboo shoots, tomato, buttermilk.	Tamarind, dried green mango, bamboo shoots.
Thickening agent Used	Leftover rice, broken rice or khudaw, rice water (pej), and raw rice paste (pithau).	Chickpea flour, rice paste, tomatoes	Coarsely ground rice powder
Region	Most parts of the state.	Sambalpur	Tribal-dominated areas like Kalahandi, Kandhamal, etc.

	Kanji	Ambil/Ambila	Letha
Community-specific (in earlier times)	Most communities including Brahmin and *Khandayat*	Some communities like Kumuti. All communities in Sambalpur.	*Kulita*, various tribal communities
Sweetening agent used	Yes, jaggery is used		Mahua flower paste
Medicinal plants used	Tempering of dried neem blossoms seen in specific variants. Drumstick leaves are used as an ingredient in a variant seen in Berhampur.	No.	Yes. Ingredients with medicinal properties like the skunk vine leaves, *bhuinanla* plants, and mahua flowers are used mostly by tribals in Kandhamal and Koraput.
Mustard paste used	Yes, in a specific variant.	No	No
Non-vegetarian ingredients used	Freshwater prawns are used in a specific version.	No	Chicken is used by a few tribal communities.
Any other seasoning used	Mustard/pancha phutana, garlic, curry leaves and dry red chilli for tempering; some people also use asafoetida; specific versions use a tempering of dried neem flowers	Mustard/pancha phutana, garlic, curry leaves and dry red chilli for tempering; some people also use asafoetida	Ground spices paste used which varies with communities and regions
No cook version if any	*Surjya Kanji* made by the widows observing *Habisa* involves keeping the fermented rice water with pieces of radish in an earthen pot under the sun		

	Kanji	Ambil/Ambila	Letha
No vegetable version if any	A specific kind of kanji made in Nayagarh used only Khudaw and curd.		The chicken version does not use any vegetables.

Note- A few decades back, most recipes had caste connotations. But as we move towards an increasingly flat world, these distinctions are disappearing for good. Any caste reference in this book is made from a historical and academic study point of view.

AMBIL/AMBILA
(A tangy and chunky vegetable soup)

Nuakhai. A festival observed by the Western belt of Odisha, parts of Jharkhand and Chhattisgarh to thank the Gods for the paddy harvest. The early maturing varieties of paddy ripen around this month. A few ears of paddy are harvested, threshed, pared and offered to the presiding deity of the respective regions (*Maa Samalei* in the case of Sambalpur, *Maa Patneswari* in Balangir, and so on) at an auspicious time on the day after *Ganesh Chaturthi.* The offering is usually in the form of a '*khiri*' or a '*chakata*,' a thick mixture of rice grains mashed with *panchamrit*. The latter is also called '*Nabanna*.' The head of the family is the first to partake in this offering. He then distributes it among other members who touch his feet while receiving the prasad.

It is a celebration where the entire clan gathers under one roof. People working in other cities return home to celebrate Nuakhai with their families. Special invitations are sent to the married daughters and sons-in-law. New clothes are distributed to every family member. Even the farm support staff and servants are given a bonus. A feast featuring the 'Nuakhai Khiri,' 'Ambil,' Pitha and a host of other dishes made from ingredients like pumpkin, taro, bamboo shoots, spine gourd, etc., is laid out on *Kurei* leaf plates in areas like Sambalpur, Sundargarh and Bolangir. Some communities, however, prefer Sal or Semul leaf plates for this celebration. This preference has is invariably linked to the native flora of the region.

The Ambil is a regular in most Sambalpur homes, and also one of the most important dishes on the Nuakhai menu.

 **Cooking time – 1 hour**

 **Ingredients:**

- 1/2 cup cubed pumpkin
- 1/2 cup cubed eggplant

- 1/4 cup cubed taro

- 2-3 okra

- One small radish

- One large tomato

- 1/3 tsp turmeric

- 1 tsp salt or to taste

- Souring agent – 1-2 pieces ambula (dried mango) (or) a small ball of tamarind

- Thickening agent – 2 tsp besan + 2 tbsp curd (or) 2 tsp rice paste

Tempering:

- 2 tsp fresh karadi (bamboo shoots)

- 7 – 8 garlic cloves

- 3 dry red chilli

- 2 sprig curry leaves

- 1/2 tsp mustard seeds

- 2 tsp mustard oil

Cooking:

- Bring 7-8 cups of water to a boil in a deep vessel. Add salt and turmeric. Add all the cubed vegetables except okra.

- Soak the souring agent in a little water.

- Take another pan. Add a little oil and stir fry the okra for two minutes. Once the other vegetables are 75 per cent cooked, add the okra.

- Add the thickening agent to the vegetables. If it is curd and besan, beat the two into a thin paste without any lumps and lower the flame when adding. Keep stirring until it gets to a boil.

- Let it boil for 5 minutes before adding the souring agent.

- Heat oil in another saucepan for the tempering. Add the mustard seeds, broken red chillis, curry leaves and garlic. Once the garlic starts to brown a bit, add the bamboo shoots and sauté for a minute or two.

- Tip the contents of this saucepan over the boiling ambil. Let it simmer for 2-3 minutes before taking off the flame.

- Serve warm.

Note – Nuakhai meals are mandatorily served on Kurei leaf plates and bowls. The leaf is known to cure piles, irritable bowel syndrome and diarrhoea. In addition, it is known to promote the 'agni' (digestive fire) in the body and balance Kapha and Pitta doshas.

KARADI-MAKHAN SAAG

(Pumpkin leaves cooked with tender pumpkin and bamboo shoots)

The importance of the pumpkin crop is evident from the fact that some tribal communities have a day earmarked for the first consumption or 'nua' of the leaves. Perhaps this reverence is because every part of the plant is edible. From the tender leaves cooked as greens to the delicious flowers that are pan-fried, even the stems make a great addition to curries. The fruits last long after the plants have died.

Cooking the first pumpkin shoots of the season with the first bamboo shoots (yet another seasonal ingredient) on Nuakhai is a reminder to be grateful and appreciate these gifts from nature.

The recipe is a pretty simple one. However, the addition of fresh bamboo shoots adds that special touch to it.

 **Cooking time – 20 minutes**

 **Ingredients:**

- 200 gm tender pumpkin leaves and stems
- 2-3 tender Taro leaves
- 50 gm fresh bamboo shoots
- 1 medium-sized tomato (or a few pieces of sundried tomato)
- 3-4 garlic pods
- 1-2 dry red chilli
- ½ tsp mustard seeds
- ½ tsp salt
- 3 tsp oil

🍽 Preparation:

- Wash and chop the tender pumpkin leaves and stems.
- If using taro leaves, chop and boil then for 2 minutes and discard the water before using in this recipe.

Cooking:

- Heat the oil in a wok. Add the broken red chilli, crushed garlic and mustard seeds.
- Once the garlic turns light brown, add the bamboo shoots and fry for 1-2 minutes.
- Add the tomato pieces along with the chopped greens and turn up the flame for 1-2 minutes.
- Sprinkle salt, reduce the flame and cover the greens for 2-3 minutes.
- Remove the lid and give it a mix. Cover and repeat the process until the greens have cooked.
- Serve warm with rice meals.

Note – If tender taro leaves are added to this recipe, it is referred to as 'Gadiya saag'. This is because both these greens tend to grow wild near water bodies.

***Sula or sundried tomatoes give a better texture and flavour to this dish.*

MUGA BARA
(Moong Fritters dunked in sugar syrup)

A feast like Nuakhai is incomplete without something sweet on the menu. Apart from pithas like Arissa, Kakara, and Manda, sweets like Ras *Bara* and Sarsatia are preferred. The Western Odisha palate and local produce dictate a marked inclination towards lentil-based preparations compared to the 'chenna-based' sweets that dominate the Coastal parts.

The clean and almost earthy flavours of the Muga Bara have a rustic appeal.

Cooking time – 20 minutes

 **Ingredients:**

- 1 cup split yellow moong dal
- 2/3 cup sugar
- 1/4 tsp salt
- A pinch of cardamom
- Oil for deep frying

 **Preparation:**

- Soak the moong dal for 4-5 hours. Drain and grind into a thick smooth paste.
- Add the salt and beat it for 3-4 minutes using your hands. Otherwise, use a whisk or a heavy spoon.

Cooking:

- Bring 1 cup of water and the sugar to a boil. Let it boil on a medium flame until the sugar syrup starts to thicken a bit. Switch off the flame. Add the powdered cardamom.

- Heat a wok. Add enough oil for deep frying. Wait until it gets to the smoking point.

- Add little blobs of the batter to the oil and fry on medium flame until it turns golden brown.

- Remove and add to the hot sugar syrup. Gently mix the muga bara with the sugar syrup for 30 seconds. Remove from the syrup and transfer to another bowl.

- Repeat the process for any remaining batter.

> *Note - *Earlier this recipe was prepared with split moong that had its skin intact. After soaking for a couple of hours, the skin gets loosened. The ladies would spread the soaked moong dal on a rough jute sack and rub it to get the skin off. Most of the skin would be removed by this process but it still retains some of the skin.*
>
> ***Other lentils that are used to prepare this Ras Bara are – black lentils (biri) and lobia (rumha).*

ARISA PITHA/GHEE PITHA
(Deep fried rice cakes)

Arisa pitha is an integral part of the *Chappan bhog* offered to Lord Jagannath. It is a must-have on the menu during harvest festivals, and an essential part of the *'bhara'* (gifts sent to the married daughter's place). The longevity of this pitha is much more than any other kind, so it is the ideal candidate for travel. There are many historical mentions of this pitha. There is a mention of two travellers from Kalinga offering the Arisa pitha to Lord Buddha.

One of my earliest food memories is that of my grandmother shaping the steaming hot dough into pitha, a task that called for speed and skill to ensure the pithas turned out perfect. She would put a blob of the dough on shiny jackfruit leaves, or banyan leaves plucked from our backyard, slightly wet her fingers with water, and work quickly to shape them. Hers were by far the best I have ever had!

⏳ **Cooking time Required - 40 minutes**

 **Ingredients:**

- 2 cups raw rice (plus a little extra)
- 1 cup jaggery
- ¼ cup water
- ghee/oil for frying
- 3-4 tsp sesame seeds

 **Preparation:**

- Wash and soak the rice for 2 hours. Drain all the water and spread it out on a cloth towel. Air dry for 2-3 hours or until the surface moisture disappears. Do not dry under the sun.

- Grind in a mixer grinder to a fine powder. Use a sieve, to separate the coarse particles. Use the finer portion to make the pitha.

Cooking:

- Heat the water in a wok. Add the jaggery and allow it to dissolve. Bring to a boil. When it is sufficiently thickened and sticky, add the rice in small amounts and mix well.

- Allow to cook, stirring the dough until it reaches a semi-solid consistency.

- Put aside the mixture to cool down to a tolerable temperature. Rub ghee on both palms and pinch out small portions. Shape the dough into a smooth ball by applying some pressure before flattening it into small circles (of 5-6 mm thickness). Sprinkle some sesame seeds on the surface of the circles and press them lightly.

- Heat oil in a wok for deep frying. Put in the pitha (one at a time) and cook for 3-4 minutes on a low to medium flame. Remove from the wok and allow to cool down.

- Arisa pitha can be stored in air-tight containers for up to a month.

Note – Use the drop test to check the consistency of jaggery before adding flour. Add a drop of the liquid jaggery to a bowl of water. If it does not dissolve but is still pliable to touch and forms a string, it is the right consistency to add the rice flour.

Always do the shaping and frying when the dough is warm (a little hot is even better) as it tends to turn brittle and develop cracks. Also, if one overcooks the dough, the pitha will disintegrate when it is dropped into the hot oil.

SARU MAGURA

(A spicy preparation of rolled and steamed taro leaves)

The fascinating faux fish curry of Western Odisha. I sometimes wonder how our ancestors got the inspiration to reimagine something as mundane as a fish curry. The likely stimulus might have been a youngster who refused to stick to the vegetarian menu on an 'osa' or 'brata.' Or it might even have been an influence carried via the trade route. The later seems more probable, given that the dish finds a mention in various cuisines across the subcontinent. Either way, the dark green chunks of steamed and fried taro leaves, buffeted with layers of spiced black lentil paste, could easily pass off as the real thing on any given day.

As the taro leaves are carefully slathered with lentil paste, stacked upon each other, given another generous coating, and carefully rolled into a streamlined shape that resembles a fish rather than a cylinder, it is tough to miss the resemblance.

 **Cooking time – 1 hour**

 **Ingredients:**

- 4 taro leaves
- 1 large onion + 1 small onion
- 2 large tomatoes
- 1 tsp cumin seeds
- 1 inch cinnamon
- 2-3 garlic cloves
- 2 dry red chillis
- ¼ tsp garam masala
- 1 ½ tbsp oil (plus extra for deep frying)
- ½ tsp turmeric
- Salt to taste

For making the paste:

- 1 cup spilt black lentil (skinless)
- 1-inch ginger
- 4-5 garlic cloves
- 1-2 green chilli
- Salt to taste

🍽 Preparation:

- Wash and soak the black lentils. Grind into a smooth paste along with the other ingredients listed along with it.

- Take the taro leaves and slather each one of them with the paste. Stack the leaves on top of each other and roll into a tight cylinder while pressing the sides to give it a streamlined shape. Slather the remaining paste over the cylinder.

- Grind the small onion, garlic cloves, cumin seeds, cinnamon and dry red chilli into a paste. Chop the large onion into medium-sized pieces.

Cooking:

- Steam the rolled taro leaves for 10 minutes. Once they have cooled down, cut across the width into pieces that are about 2 cm thick.

- Deep fry the pieces until they turn brown.

- Heat another wok. Add 1 ½ tsp oil and toss in the onions. Sauté them until they turn light brown. Add the masala paste and cook until the raw smell goes off. Add the turmeric and mix it for 20-30 seconds.

- Add the chopped tomatoes and sprinkle some salt over them. Cover and cook until they start to turn mushy. Add the garam masala and cook for 2 minutes.

- Add about 1 ½ cup water at this stage and bring it to a boil. Adjust the salt and let it simmer for a few minutes before adding the fried chunks.

- Cook for 1-2 minutes on a low flame before switching it off.

- Serve warm with rice or even roti.

Note – A variation of this curry is also prepared with mustard paste and dried green mango instead of the onion tomato gravy.

1981. My mother, who belongs to Mayurbhanj, discovered a new ingredient along with a new family. Tiny nuts that smelled and tasted divine. A whole sack had been procured for the wedding feast, to spruce up the kheer and the pulao. John, one of my grandfather's associates and a friend from his 'Shikar' days, had made it possible. He belonged to the tribes who called the dense forests of the Western belt their home. His knowledge of the forest terrain was impeccable. And he had access to the most precious forest resources. Chara was just one of those.

Mostly picked by gangs of teenage boys these days, the tiny berries are delicious but have very little flesh. Once dried, the hard shells are cracked in a 'dhenki' and then split using a chakki. Next, the hard shells are mostly removed by winnowing. The remaining bits and pieces of shells are painstakingly handpicked to reveal these tiny little gems. Trust the forest inhabitants, the original 'foragers' to discover and reclaim every little mite of nutrient from things that would be discarded by city folks without a thought. Not just char, even the fruits of Harida, Baheda and Tamarind have delicious kernels which were once consumed by people who had knowledge about them.

CHAR MANJI LADDU
(Charoli nut Laddoo)

While most people in Western Odisha love the *'Char koli,'* a sweet-sour berry, very few know about the seed extracted from it. It was left to the resourceful tribal women to carefully break the shell and extract the kernel which sells at a much higher price than the berries themselves. Added to *Muan, Khiri,* and pulao made in these parts of the state, these little nuts were among the 'indigenous dry fruits' along with the *'char magaj'* or watermelon seeds.

⏳ **Cooking time – 20 minutes**

 **Ingredients:**

- 1 cup charoli
- 2/3 cup jaggery

🍳 **Cooking:**

- Heat a pan. Add the seeds and toast for 3-4 minutes on a low flame. Remove to a plate and allow to cool down.

- Add 2-3 tbsp of water to the pan. Add the jaggery and allow it to melt.

- Keep stirring the jaggery until it has reached the right consistency. (Use the drop test mentioned in Arisa Pitha recipe)

- Add the toasted seeds and mix them. Switch off the flame and keep it aside until it is bearable to touch. Do not let it cool down completely as it will turn brittle and cannot be shaped.

- Dip your fingers in a bowl of water, pinch out small portions of the mixture and shape into laddus.

- Store in an airtight container.

- *[Tip- rub a little ghee/oil on a plate and spread out the mixture into a thin layer to make charoli chikkis.]*

SANKHA SARU BAIGANA TARKARI
(Taro and eggplant cooked with a light mustard base)

Taro is an irreplaceable ingredient in Odia dishes like *Dalma*, *Santula*, *Besara* and *Ghanta*. Although used in a smaller proportion as compared to other vegetables, it lends a cohesive quality to the preparation. Once cooked, it turns sticky and holds the lentils and vegetables together. This is why one should not add too much of this vegetable to any curry or overcook it if one does not want to end up with a gloopy dish.

Apart from the culinary aspect, taro offers numerous health benefits. It nourishes the digestive system, controls sugar levels, boosts the immune system, and speeds up blood circulation. Little wonder this vegetable is widely used during fasts like Navratri and even the 'no onion no garlic' days which are an integral part of Hindu culture.

A few decades ago, the taro plant, along with the plantain and drumstick, was an integral part of every garden/backyard in Odisha. The tubers were dug up only after the plants died (otherwise they tend to be itchy) and stored for use throughout the year. My parents still grow taro in their garden, although not in large quantities. It is enough to last a few months. The 'Sankha Saru' is a large variety of Taro and is so called as the shape resembles a conch. Apart from being used in regular Odia dishes, it is often dipped in a rice batter and pan-fried. But when the vegetable supply is low, it is made into a light curry with tomatoes and badi.

 **Preparation time – 30 minutes**

 **Ingredients:**

- 200 gm Taro cubes
- 1 large-sized eggplant
- 2 medium-sized country tomatoes

- 1/2 of a small onion
- 1 dry red chilli
- 2 pinch mustard seeds
- 1 pinch cumin seeds
- 2 pinch turmeric powder
- A handful of badi (dried lentil dumplings)
- 3 tsp vegetable oil
- Salt to taste

For the mustard paste:

- 2 tsp mustard seeds
- 2 dry red chillis
- 2-3 garlic flakes

Preparation:

- Grind the mustard seeds, garlic and red chilli into a fine paste.

Cooking:

- Heat 2 tsp oil in a wok. Add the badi and fry on a low flame until they start turning red. Remove and keep aside.

- Add the remaining oil to the same wok. Once hot, add the mustard seeds, cumin seeds and broken red chilli. Once the seeds start spluttering, add the coarsely chopped onion.

- Once the onion turns translucent, add the chopped tomatoes. Sprinkle a little salt over them and cover with a lid for 2 minutes to soften them.

- Remove the lids and smash the tomatoes. Cook for another 2-3 minutes.

- Dissolve the mustard paste in 1 cup water and pour slowly into the wok. This ensures that the sediments of the mustard paste do not go into the curry and turn it bitter.

- Now add the taro cubes, salt and turmeric. Cover with a lid for 3-4 mins. Add the eggplant cubes to the wok when the taro is half cooked. Cover it again and let it cook until the taro is just done. Do not overcook as the taro will turn sticky.

- Crush the badi lightly and add to the curry just before removing it from the flame.

- Serve with rice meals.

Note - Taro tends to absorb water and so does the lentil dumplings. So do not worry if there is any excess liquid remaining. It will be soaked up in some time.

During the winters, when flat beans and freshly prepared Sukhua are available in abundance, another version of this curry is prepared by adding these two ingredients. Substitute half of the taro used with flat beans and skip the badi while preparing this version.

CHUDA GHASA

(A sweet and crumbly dish made with flattened rice and coconut)

Flattened rice is traditionally made by the fishing communities to supplement their income during the monsoon months when fishing activities are on hold. This period also coincides with the harvest of the early ripening paddy varieties, which are suitable for this purpose. The flattened rice available during this season is naturally sweeter. As it ages, the simple sugars convert into more complex sugars. Hence, flattened rice is traditionally prepared and consumed during this time of the year.

Chuda Ghasa is a popular offering prepared in the pandals during Ganesh Chaturthi.

 **Preparation time – 20 minutes**

 **Ingredients:**

- 1 cups of beaten/flattened rice
- 1 cup finely grated coconut
- 2-3 tbsp ghee
- 4-5 tsp sugar
- A tiny bit of food-grade camphor
- A pinch of black cardamom powder
- 1-2 pinch freshly crushed black pepper
- A few slices of coconut

- Grind the flattened rice in a mixer-grinder to a coarse consistency. Transfer it to a plate/flat surface. Add the sugar and ghee. Sprinkle a few drops of water.

- Rub the mixture between the palms so that that warmth melts the ghee and it forms a texture that resembles breadcrumbs.

- Add the grated coconut, powdered spices and the powdered camphor. Sprinkle a little more water to moisten the mixture. Mix thoroughly. Take a fistful of the mixture and press it between your palm and fingers. If it holds shape, it is ready.

- One can add more ghee if it feels too dry. *In the pandals, adding some chopped cucumber/chopped apple/banana slices/ sweetened boondi serves the purpose.*

- Consume within the same day.

Note – Chuda Ghasa is one of the offerings during Bahuda Jatra. On regular days, it is served with Dalma as a popular breakfast option in Puri.

CHUDA KADALI CHAKATA

(Flattened rice mashed with banana and curd)

Soaked flattened rice mixed with ripe banana, jaggery, and milk/curd is a no-cook breakfast that has sustained many generations of Odias. And it is still relevant today as the perfect solution to beat the mad morning rush. It is a natural probiotic and helpful for maintaining gut health. There are many variations to this dish, with the poor farmers making one with the addition of jaggery and occasionally a ripe banana, while the Brahmin families are known for making more elaborate versions that mirror the patronage once enjoyed by them.

Unfortunately, this humble dish is being elbowed out by fancier cereals or 'ready to eat' mixes laced with sugar and preservatives.

I'm sharing a recipe for the elaborate version.

 **Preparation time – 5 minutes**

 **Ingredients:**

- 1 cup beaten/flattened rice
- ¼ cup finely grated coconut
- 1 ripe banana
- ¼ cup fresh curd
- 2 tbsp chenna
- 2-3 tsp jaggery/sugar
- A pinch of salt

Preparation:

- Wash and immediately strain the flattened rice.
- Transfer to a bowl. Add the banana and mash it. Add the rest of the ingredients and mix it.
- Serve immediately as it tends to oxidize fast due to the presence of ripe bananas.

KAKHARU BUTA DALI
(Pumpkin and Bengal gram dal)

A regular dish on the Odia breakfast and dinner menu, *Kakharu buta dali* goes well with roti, paratha, puri, and even upma. The locally grown pumpkin crop is harvested around late monsoon or early winter, and it finds its way into a number of dishes prepared during the winter months. If the skin is still green, the pumpkin has been harvested while it is tender. Tender pumpkin is made into delicious *Bhaja* or added to the greens as a bulking agent.

If the skin is an ashy orange, the pumpkin is fully ripe. This state is ideal for making dishes like Dalma, *Ghantaw, Besara, Mahura,* and *Sakara.* A well-ripened pumpkin can be preserved for a couple of months without refrigeration.

 **Cooking time – 30 minutes**

 **Ingredients:**

- 1 ½ cup chana dal
- 1 cup cubed pumpkin
- ½ cup potatoes
- ¼ cup freshly grated coconut
- 1 tsp crushed ginger
- 1 tsp roasted cumin-chilli powder
- 1 tbsp ghee
- 1 tsp sugar
- 2-3 dry red chillis
- ½ tsp cumin seeds
- 1 bay leaf
- ½ tsp turmeric
- 2/3 tsp salt

🍽 **Preparation:**

- Soak the chana dal for 3-4 hours. Wash and transfer to a pressure cooker, add the pumpkin and potato pieces along with 3 cups water. Add turmeric and salt. Close the lid and allow to cook for 2-3 whistles on medium flame.

- Remove from fire and allow steam to escape. Open the lid and check the dal. The dal should be cooked and just starting to turn mushy. [Adjust the consistency of dal at this stage if required. Remember it tends to thicken as it cools down]

- Heat the ghee in a wok. Add the bay leaf, red chillis, cumin seeds, and finally ginger.

- Sauté for 30 seconds and pour over the boiled dal.

- Add the sugar and let it simmer for 2-3 minutes. Finally, add the roasted cumin-chili powder and grated coconut and remove from the flame. Give a mix and serve hot.

> *Note - One can also add vegetables like ridge gourd, sweet potato and even green papaya to this preparation.*

KARADI LEMBU PAGAW

(A local condiment made with bamboo shoots and native lemon)

Another version of the pagaw rustled up with ingredients found during the monsoons. The fresh bamboo shoots have a nice bite but they lack the signature tang that develops with fermentation. A squeeze of fresh lemon and a spicy green chilli is all one needs to make this pagaw that never fails to tickle the taste buds.

The local varieties of limes available during monsoon have an irresistible aroma and take this condiment to the next level.

 **Preparation time – 5 minutes**

 **Ingredients:**

- 1 tbsp fresh bamboo shoots
- ½ of a lemon
- 1 green chilli
- Salt to taste

Preparation:

- Squeeze the lemon over the bamboo shoots. Mash in the green chilli and salt.
- Serve it with hot parboiled rice and dal.

MAKA BARA
(Fresh corn pancakes)

The tribals of Odisha grow a few native varieties of corn which are a secondary source of carbohydrates for them. During the lean period, corn is transformed into a vital source of food. Fresh corn is ground into a coarse paste with minimal seasoning like green chilli, and made into a thick pancake or Chakuli. Corn is also the preferred food for small children.

During the subsequent months, the corn is dried, powdered, and stored for usage throughout the year. Though there is no evidence of nixtamalization in these regions, it does not seem to cause any malnutrition because it is not the primary food component. It is usually cooked as a gruel along with other cereals and legumes.

Cooking Time – 15 minutes

Ingredients:

- 1 cup fresh corn
- 1 green chilli
- 2 garlic cloves
- 2 tsp oil
- Salt to taste

Cooking:

- Grind the corn into a coarse paste along with the chilli and garlic. Add salt and mix.

- Heat a griddle. Season it with a few drops of oil.

- Add small dollops of the paste and spread them into small discs about 1 cm thick. Drizzle oil around the circumference.

- Let then cook on a low flame till the bottom side is reddish brown. Flip it over and cook on the other side till brown.

- Serve with meals or as a snack.

Note - The husk or outer layers of corn are sometimes utilized by the tribals for wrapping and cooking food. Rice paste or millet paste is sandwiched between the layers and cooked on embers to make a primitive kind of pitha.

ASWINA (SEPTEMBER – OCTOBER)

Enter Sharad Rutu. The days are neither too hot nor too cold. A hint of winter is in the air. Wide swathes of 'Kashatandi' flowers swaying in the gentle breeze perk up the landscape. The moonlit nights are nothing less than magical. The once verdant paddy fields are fast turning into gold. Regular weeding and fertilization continue for the late-ripening varieties, even as the early varieties are harvested. More phased breaching of the bunds takes place as the paddy gets ready for harvest. Sowing work commences for the winter vegetables. Chillis, garlic, onion, tomato, and mustard are some of the crops sown during this month.

A very late variety of mushroom, called Nada Chattu, grows during this month. These mushrooms have an unusually long stem that stays underground, while a small cap is visible above the soil. It requires skill to pull them out carefully without breaking the meaty stem.

A significant agricultural festival, Garbhana Sankranti, falls during this month. As most paddy plants are in the reproductive phase, this period is compared to a woman's pregnancy. Hence, a special ritual is observed to pray for a plentiful harvest. 'Ghanta', a mix of several seasonal vegetables and pulses is cooked in most homes to mark this occasion. It is consumed by all family members and shared with friends and neighbours.

Major festivals like Aswina Navtratri and Pua Jiuntia fall during this month. A variety of dishes like Khiri, Khechudi and Tikhri are prepared during Navratri. Women keep a fast on Pua Jiuntia, and a number of vegetables are offered to the deity Dwitibahana along with Tikhri and Jagar. These offerings are consumed on the next day by the family members. The vegetables used for the offering are cooked into a 'Ghanta.' Like Chaitra Navratri, Aswina Navratri is also marked with animal sacrifices in most Shakti or Devi temples. In Bonaigarh, the local deity-, Kanta Kumari, is worshipped during these nine days.

In the coastal belt, the last day of this month is observed as Kumar Purnima with the belief that girls will find a handsome husband by praying to the Moon God. The day starts with an offering of Khai, cucumber, tender ridge gourd, coconut, banana and other fruits to the Sun God. These offerings are mashed together with chenna, pieces of sugarcane, sugar palm sprouts, and sugar during the evening. The mixture 'Chanda Chakata' is shaped into a crescent and offered to the Moon as it appears on the horizon. The sounds of the conchs blowing, bells ringing, and the 'hulahuli' arising from the neighbourhood creates a beautiful atmosphere. In the older days, girls from the village used to gather near a pond for this ritual. This practice was undoubtedly created to forge a sense of sisterhood and keep the community together.

Another festival observed during this month is Janhi Osa. The bright yellow flowers blooming on trailing ridge gourd vines dot the landscape in rural Odisha in this season. Unmarried girls collect these flowers and decorate the 'Tulsi Chaura,' a small structure built around the sacred 'Tulsi' plant, throughout the month. Beautiful patterns called 'Muruja' are created with natural colours, and 'Janhi Osa' song is recited by the girls. Offerings consist of Lia, Ukhuda and local fruits on all the days except for the last one when various kinds of 'pitha' are offered. There is a restriction on consumption of non-veg and ridge gourd during this period. In recent years, the custom seems to be fading away.

What's on the menu this month

PATALGHANTA BHENDI HENDUA

(Tomatoes and okra cooked with dried bamboo shoots)

Hendua, or dehydrated bamboo shoot, is one of the lesser-known ingredients from Western Odisha. It has a sharp and distinctive smell and lends tanginess and flavour to a dish. Since it provides a gustatory sensation quite unlike anything, one can either love it or hate it. But it is almost impossible to ignore. And a little goes a long way so one needs to use it judiciously. There are variations to this recipe as people add their tweaks and tricks to it.

This version was shared by a close friend's mother.

⏳ **Cooking time – 15-20 minutes**

 **Ingredients:**

- 3 large tomatoes
- 5-6 ladies finger / okra
- 3-4 green chillis
- 1 ½ tsp mustard-garlic paste
- ¼ tsp mustard seeds
- 1 tbsp hendua
- 2-3 pinch turmeric
- 3 tsp oil
- Salt to taste

🍽️ **Preparation:**

- Chop the tomato into small pieces. Cut the okra into inch-long pieces.
- Wash and soak the hendua in ¼ cup warm water for 5 minutes. Drain and squeeze out the remaining water.
- Dilute the mustard paste with ½ cup water.

 Cooking:

- Heat the oil in a wok. Add the mustard seeds and the slit green chillis.

- Once the chillis start to brown, add the hendua and fry for 1-2 minutes.

- Add the chopped okra and fry lightly for 2-3 minutes. Finally, add the chopped tomatoes, reduce the flame and allow it to cook until the tomatoes have turned mushy.

- Add the diluted mustard paste, turmeric and salt, and cook on medium flame for 4-5 minutes until any raw smell/taste has gone off.

- Serve it with white rice.

An evergreen clump of banana and plantain plants was the obligatory sight in every Odia house in earlier days. This is true even today for smaller towns and villages where most houses have a small garden patch. The presence of the banana grove is directly related to its sheer utility. Every part of the plant, from the stem to the flower and the fruit, makes it to the kitchen and beyond.

While the flower, fruit, and stem are transformed into an array of incredible dishes, the leaf serves as a receptacle for serving them. Ripe bananas are possibly the handiest snack one can find in the tropics while the overripe ones go straight into malpua, kakara and even a delicious chakata (mashed dish made with banana and dairy products). The plant is highly revered, and a part of every marriage, pooja or 'homa' conducted in homes and temples. Even the Gods are served 'bhoga' or offering on the shiny leaves. It is a handy substitute for offering 'pinda' or 'pitru bhojana' if jackfruit leaves are not readily available. Even the curved outer fibrous portions of the stem are turned into makeshift slippers (during Rajaw) and boats (during Boita Bandana).

Banana varieties like Patakapara, Amruta keli, Champa, Chini Champa, and Kaathiya were cultivated in most homes along with the Bantala Kadali (Plantain). And people knew which one's inflorescence could be cooked directly and the ones that needed additional prepping make it palatable.

KADALI BHANDA PATUA

(A spicy dish cooked with plantain/banana inflorescence)

If one finds prepping the banana stem tough, this ingredient cranks up the difficulty level by a good number of notches. Peeling the banana inflorescence and cleaning the flowers is a task that needs to be taken up at leisure. In this recipe, I have used the banana heart or the innermost part of the inflorescence while the outer layers went into making crispy 'baras.' One discerns that one has reached the heart or innermost part of the inflorescence, where it becomes increasingly difficult to peel off the bracts.

 **Cooking time – 20 minutes**

 **Ingredients:**

- 2 banana hearts
- 1 medium-sized potato
- 2 tsp mustard seeds (I use the light brown ones)
- 1 tsp poppy seeds
- 2 fat garlic cloves
- 1-2 hot green chilli
- 3 tsp mustard oil (+ 1 tsp for drizzling while serving)
- 1/4 tsp turmeric
- 1/4 tsp salt to taste

Method

- Soak the mustard and poppy seeds for 2-3 hours.
- Transfer to a mixer/chutney jar along with the green chilli and garlic pods. Chop the banana heart and add to this jar. Grind into a smooth paste.
- Wash and chop the potato into thin long pieces.

- Heat the oil in a heavy-bottomed wok. Break a green chilli and add it to the hot oil.

- Add the chopped potatoes and sauté for a minute on high. Tip the contents of the chutney jar into the wok. Add the salt and turmeric. Sauté for another minute before lowering the flame and covering it with a heavy lid.

- Open the lid after 5-6 minutes and give it a mix while taking care to scrape the bottom. If it looks too dry, sprinkle a little water over it. Cover once again and leave it for 3-4 minutes. Open and check if the raw smell is gone. This means the dish is ready.

- Remove from the stove. Serve hot with a drizzle of mustard oil on top.

Note – In some families, poppy seeds are not used in this recipe. Also, adjust the amount of green chilli as per one's tolerance levels.

I prefer using the inflorescence of a local variety called Champa as it is not at all bitter.

SARU PATALGHANTA KHATTA

(A tangy dish cooked with taro and tomatoes)

Sometime towards the end of this month, the first of the season's tomatoes are available in the local markets. These tart ones are perfect for making a saliva-jerking 'Khatta.' In Odia, 'Khatta' translates to 'sour.' In the Western districts, it stays true to the word. In contrast, the coastal version seems like a masquerade with the addition of enough sugar to reduce the tartness to a whimpering note. The irony is not lost on our guests.

I'm sharing the Western Odisha version, which is what one needs during this time of the year to rouse those tastebuds after a bout of seasonal flu.

Cooking time – 20-25 minutes

Ingredients:

- 200 gm taro
- 200 gm country tomatoes
- 2 tsp mustard seeds (+ ½ tsp for tempering)
- 1/2 tsp cumin seeds
- 2 dry red chillis
- 10-12 garlic cloves
- 2 green chillis
- 2-3 tsp mustard oil
- 2/3 tsp salt
- 1/2 tsp turmeric

🍽 Preparation:

- Soak and grind the mustard seeds, cumin seeds, garlic and dry red chilli into a fine paste.

- Boil the taro and keep it aside until it cools down. Peel and cut into big chunks.

🫕 Cooking:

- Heat a wok. Add the mustard oil and let it heat until smoking.

- Add the mustard seeds and slit green chilli.

- Once the seeds start popping, add the diced tomatoes. Add salt and turmeric.

- Cover for 2-3 minutes to soften the tomatoes. Open the lid and crush the tomatoes with the back of a heavy spoon/ladle. Cook for a while until the tomatoes turn into a paste.

- Add the mustard paste diluted with about 1 cup water. Bring to a boil and let it simmer for 2-3 minutes before adding the boiled taro chunks.

- Adjust the amount of the water depending on the desired consistency and the amount of gravy to be retained. Let it simmer for 5-6 minutes before switching off the flame.

- Serve hot with rice meals.

Note – Some folks in western Odisha prefer adding Karadi (bamboo shoots) or Hendua (fermented and dried bamboo shoots) to this dish.

****Both karadi and hendua are usually added to the oil right after the tempering and sautéed for 1-2 minutes as it helps to release the aroma of these ingredients.*

MUGRI LADDU

(Sweetened laddoo made with cowpeas)

The local produce of a region has a marked influence on the dishes prepared in that geography. Unlike the coastal parts where dairy is surplus and most sweets are dairy-based, lentil-based sweets are the hallmark of Western Odisha cuisine. Sadly, most of them are barely mentioned beyond their geographical boundaries.

Mugri Laddu is one such preparation that is made from red cowpeas, which have a naturally sweet taste and a creamy texture. Called 'rumha dali' or 'jhunga' in the local dialect, cowpeas are among the lentils cultivated in Western Odisha. They can withstand drought conditions better than most lentils, a bonus in these arid regions. Cowpeas are cooked as a dal or added to various preparations.

But on special occasions, they are used to cook sweets like murgi ladu or ras bara.

 **Preparation time – 30 minutes**

 **Ingredients:**

- 1 cup rumha dali (lobia)
- 1/4 cup arwa chaula (raw rice)
- 1 cup jaggery
- Oil for deep frying

Preparation:

- Soak the rice and cowpeas. Grind into a smooth paste.
- Heat the oil. But don't let it smoke. Use a 'jali chattu' or perforated spoon/ladle like the one used for making boondi.

- Hold the perforated ladle near the oil. Drop a little batter on it and press using a serving spoon. Fry small batches at a time to avoid them from sticking together and to make them crisp.

- Heat another wok. Add the jaggery and a little water. Bring to a boil. Once the foam starts to form, check for readiness by dropping some in a bowl of cold water. Once it starts to hold shape, immediately remove the wok from the stove. [Use drop test mentioned in earlier recipes]

- Add the boondi and mix thoroughly. Once it is bearable to touch, moisten hands with water and divide them into sections before shaping each one into a ball.

- Store in an air-tight container once the balls have cooled down completely.

DUDURA PITHA
(A deep-fried rice and lentil cake)

A traditional deep-fried pitha prepared in Western Odisha. It is made on festive days, especially during Nuakhai and Navratri. It is offered to Maa Samaleswari, the presiding deity of Sambalpur and a much-revered Goddess in Western Odisha and neighbouring Chhattisgarh.

⏳ **Cooking Time – 30 minutes**

 **Ingredients:**

- 1 cup aromatic rice
- ½ cup split moong dal
- ¼ cup finely chopped coconut
- ½ cup jaggery
- 1 tsp crushed fennel seeds
- A pinch of baking soda (optional)
- Oil for deep frying

🍽️ **Preparation:**

- Wash and soak the rice and dal for 4-5 hours. Grind into a smooth paste having a slightly thick consistency.
- Transfer to a mixing bowl and add the jaggery, coconut and fennel. Mix it till the jaggery is completely dissolved. Let it rest for 1-2 hours.
- Whisk for 2-3 minutes.

- Heat enough oil in a wok for deep frying. Once the oil is hot, slowly pour a ladle of the batter into the wok. Allow it to cook on a medium flame till it starts to puff up. Do not touch it before it is completely puffed.

- Slowly flip it over and let it cook on the other side as well. Remove from the wok and keep aside.

- Repeat the same process for the remaining batter.

> *Note – Some people use black lentils instead of split moong to make Dudura pitha.*

KHUDAW PITHA
(A deep-fried cake made with broken rice)

Khudaw Pitha is almost exclusively made by the Agharia community in Western Odisha. Usually prepared during the Pitru Shradha observed in the month of Aswina, it is a stellar example of the diversity that exists within the boundaries of Odia cuisine. Shaped by varying geographies and communities over centuries, these micro-cuisines are fast disappearing as people no longer take pride in their identity.

 **Cooking time – 1 hour**

Ingredients:

- 200 gm Jaggery (approx.)
- 250 gm *Khudaw* (broken rice)
- 50 gm *Khaee* (popped rice)
- 3-4 tbsp curd
- 2-3 tsp oil
- 1/8 tsp salt
- Extra oil for deep frying

Cooking:

- Take the popped rice in a mixing bowl and add 3-4 cups of water. Soak for 30 minutes.
- Add the jaggery to a wok along with 1 cup of water approximately. Let it melt on a low flame and turn into a syrup.
- Take the broken rice in a big mixing bowl. Sprinkle the salt over it.
- Heat 3-4 tbsp oil and pour over the broken rice. Mix until it reaches breadcrumb consistency.

- Next, add the curd and the soaked popped rice after squeezing out all the water. [Add the soaked popped rice in small batches and keep checking the mixture so that it does not become too wet.]

- Take small portions of the mixture and make balls out of it.

- Deep fry the balls on low flame until they turn brown on all sides. Do not crowd the wok.

- Remove the fried balls from the wok and put them in the warm jaggery syrup for 5 minutes. Remove and keep aside.

- Can be consumed once it has cooled down.

> The Aghria community is a group of Hindu settlers who migrated from the Northern parts of the country around the year 1550 AD due to persecution by the Muslims. They describe themselves as the descendants of the historical character of Bidur (from Mahabharata). They are settled in Odisha and Chhattisgarh. Most community members are rich landholders or merchants in today's time. While they have assimilated most Odia customs, their cuisine, although sourced from local ingredients, retains a distinctive quality. The word 'Aa-gharia' or one without a home, is a reference to their archaic status as asylum-seekers.

PEJ PITHA

(A kind of rice cake made with rice and rice starch)

Pej - the excess water drained off after cooking rice. Bursting with nutrients. Too precious to go down the drain. It was once consumed by toiling rural folks, babies, people with an upset tummy, cattle, or even poured into the roots of plants. The more sophisticated folks used it as 'mandaw' or starch to crisp their dhotis and cotton sarees.

Starch, in any form, had never been tagged as the villain in Indian cuisine until people realized they could make easy money by promoting protein at the cost of carbohydrates.

The usage of 'pej' in a pitha (or even in the mandia pej) proves beyond doubt that ours has always been a culture of sustainability. Raw rice and parboiled rice are used together in this recipe which is very hyper-local and limited to a small part of Bonaigarh.

⏳ **Cooking time – 30 minutes**

 **Ingredients:**

- 1-2 cups Pej (from parboiled rice)
- 1 cup raw rice
- 3-4 tbsp oil (needs a generous amount of oil)
- Salt to taste

 **Preparation:**

- Wash and soak the raw rice for 3-4 hours.
- Discard the water used for soaking and grind it into a smooth paste.
- Dilute this rice paste with the cooled pej from the parboiled rice to get a watery batter.
- Add salt to this batter.

Cooking:

- Heat a wok. Add 1-2 tsp oil to it. Add 1-2 ladles of the batter. Drizzle a little oil on the sides.

- Cover and cook until the bottom layer is done (It will develop a golden colour).

- Flip it carefully, drizzle more oil on the sides and cover it again until done.

- Once it develops a golden colour on both sides and feels a little firm to handle, it is done. Remove from the wok.

- It will be very soft even after it is cooked. Let it cool down a bit before eating as it tends to trap a lot of heat due to its texture.

> *Note – Parboiled rice is consumed daily in most Odia homes. This is one of the preferred ways to consume the excess water used for cooking the rice. Adding it to the Kanji is another way to use it up.*

USNA CHAKULI

(Par-boiled rice pancake)

Unlike the rest of the state, Chakuli is also prepared with parboiled rice in Sundargarh and some of the nearby areas. Parboiled rice is preferred as it is easier to digest and also a cheaper alternative to the raw rice-black lentil combination, which is the regular version. And not just Chakuli, this preference for parboiled rice is evident in dishes like the Pej pitha, Bhabra pitha and even the Usna Jau consumed in these parts.

The Usna chakuli batter is of thinner consistency as compared to regular Chakuli batter and a little milk is added just before cooking for extra crispiness.

 **Preparation time – 30 minutes**

 **Ingredients:**

- 1 cup parboiled rice
- 2 tbsp milk
- 1/3 tsp salt
- Oil for cooking the chakuli

Preparation:

- Wash and soak the parboiled rice for 6 -7 hours. Parboiled rice usually takes longer to soak than raw rice.
- Grind into a smooth paste and keep aside for 2 hours.
- Add the milk and salt. Adjust the water to get a consistency which is a little thinner than the dosa batter.

Cooking:

- Heat a griddle. Season it with a few drops of oil.

- Add a ladle of the batter and quickly turn the griddle to spread the batter (it's like making crepes).

- Drizzle a little oil on all sides and wait for 2-3 minutes.

- Flip it over and cook on the other side as well.

- Serve warm with milk or molasses.

Note – In the villages, a flat earthen vessel called 'palama' or 'tai' is used for making different kinds of chakuli or even the Chittau/ Bhabra pitha

MANDIYA TIKHRI

(A thick custard made with finger millet)

Tikhri is a millet-based sweet with a custard pudding-like texture and consistency. Different kinds of Tikhri are usually prepared as an offerings during fasts like Navratri and Pua Jiuntia. They are consumed to keep the stomach cool during the long hours of fasting undertaken during those nine days.

Mandiya Tikhri is also prepared throughout the year, especially as breakfast during the hot summer months. It is cooked in the evening and left to ferment overnight. It is partaken in the morning, as it is, or with curd and jaggery. It helps keep the stomach cool and provides energy.

This is the recipe for the festive version which is always consumed fresh (not fermented).

 **Cooking time – 20 minutes**

 **Ingredients:**

- 1 cup ragi flour
- 3 cups water
- 1 cup jaggery (adjust as per preference)
- 1-2 bay leaves
- A pinch of cardamom powder (optional)
- 1/2 tsp ghee
- 1/4 tsp salt

🍽️ Preparation:

- Mix the ragi flour with 3 cups water. Strain the liquid portion and discard the solids.

- Transfer the liquid into a thick-bottomed wok and add the salt, jaggery and spices.

🍲 Cooking:

- Bring to boil on a low flame while stirring continuously as it tends to catch at the bottom very easily.

- After 8-10 minutes, it starts turning thick and glossy. Add the ghee at this point and cook for another minute or two.

- Switch off the flame and pour onto a greased mould or plate. Once it has cooled down completely, cut it into diamond-shaped pieces.

- Serve it warm or cold.

Note – ** A raw paste of finger millet diluted with water is considered a home remedy for the loosies which are rather common during the hot dry summers.

***Easy tip to dissolve finger millet flour - Add finger millet flour to water (1:4 ratio) and let it stand for 30 minutes. It will dissolve without any lumps. Give it a good stir before using it in the recipe.

MUNG TIKHRI

(A custard made with split moong)

Another version of the Tikhri, this one is made from split moong dal.

Moong is one of the hardiest pulses, which makes it a good choice for the dry climate of Western Odisha. Apart from its adaptability, the blood-sugar regulating and gut-friendly properties of green moong make it an ideal ingredient for inclusion in the 'fasting' menu. Traditionally, split moong dal was prepared by coarsely grinding the whole mung beans in a milling stone. The split lentils were soaked in water and rubbed to loosen/dislodge the skins. The skins being lighter in weight, floated to the surface and were removed by decantation.

 **Cooking time – 20 minutes**

Ingredients:

- 1 cup split and skinned moong dal
- 2 cups water
- 2/3 cup sugar
- 1-2 bay leaves (Teja patra)
- A pinch of cardamom powder (optional)
- 1 tsp ghee
- 1-2 pinch of salt

 **Preparation:**

- Wash and soak the moong dal for 2-3 hours.
- Grind into a smooth paste with ½ cup water.

- Take 2 cups of water in a thick-bottomed wok. Add the salt, sugar and bay leaf. Bring to a boil. Let it boil for 2-3 minutes.

- Pour the moong dal batter slowly into the wok while stirring continuously.

- After 10-12 minutes, it starts turning thick. Add the ghee at this point and cook for another minute or two.

- Switch off the flame and pour onto a greased mould or plate. Once it has cooled down completely, cut it into diamond-shaped pieces.

- Serve it warm or cold.

PALUA KHIRI

(A thin custard made with arrowroot chunks and milk)

A light kheer made from arrowroot chunks, it is considered to be one of the best foods for keeping the stomach cool. It is also useful for addressing problems like acidity that crop up during or after long fasts.

If is often given as food during fever and dysentery due to its anti-inflammatory and electrolyte balancing properties. It also has more protein and other nutrients in comparison to any other starchy root vegetable.

 **Cooking time – 20 minutes**

 **Ingredients:**

- ½ cup Arrowroot chunks
- 2 cups water
- ½ cup milk
- 2/3 cup sugar (adjust as per preference)
- 1-2 bay leaves

Preparation:

- Soak the arrowroot chunks in 3 cups of water for 1-2 hours in a big mixing bowl. Discard this water by gently decanting it. It gets rid of any impurities present in the arrowroot.

- Add 3 cups water to the remaining arrowroot slurry and give it a good stir.

Cooking:

- Transfer to a thick-bottomed wok. Add the torn bay leaf. Bring to boil on a low flame while stirring continuously as it tends to catch at the bottom very easily.

- After 8-10 minutes, it starts to thicken slightly. Add the warm milk and sugar at this point.

- Switch off the flame and allow it to cool down completely.

- Serve cold.

Note – Arrowroot is one of the best foods for the stomach as it is very easy to digest. It also helps keep the stomach cool and hence, palua Khiri, palua tikhri and even palua manda are popular during fasts.

** Arrowroot diluted with water and sweetened with a little rock sugar is considered a home remedy for the loosies

DWITIYA GHANTA
(A mixed vegetable and sprouted lentil preparation)

Dwitibahana Osa is a fast observed by women in Odisha for the well-being of their children. Childless women also follow this ritual in the hope of conceiving a child. The presiding deity 'Dwitibahana' is offered a variety of seasonal vegetables and sprouted legumes/pulses to appease him. On the next day, these offerings are made into the 'Ghanta,' a mixed vegetable delicacy. Not only is it consumed by the fasting women and their families, but 'Ghanta', which is made in huge quantities, is distributed among the neighbours too.

The concept of fasting revolves around detoxifying the body to get rid of the accumulated toxins and improving the metabolism, which leads to better tissue health. Consumption of seasonal and nutritious food after the fasting period leads to better absorption of nutrients. The seasonal vegetables, sprouts, plantain and raw papaya used in this preparation are rich in folic acid is usually prescribed by doctors to women who are trying to conceive. Looking at it from a broader perspective, this festival was designed to help women achieve optimal health, which, in turn, increased the chances of conceiving. The usage of such a large number of ingredients ensured that any nutritional gaps were closed.

Another aspect of this dish is that it is symbolic of fertility. This is conveyed by using sprouts and mature vegetables that have gone to seed.

 **Cooking time – 1 hour**

 **Ingredients:**

- 1 cup diced pumpkin
- ½ cup ash gourd cubes

- ½ cup plantain cubes
- ½ cup yam cubes
- ½ cup colocasia cubes
- ½ cup raw papaya pieces
- ½ cup eggplant cubes
- ½ cup string beans (cut into 2" pieces)
- 2-3 pieces Elephant apple (Oau) [Use tomato as a substitute if not available]
- 1 cup ripe cucumber (deseeded and cubed)
- ½ cup teasel gourd (cut into half)
- 4 cups sprouts (yellow peas + chick peas + green moong + Bengal gram),
- 1 coconut (half grated and half chopped)
- 2-inch ginger
- 1 ½ tsp turmeric
- 3-4 tsp jeera-lanka gunda (roasted cumin chili powder)
- 4 tbsp ghee
- 4-5 dry red chilli
- 1 tsp cumin (or)1 tsp pancha phutana
- 2-3 bay leaves
- 3-4 tsp sugar
- Salt to taste
- 1/2 tsp black pepper powder (adjust as per preference)

Garnishing:

- 2-3 tbsp grated coconut
- 4 tbsp chopped coriander leaves

Cooking:

- Put all the vegetables into one pressure cooker. Add salt and turmeric and cook for 1 whistle. Remove from flame and keep aside until steam escapes.

- Put the sprouts and chopped coconut slices into another pressure cooker. Add salt and turmeric and cook for 2 whistles. Remove from flame and keep aside until steam escapes.

- Heat 2 tbs of ghee in a large wok. Add the jeera, bay leaves and broken red chilli. Fry for 1 min.

- Add the boiled vegetables and sprouts. Add crushed ginger.

- Mix well and cook covered for 4-5 minutes.

- Add the pepper powder, sugar, jeera-lanka gunda and grated coconut. Mix together and remove from the flame.

- Garnish with remaining grated coconut and coriander leaves. Sprinkle the remaining ghee over the ghanta.

- Serve with rice/roti/paratha or even by itself.

Note – Some people add a masala paste of cumin, coriander seeds, ginger and cinnamon to this recipe.

Recipes handed down across generations are echoes of a bygone era. They speak volumes about the collective experiences of the people, their daily habits and their attitude towards life, even as they capture the tectonic shift that takes place over generations.

Misamisi saag or 'mixed greens' is one of those recipes that sings eloquent stories around a life that involved foraging. Whether it was a visit to a water body for daily ablutions or making daily rounds of the rice fields, the women were instinctively trained to keep an eye on edible stuff that could supplement the family's everyday meals. Lovingly gathered into a cosy knot at the corner of the cotton saree, it was speckled with a special kind of love and inherited wisdom. These ladies knew their food like the back of their hands.

A creeper plucked here, a fistful of leaves foraged there, a little something sourced from the backyard, everything was cooked together with a bulking ingredient like pumpkin, taro or eggplant. When boiled down to a watery consistency and topped with a flavourful tempering, it turned into a dish that was nutritious and would pair very well with the 'Bagada chaula' bhata or the coarse red parboiled rice that was consumed on an everyday basis. Foods like these were something of a necessity in large families with lots of mouths to feed.

But with access to electricity and with mass migration leading to a decline in farming, the habits that sustained such foraging practices gradually declined. The foraging ladies were then limited to their own backyards and kitchen gardens. But as they say, old habits die hard. Pumpkin leaves, radish leaves, colocasia leaves and stems, amaranthus leaves and stems (and root too), spinach, potato leaves, sweet potato leaves, and even the so-called weeds like kenna saag, nuni saag and puruni saag were happily thrown into the pot along with whatever primary greens or vegetables were being cooked on the day.

The addition of vegetables is primarily done to bulk up the dish, reduce or downplay the bitter notes carried by any of the greens and add texture or crunch to the final preparation.

There are primarily 4 categories into which all the 'misamisi sagaw' recipes can be divided:

With the addition of vegetables and without mustard paste – Greens used primarily are cauliflower leaves, spinach, mustard greens, radish greens, amaranthus leaves and drumstick leaves. Vegetables used are ridge gourd, okra, pumpkin, yard long beans and eggplant.

With the addition of vegetables and mustard paste - Greens used primarily are tender taro leaves, pumpkin leaves, ash gourd leaves, bottle gourd leaves, amaranthus leaves, Malabar spinach leaves and potato/sweet potato leaves. Vegetables used are pumpkin, taro and eggplant

A stir fry with lots of garlic and onions – different kinds of amaranthus, drumstick leaves, sunsunia saag, barada saag, kenna saag and even tender water spinach leaves.

With the addition of coarsely powdered lentils or rice (Chuna paka) - Greens used primarily are channa sagaw, ash gourd leaves, pumpkin leaves, drumstick leaves, some kinds of amaranthus and in others like potato leaves, sweet potato leaves, ivy gourd leaves, snake gourd leaves, purslane, kansari, Malabar spinach, and taro leaves are added in a small quantity. The mixed greens are cooked in a pot with water. Roasted and finely ground lentils like mung, black lentils, and horse gram are added to it and allowed to cook together for a few minutes. Finally, everything is mashed coarsely and removed from the flame. A tempering is added over it at the end.

MISAMISI SAGAW

(Mixed greens cooked in a rustic style)

'Chuna-paka sagaw' or 'ghura saag' as people call it in Odisha, is one of the best methods of cooking the seasonal greens as the dish exhibits a certain wholesome quality. Cooked in a covered earthen pot, they retain every bit of their aroma and nutrients.

The consistency and composition of this dish is such that it eliminates the need for another side dish. Chuna-paka sagaw and hot rice are relished with a little 'pagaw' on the side.

 **Cooking time – 40 minutes**

 **Ingredients:**

- 1/2 cup young radish leaves
- 1 cup amaranthus leaves
- 1 cup pumpkin leaves
- ½ cup potato leaves
- ½ cup ash gourd leaves
- ½ cup spinach
- 1 cup pumpkin (cut into small pieces)
- 1 cup eggplant (cut into small pieces)
- 1 medium-sized potato (optional)
- 2/3 cup roasted black lentil/horse gram (coarsely powdered)
- Salt to taste

For tempering:

- 2-3 dry red chillis
- ½ tsp mustard seeds
- 10-12 garlic cloves (slightly crushed)
- 2 tsp mustard oil

🍽 Preparation:

- Bring 3 cups of water to a boil in a deep vessel.   Add   the pumpkin and potato along with the finely chopped greens. Boil it on high flame.

- Once the vegetables are half done, add the eggplant cubes. Boil for 3-4 minutes on high before adding the powdered lentils. Cover the vessel and lower the flame. Let it cook for 7-8 minutes.

- Uncover the vessel and use a heavy ladle to mix everything into a pulp. Let it simmer for some more time until the excess water is absorbed and it thickens to a slurry.

- Heat a wok. Add the oil. Add the broken red chilli and mustard seeds. Once the seeds start spluttering, add the crushed garlic. Allow the garlic to turn a light brown.

- Pour it over the simmering greens and mix.

- Serve hot with rice meals.

Monocropping is a relatively new concept that works on the idea of capitalism. It shows no regard for the natural ecosystem where flora and fauna complement each other. Some plants are known to fix the nitrogen levels of the soil. Others keep pests at bay. And then, there are some more which acts as protective barrier for other plants. The old ways of farming capitalized on this knowledge and hence, farmlands were rich ecosystems that yielded much more than one major crop. The paddy-fish co-cultivation is a stellar example of such an ecosystem. 'Bila maccha' or fish found in rice fields that were irrigated with water from flooded rivers were a common thing in the era before green revolution. These paddy fields also yielded a rich variety of greens throughout the year. Many of the foraged greens that went into a misamusi sagaw came from such fields.

MAHUKA SIMBA RAEE

(Sword beans cooked with a dash of mustard paste)

Mahuka Simba or Sword beans are consumed in the rural pockets of coastal Odisha. These beans are harvested at a tender stage before they develop the tough fibres, turning them inedible. Sighting these beans at the local markets is becoming increasingly rare as the diversity on our plate shrinks, and small-time sellers fail to find buyers for local produce like this.

 **Cooking time – 30 minutes**

 **Ingredients:**

- 200 gm sword beans
- 1-2 tsp mustard paste
- 1 medium-sized tomato
- 5-6 garlic cloves
- 1-2 dry red chilli
- 1/8 tsp mustard seeds
- 3-4 tsp mustard oil
- 1/5 tsp turmeric
- Salt to taste

Cooking:

- Cut the sword beans into small pieces.
- Boil 3-4 cups of water in a saucepan. Add the sword beans, a little salt and turmeric. Let it boil for 5 minutes. Discard this water.
- Heat a wok. Add the oil. Once it is hot, add the broken red chilli and mustard seeds. Once it starts spluttering, add the garlic and sauté it until it turns golden.

- Add the boiled beans, finely chopped tomato and the mustard paste. Add salt and a little turmeric. Sauté for 2-3 minutes.

- Add ½ cup water and bring to a boil. Simmer until almost all water evaporates.

- Serve warm with rice.

KARTIKA (OCTOBER – NOVEMBER)

The onset of *Hemant Rutu.* The days are pleasant, but the nights are getting colder. Almost all the paddy has ripened, and the fields gleam like gold under the bright sun. It is a busy time for farmers and their farm hands as harvesting of paddy, lentils, and groundnuts is underway. Sowing of other winter crops, sugarcane, and potato happens during this month.

It is the holiest month according to the Odia Calendar, and there are multiple restrictions regarding food, and even general behaviour. Many people give up non-vegetarian food for the entire month. Certain vegetables and lentils are barred from the kitchens during this period. While it might appear religious and even superstitious on the surface, the rationale behind it is sound. The diet recommendations and prohibitions help cleanse and season the body to deal with the colder months when the 'agni' or the digestive fire is at its peak. The day starts with an early morning dip, or 'buda,' in a water body. It is well established that showering with cold water improves blood circulation and boosts metabolism. The diet that follows is easy on the stomach, helps manage the Agni and keep it going strong.

This month is characterized by the '*Habisa*' rituals. The word has a Vedic origin and is used to refer to food offerings used in fire sacrifices. However, the term is also used in the context of the human stomach being a sacrificial fire-pit and the 'agni' being the universal fire. Hence, any food item that conforms to a certain standard of purity can be categorized as 'Habisa.' Devotees observing 'Habisa,' keep a partial fast on Mondays and visit Shiva temples. They eat a single meal consisting of '*arua*' and Habisa Dalma, a frugal preparation that adheres to local and seasonal ingredients.

Kartika Purnima, the holiest day in the Hindu Calendar, is the major festival celebrated this month. *Boita banadana*, the symbolic sailing of boats in various water bodies, is done on this day to commemorate the rich maritime trade history of Odisha dating back to the 3rd Century B.C. Sadhabas, a sea-faring business community used to sail to the far-off islands of South-East Asia and China in huge ships called *Boitas* during this month and return during the summer months. Diamonds, elephants, ivory, sandalwood, paper, betel nuts, rice, fine textiles, and fabrics were some of the commodities traded by them. They took advantage of the trade winds blowing along the equator to sail across the seas. The retreating monsoon or North East monsoon blowing from mid-October to January was leveraged for the onward journey, while the advancing South West monsoon wind blowing from June to September was leveraged for the return journey. They followed a path along the coastline until Sri Lanka and then, sailed further along the equator. This short stoppage allowed them to load fresh water and food into the boats. During the later centuries, Buddhism travelled to Sri Lanka and the rest of the world by this sea-route.

Traditionally, the boats floated on Boita Bandana are made from eco-friendly materials like the outer concave layers of banana stem and 'sola' (Indian cork.) But nowadays, colourful boats made with paper and thermocol have taken over. Even today, festivals like Boita Bandana, *Khudurukuni osa* and fairs like *Bali Jatra* remind the Odia people of the past glory of their ancestors. But unlike the well-documented 'Columbian exchange,' which witnessed the migration of flora and fauna across continents, the exchanges of the Sadhabas remain largely undocumented.

The primary marriage season in Odisha starts from this month. With money flowing in through the sale of the harvest, the marriage expenses are easier to manage.

What's on the menu this month

Panchuka or the five days of abstinence in the Odia calendar. As the holy month of Kartika draws to a closure, the religious fervour goes up by a few notches, and folks who had not given up nonvegetarian food for the entire month turn vegetarian. Even onion and garlic are off the menu. For some folks, Panchuka begins on the day of 'Anla Nabami' while others adhere to it from the day of Ekadashi. It is purely a matter of personal belief rather than something which is backed by evidence. And belief mingled with a need for validation can sometimes give rise to urban legends. Like the one which says that even the crane gives up fish during these five days. A story that is likely attributed to another mythological tale that mentions Lord Vishnu awakening from his slumber after four months on the day of Ekadashi and taking the disguise of a fish to reclaim the Vedas stolen by the asura, Hayagriva.

But 'Panchuka' or for that matter, the month of Kartika, is not just about abstaining from food. While it explicitly calls for giving up non-vegetarian food, certain vegetables, grains, and all greens except Agasti are also forbidden; that is just about the easy part of it. It is marked as a period of abstinence from everything that keeps one from attaining Moksha – right from consumption of intoxicating substances to restraining one's speech and sexual conduct. People are expected to immerse themselves in the scriptures or chant the name of the Almighty. So, one can say that in some ways, it is similar to 'Paryushan Parva' of the Jains. Both are a time to introspect on one's actions and purify oneself from the accumulated sins. However, with the passage of time, the significance of Panchuka or even the month of 'Kartika' has been reduced to a period that calls for dietary restraints or if one is more religiously inclined, reading the Kartika Mahatyma on a daily basis.

Coming back to the food practices followed during the month of Kartika, it is interesting to note how different regions have modified the ingredients used in the Habisa Dalma, an almost iconic dish prepared during this time of the year. Shorn of the golden glow of turmeric, this spartan dish is symbolic of the 'Habisyali' widows who flock to Puri to perform the most rigorous version of this 'Vrat,' subsisting on just a single meal taken before sunset for an entire month. With a little effort, one is able to uncover regional variations of this iconic recipe. I am unwilling to dwell on the topic of authenticity at this point for obvious reasons. The variations are, perhaps, an attempt to assimilate more of the seasonal produce of a particular area. But that does not explain why certain commonly available ingredients have gone missing from it. Making it appeal to the taste buds? Possibly. Substituting with newer ingredients available to one? Why not? For example, most of us cannot imagine the ideal Habisa meal without the 'Kandhiya Pagaw', a kind of citrus mashed together with salt and green chillis. But chillis are themselves a 'New World' ingredient and were not available a few hundred years ago. What did our ancestors use instead? A good amount of ginger perhaps to provide the right amount of heat minus the 'excitement' offered by the chillis.

The most striking departure has been the discovery of a version that I would like to call the Sagaw dalma, another Karthik month specialty in some parts of the state but one that uses 'Kosala saga.' It's most interesting because the 'Kartika Mahatmya' explicitly prohibits any kind of green except for the Agasti or Agastya Sagaw (leaves of the Hummingbird tree.) Digging a little deeper or rather, after asking a dozen of questions, I figured out that most people in that particular region were not aware of the Agasti plant. But that hardly explains the usage of Kosala leaves in the Kartika dalma, except for pointing to the most primitive practice of offering the first harvest of any crop to the Gods. Supporting this theory is the presence of another version of Habisa dalma around Salepur (the rasagola hub). This version uses ash gourd which is clearly prohibited in the text.

Dietary restrictions imposed as per the Kartika Mahatmya are – avoid Horsegram, masoor, black lentila, any kind of non-vegetarian food, ash gourd, vegetables and fruits with spines/thorns (teasel gourd and bitter gourd probably), dark coloured vegetables, brinjal (karka bheji), citrus (lembu, jambila), betelnut, burnt food, leftovers, red rice,and black rice.

Permitted Edibles – Taro, plantain, cucumber, Agasti leaves, Agni Apaka luna (Himalayan salt), coconut, Dhatri phala (amla), and ginger.

HABISA DALMA
(A frugal dal cooked with selected vegetables)

Devotees of Lord Shiva, also known as *Habisiyalis*, observe a fast and eat once a day before sunset on the Mondays of this month. Their meals consist of *arua, habisa dalma,* and *aau khatta*. This is a special kind of Dalma prepared without turmeric and even without the final tempering. Split green moong dal is the primary ingredient. Only a few vegetables are sanctioned for this recipe which are mentioned explicitly in the Kartika Mahatmaya.

⧗ **Preparation time – 20-25 minutes**

 **Ingredients:**

- 1 1/2 cups split moong dal
- 1/2 cup taro (cubed)
- 1/2 cup plantain (cubes)
- 1/2 cup yam (cubed)
- 1-2 pieces elephant apple (slightly crushed)
- 1 tsp cumin seeds
- salt to taste
- 2 tsp ghee
- 1 ½ inch ginger
- Grated coconut for garnishing

Cooking:

- Bring 4 cups of water to boil in a deep vessel.
- Wash and add the dal to the boiling water. Add all the vegetables except the elephant apple. Crush the ginger and add it to the boiling lentils and vegetables.

- Once the dal is 80 per cent cooked, add the crushed elephant apple along with the salt.

- Once the dal and vegetables are completely cooked, remove from the flame. Sprinkle cumin seeds over it. Heat the ghee in a separate pan and drizzle over the Dalma. Finally, add the grated coconut.

- Serve hot with aromatic small-grained rice, *sagaw bhaja*, *Oou Khatta* and a dollop of ghee.

PRASARUNI PATRA CHAKULI
(Skunk vine leaves crepes)

A whiff of the chemistry lab. Or rather rotten eggs. That is the first thing that comes to mind when one crushes a skunk vine leaf between the fingers. Known for its medicinal value rather than culinary usage, *Paederia foetida* is a hardy creeper that proliferates easily. Primarily consumed in cases of bodily discomfort (joint pains/arthritis), it has been pushed to the fringes of mainstream cuisine. But it was not always the case. The previous generations, who understood the importance of food as medicine, made it a point to add such leaves/stems/roots to everyday food as prophylaxis. Building immunity one step at a time – that's how they would describe it to the younger generation. And this philosophy encompassed not just food but routine things like brushing one's teeth with neem twigs(Dantakathi), taking a dip in the river at the crack of dawn during the onset of winter and paying heed to the body's circadian rhythm.

Made into a bhaja or a chakuli or thrown into a simmering pot of curry, a few leaves of skunk vine consumed every day during the monsoon and winters give immense relief from stomach-related ailments or body pains. A lip-smacking chutney can be made by grinding the leaves with mustard seeds, garlic pods, and green chilli and cooking it down with a piece of dried green mango (*Ambula*). A few crushed leaves can be dropped into *santula* every now and then to derive maximum benefit from this plant.

The *Prasaruni patra chakuli* is one easy beginner-level recipe and one cannot go wrong with it. Made with skunk vine leaves, garlic, cumin, green chilli, and a handful of soaked 'arua' rice, it is best eaten hot. While the smell might seem off-putting initially, it tastes good upon eating. And there is nothing like this powerful anti-inflammatory ingredient to manage those aches and pains regularly without medication. Hence, it is a must-have during the cold winter months.

⧖ **Cooking time – 20 minutes**

🥣 **Ingredients:**

- ½ cup raw rice (one can also use parboiled rice but it needs a longer soaking time)
- 1 cup tender skunk vine leaves (stems snipped off)
- 2 garlic pods
- 1 green chilli
- ¼ tsp cumin seeds
- ¼ tsp salt
- 2-3 tsp oil for frying

🍽 **Preparation:**

- Wash and soak the rice for 30 minutes to 1 hour. Drain off the water and transfer to the chutney jar. Add the remaining ingredients except salt and oil.
- Add a few teaspoons of water and grind into a smooth paste. Add salt and adjust the consistency of the batter. *It might turn black due to oxidation while grinding but that does not affect the taste.*

🍲 **Cooking:**

- Heat a griddle and sprinkle a little oil over it. Pour a ladle of the batter and spread it into a slightly thick layer. Drizzle more oil on the sides. Cook on a low flame on both sides for 2-3 minutes each or until done. Remove from the griddle.
- Repeat with the remaining batter.
- Serve it hot with rice meals.

PRASARUNI PATRA BARA
(Skunk vine leaf patties)

These delicious pan-fried fritters are yet another way to include these beneficial leaves in one's diet. The addition of potatoes gives it a nice texture and provides volume as well.

 **Cooking time – 20 minutes**

 **Ingredients:**

- ½ cup raw rice (one can also use parboiled rice but it needs a longer soaking time)
- 1 cup tender skunk vine leaves (stems snipped off)
- 2 garlic pods
- 1 finely chopped green chilli
- 1 finely chopped medium-sized onion
- 1 finely chopped medium-sized potato
- ¼ tsp cumin seeds
- ¼ tsp salt
- 2-3 tsp oil for frying

Preparation:

- Wash and soak the rice for 30 minutes to 1 hour. Drain off the water and transfer to the chutney jar. Add the skunk vine leaves, garlic pods and cumin seeds.
- Add a few teaspoons of water and grind into a thick smooth paste. Transfer to a mixing bowl. Add all other remaining ingredients except the oil. Mix it well for 1-2 minutes.

- Heat a griddle and sprinkle a little oil over it. Take a tablespoon and pour 5-6 spoonfuls of the batter at a little distance from each other. Drizzle more oil over the griddle. Cook on a low flame on both sides for 3-4 minutes each or until it's done. Remove from the griddle.
- Repeat with the remaining batter.
- Serve it hot with your rice meals.

PRASARUNI PATRA JHOLO
(Skunk vine leaves stewed with selected vegetables)

'Baigana-Saru-Bilati' aka Eggplant-Taro-Tomato are the unsung heroes of the winter produce. They are steamed/fried/roasted/curried individually or in combination with other winter ingredients. *'Baigana-Saru-Bilati'* cooked with mustard-based gravy often finds a place in the lunch menu, while the more mellow ginger-cumin-chilli version accompanies the rotis and *chakuli* for dinner.

 **Cooking time – 30 minutes**

 **Ingredients:**

- 1 ½ cup eggplant (diced into 1-inch cubes)
- ½ cup taro/*saru* (cut into smaller cubes)
- 2 medium-sized tomatoes
- 1 small potato (cut into smaller cubes) (if you find taro itchy substitute it with potato)
- A fistful of the skunk vine leaves
- 1 medium-sized onion (chopped into small pieces)
- 6-7 garlic cloves
- 2 dry red chillis
- ¼ tsp mustard seeds
- ½ tsp salt
- 2-3 tsp mustard oil

To grind into a smooth paste:

- 2 tsp mustard seeds
- ½ tsp cumin seeds
- 2-3 garlic pods

Preparation:

- Grind the mustard, cumin and garlic into as smooth paste with a few spoons of water.

Cooking:

- Heat a wok. Add the oil and let it smoke a bit.

- Add the taro pieces and fry them for 3-4 minutes. Remove and keep aside.

- Add the broken red chilli and mustard seeds to the wok. Once it splutters, add crushed garlic and fry until it turns golden.

- Add the onions and fry until it turns translucent.

- Add the tomato and sprinkle a little salt. Close with a lid for 2-3 minutes until the tomatoes become mushy.

- Now add the mustard paste with 1 1/2 cup water. Bring it to a good boil.

- Throw in the eggplants, potatoes and taro. Cover and cook on high flame for 2-3 minutes.

- Remove the lid and add the skunk vine leaves. Cover it again and cook on medium-high flame until the veggies are done but not completely mushy. There should be a little gravy left even after the veggies are cooked.

- Remove the skunk vine leaves at this stage and discard them.

- Serve this curry hot with a rice meal.

This particular dish (ginger-cumin-black pepper version) is recommended for post-partum recovery. It is said to take care of the aches and pains in the body, and correct the digestive issues that usually crop up during pregnancy.

PANI SANTULA
(Soupy mixed-vegetable preparation)

Pani Santula, a watery medley of boiled vegetables, is one of the healthiest sides that one can have with rotis. Most people, especially older folks, consider it as a must-have component of their dinner as it contains a good dose of fibre and nutrients while being light on the stomach. It uses minimum spicing and one can also make it without adding any onion or garlic.

 **Preparation time – 20 minutes**

 **Ingredients:**

- 1 cup red pumpkin
- 1/2 cup raw papaya
- 1/2 cup plantain
- 1/2 cup yam
- 1/2 cup taro
- 1 small eggplant
- 1 cup chopped yard long beans
- 1/3 cup beans
- 1 medium potato
- 1-2 tomatoes
- 1 large roughly chopped onion
- 3-4 crushed garlic flakes
- 1 tsp pancha phutana
- 2-3 dry red chillis
- 1 tsp roasted cumin-chilli powder
- Salt to taste

- ½ tsp turmeric

- 2 tsp oil/ghee for tempering

- 2 tbsp chopped coriander leaves

Cooking:

- Boil 4 cups water along with a little turmeric and salt to taste.

- Add the pumpkin, papaya, raw banana, yam, taro and potato. After 3-4 minutes, add the remaining veggies. Cover and boil until they are cooked but not mushy.

- Heat the oil/ghee in a pan. Add the broken chilli and pancha phutana followed by the onion and garlic.

- Once the onion turns translucent, pour the tempering over the boiled veggies. Sprinkle cumin-chilli powder and boil on high for 20-30 seconds. Remove from flame, garnish with cilantro and serve immediately with hot rotis.

Note - It does not taste well if refrigerated and re-heated.

MATI ALU BHAJA

(Pan-fried yam fritters)

Mildly spiced slices of yam, fried to a crisp, make for an amazing side with simple rice and lentil meals. The key to getting them right is to choose the yams with perfectly white flesh [as opposed to a dull yellow] and steam them to just the right extent before frying them. Use a thick iron skillet on a low flame for best results.

A little extra oil is recommended!

 **Cooking time – 15 minutes**

 **Ingredients:**

- 200 gm yam (*Mati Alu*)
- 2 tbsp rice
- 3 tsp mustard seeds
- 2 green chillis/red chillis
- 3-4 garlic cloves
- 5 tsp mustard oil
- 1/6 tsp salt
- 1/3 tsp turmeric

Preparation:

- Grind the mustard seeds, garlic cloves and chilli into a fine paste.
- Soak the rice for 2 hours and grind separately into a thin watery paste. Add a pinch of salt to this paste.
- Peel and cut the yam into 6-7 mm thick pieces.

Cooking:

- Take the yam pieces in a wok. Add the mustard seed paste along with salt and turmeric. Pour just enough water to cover the pieces.

- Cook on a medium flame for 5-6 minutes or until it's 80-90 per cent cooked. Remove from flame and discard the excess water.

- Heat a thick pan. Drizzle a little oil on it.

- Dip the boiled yam pieces in the rice paste and place on the pan. Drizzle a little more oil around the sides. Let them cook on one side.

- Flip them over and fry on the other side until lightly crisp.

- Serve hot with rice meals.

Palua. East Indian Arrowroot. Curcuma Angustifolia. Those white roots that play peek-a-boo among the wicker baskets overflowing with bright hued winter produce at the vegetable markets. Not exactly the most sought-after vegetable, the probability of finding it goes up if you check out those obscure little stalls instead of scouring the main ones. And not without reason. These are very much local and foraged by villagers who have identified the thickets that often grow wild on mountain sides. The West Indian Arrowroot or Maranta Arundinacea is by contrast a commercially cultivated crop that supplies most of the world's arrowroot needs. From being the thickening agent used in sauces, jellies, soups and curries to being added to a host of baked goodies, the powdered starch extracted from the underground stems is in huge demand. Except in Odisha, where the locally grown Curcuma Angustifolia has a monopoly of sorts. And that too as a 'cure' for all stomach related problems.

The processed arrowroot chunks seem to crop up at different places of Odisha in their strikingly different avatars. From a beautifully flaky Palua ladoo to a Palua khiri served on Shivratri and Janmashtami (rejuvenates the body after a fast,) and a cooling Jhiliri panna served during summers, I have ended up digging into a range of arrowroot-based recipes over the years. Yet, one thing stood out. Most of the arrowroot consuming population swore by its use as a home remedy for diarrhoea. A tablespoon of the raw powder dissolved in a glass of water taken at regular intervals seems to do the trick as it contains a large proportion of insoluble fibres. Moreover, being a demulcent, it soothes the stomach membranes and also maintains electrolyte balance.

PALUA KANDA BHAJA
(Pan-fried arrowroot tubers)

Arrowroot tubers are available in parts of Odisha for a brief period during the months of Aswina and Kartika. While the extracted starch or arrowroot chunks are used in recipes or as a traditional remedy for stomach-related disorders, their use as a vegetable is limited to a small area. They are eaten as a bhaja or added to the dalma and ghanta as a seasonal vegetable.

In villages, tender tubers are roasted or boiled and eaten like sweet potatoes before the fibres develop.

 **Cooking time – 15 minutes**

 **Ingredients:**

- 200 gm Arrowroot tubers
- 3 tsp mustard seeds
- 1 tsp cumin seeds
- 2 dry red chilli
- 5 tsp cooking oil
- Salt to taste
- 1/5 tsp turmeric

Preparation:

- Grind the mustard seeds, cumin seeds and chilli into a fine paste.
- Peel the outer layers of the arrowroot and cut the tubers into 1 cm thick roundels.

Cooking:

- Take the arrowroot pieces in a wok. Add the mustard paste along with salt and turmeric. Add 1 cup water.

- Cook on a medium flame for 10 minutes or until it's cooked completely. The mustard paste should form a thick layer around the pieces.

- Heat a pan. Drizzle a little oil on it.

- Place the boiled arrowroot pieces on the pan. Drizzle a little more oil on the sides.

- Flip it over and fry on both sides until it's lightly crisp.

- Serve hot with rice meals.

> *Note – Saru bhaja (taro fry) is also prepared during the winter using the same recipe as above.*

TAMPA
(A finger millet-based dessert)

Even as we rediscover millets like *Mandiya*, *Kodaw*, *Gangei*, and *Suan*, traditional recipes that leverage these ingredients are being obliterated. In the quest to create something that is catchy and that can be marketed easily, conventional millet-based foods are being overlooked.

Tribals in Odisha make a gruel out of rice, lentils and millets. Most of them drink large quantities of a fermented finger millet drink during the summer months. Parts of Southern Odisha mix the millet flour into the hot 'pej' or water discarded after cooking rice, and later consume it with curd. Western Odisha makes a cooling porridge with ragi that is partaken during the summer. Finger millet is turned into crispy '*Chakels*' for breakfast and Tikhri for fasts.

Tampa is a finger millet recipe popular in the Southern districts of Odisha and is prepared on special occasions like *Nagula Chaturthi*.

⌛ Cooking time – 20 minutes

- 1 cup Ragi flour
- 2 cups water
- ½ cup milk
- ½ cup coconut (grated, chopped)
- ¼ cup roasted peanut or cashews
- 1 cup jaggery
- 1-2 bay leaves
- ½ tsp black pepper powder
- 3-4 tsp ghee
- 1-2 pinch of salt

Preparation:

- Mix the ragi flour with one cup of water.

Cooking:

- Take the remaining water in a thick-bottomed wok and bring it to a boil.

- Add the salt, coconut, nuts, spices and jaggery along with 1 tsp ghee. Boil it for 5 minutes.

- Reduce the flame and add milk. Bring it to a boil.

- Add the ragi slurry, mix well to prevent lumps and cook on a medium high flame for 3-4 minutes. Then, lower the flame and cook for 8-10 minutes.

- Finally, add the remaining ghee and mix. Switch off the flame and pour onto a greased mould or plate. Pat it down to flatten it and spread it out. [*It will be very hot at this stage so moisten the fingers with a little water and work fast to avoid burns*]

- Serve warm.

Note – The major difference between Tikhri and Tampa comes from the straining of the solids (powdered skins). The removal of the skins gives the Tikhri a melt-in-the-mouth texture. Also, less water is used in Tampa giving it a grainy 'halwa' like texture whereas the Tikhri is akin to a pudding.

Also sharing a tribal version of this recipe:

⌛ Cooking time – 20 minutes

🥣 Ingredients:

- 1 cup ragi flour
- 1 cup onion cut into long pieces
- 1/3 cup jaggery
- 1/3 tsp salt
- 2-3 tbsp Mustard or Mahua oil
- ¼ cup dried mahua

🍳 Cooking:

- Heat the oil in a wok. Add the onions and fry them until they start to caramelize on the sides. Add about 2 cups of water.
- Once the water starts to boil, add salt and jaggery. Also, add the soaked and cleaned mahua flowers.
- Let it boil for 4-5 minutes on low flame. Add the ragi flour, mix and cook for 3-4 minutes until it starts to come together like a dough.
- Remove from the flame and serve warm.

KAINTHA CHUTNEY
(Wood apple condiment)

Kaintha is a sour fruit that ripens at the beginning of winter and is usually made into chutneys. It is rich in vitamin C, stimulates digestion and clears the throat. Among the many uses listed in ayurveda is the ability of the pulp extract to turn milk into curd. Hence, it is also called *Dadhiphala*.

The chutney is a breeze to make and quite addictive in taste. It belongs to that much-overlooked category of 'sour ingredients', which are not 'souring agents.' Such ingredients are sought out by women only to be turned into the most ingenious 'pagaw' or '*chakata.*'

 **Preparation time – 10 minutes**

 **Ingredients:**

- 1 ripe kaintha
- 3-4 tsp jaggery (or to taste)
- 1 chopped green chilli
- 1/8 tsp jeera lanka gunda (roasted cumin chili powder)
- 1/8 tsp salt (or to taste)
- 2-3 pinch black salt
- 1-2 garlic cloves (finely crushed, optional)

🍽 Preparation:

- Break open the shell. Scoop out the flesh into a mixing bowl.

- The pulp contains small seeds which are also consumed.

- Add the remaining ingredients and mash everything together. Adjust the salt/chilli/ jaggery if required.

- Serve with meals or thin it out to a sauce-like consistency for serving with snacks.

Note - Ambula, Amba sula, Basi Torani, Karadi, Hendua, Lembu, Kamala/Tabha, Oou, Ambada, Dahi, Ghola dahi, Tentuli and Patalghanta are the popular souring agents. Other sour ingredients like Champuta, amba sadha, kaintha, karamanga, Kandiya are not leveraged for adding 'tartness' to other preparations, rather they are turned into a pagaw.

KHATTA PALANGA CHUTNEY
(Sorrel leaves relish)

My grandmother had an old tin stowed away in the corner of her room. It was fondly referred to as her *'bihana baksa'* or seeds tin. She used to collect the seeds from the plants once they had reached the end of their life cycle, dry them in the sun and carefully wrap them in small pieces of paper sans any labelling. These small parcels were stored carefully until the next sowing season. I used to watch each step with the eagle-eyed curiosity of a child. Over the years, I acquired the skill to identify most of the seeds without assistance. But during the initial days, I used to get them all mixed up. The only exception to this was the *'Khatta palanga'* whose seeds were still enveloped with the pretty flowers when we dried and stored them. It made the identification a breeze. Even today, I marvel at the knowledge of those farmers who were able to identify hundreds of such seeds at a glance. They might have been uneducated but it is impossible to overlook their expertise.

Khatta palanga leaves have a sour taste (similar to the *'Gongura'* leaves used extensively in Andhra cuisine). This chutney combines the tartness of these leaves with sugar/jaggery to create a side dish that gets ready in no time at all!

 **Cooking time: 15 minutes**

 **Ingredients:**

- 3 cups khatta palanga saga (loosely packed)
- 1 small onion (chopped into medium-sized pieces)
- 1/3 tsp red chilli powder (optional)
- 2 whole red chillis
- 1/5 tsp pancha-phutana
- 3-4 tsp sugar/jaggery

- 1 tbsp oil

- Salt to taste

🍳 Cooking:

- Wash the greens and cut it into large pieces.

- Heat oil in a wok. Add the pancha-phutana. Break the red chilli into 2-3 pieces and add to the wok.

- Add the onions and fry until it turns translucent.

- Add the chopped greens. Sprinkle salt and chilli powder. Cover with a lid and stir at intervals.

- Cook until the leaves soften and turn mushy. Add sugar/jaggery and mix. Cook until the

- sugar/jaggery melts and the greens acquire a chutney like consistency. Remove from the fire.

Note – Gongura leaves are consumed in some parts of Odisha and they are also referred to as 'Khata palanga.' But some people call it khatta bhendi given that the plant morphology is similar to that of ladies finger or Bhendi.

OOU KHATTA
(Elephant apple relish)

Elephant apple is one of the indigenous souring ingredients available in Odisha, especially in the Coastal parts. It is turned into a sweet-sour Khatta or added to dishes like Ghanta and Habisa Dalma.

The taste is a curious mix of sour and astringent accents when the fruit is young. As it ripens, it develops a sweet-sour profile, and the astringency recedes. Traditional wisdom attributes it with vata pacifying and agni-improving properties, which make it an ideal component of the 'end of monsoon' meal.

 **Preparation time – 35 minutes**

 **Ingredients:**

- 1 elephant apple
- 1 tsp cumin seeds
- 1 tsp mustard seeds
- 2 dry red chillis
- Salt to taste
- 2/3 cup sugar
- 1/2 tsp turmeric
- 1/3 tsp chilli powder
- 1/2 tsp roasted cumin-chilli powder
- 1 tsp pancha phutana (use mustard+cumin seeds if not unavailable)
- 3 tsp cooking oil
- ¼ cup freshly grated coconut
- 2 sprig curry leaves

🍽️ Preparation:

- Cut through the oou with a sharp knife and separate the petals. Discard the inner core. Peel the outer skin and cut into long strips about 1 cm wide. Use a pestle or small stone to slightly crush the pieces.

- Grind the mustard and cumin seeds into a smooth paste.

🍲 Cooking:

- Boil 3-4 cups of water with salt and turmeric. Add the crushed Oou to this and boil for 5 minutes. Discard the water.

- Heat the oil in a wok. Add the panchaphutana and broken red chilli. Allow it to splutter. Add the curry leaves and sauté for 1-2 mins.

- Add the boiled Oou to the wok and stir fry for 3-4 minutes. Add the mustard-cumin paste and fry for 1 minute. Add 2 cups of water along with salt, turmeric and chilli powder. Cover with a lid and allow it to cook on a medium flame for 10 minutes.

- Add the jaggery. Cook until the jaggery dissolves into the gravy. Add the coconut and cumin-chilli powder, mix once and remove from the flame.

- Serve at room temperature with rice meals.

KOSALA SAGAW BHAJA
(Stir-fried winter greens)

Sagaw Bhaja is a regular dish on the Odia menu. It is prepared with a wide variety of green leafy vegetables available locally, and the add-ons provide a lot of versatility to this recipe. My grandmother would often state that the best sagaw bhaja is one in which the leaves are not bunched together. She shared that the trick is not to crowd the vessel. And she made sure that I perfected this recipe.

Usually, onions and garlic are added to this recipe, but during a fast, we rely only on pancha phutana, red chillis, and freshly grated coconut to bring alive the flavours of this dish. One has to ensure that the cooking fat is heated to the right temperature so that the spices release all their flavours. During *Kartika Masa*, this is a must-have on Mondays along with a Habisa Dalma and Oou khatta.

 **Preparation time – 15 minutes**

Ingredients:

- 4 cups of finely chopped kosala greens
- 2/3 tsp pancha phutana
- 2 red chillis
- 1/2 cup freshly grated coconut
- 3 tsp oil
- 1/6 tsp salt or to taste

Cooking:

- Heat the oil in a wok.
- Add the broken red chilli and pancha phutana. Allow it to splutter.
- Add the chopped greens in small batches and stir on high flame for 1-2 minutes.

- Lower the flame, cover and cook for 1 minute on medium to high flame. Remove the cover and stir gently to prevent the leaves from bunching/sticking together.

- Repeat the above step alternatively until sagaw is done and excess water evaporates. Add the salt and mix in. Switch off the flame and sprinkle freshly grated coconut. Mix thoroughly.

- Serve hot with Arua anna, Habisa Dalma and Ouu khatta.

Note – If it is freshly plucked and tender sagaw, do not cover it while cooking, else it will be steamed instead of being stir-fried.

*– **In my native, the Kosala sagaw bhaja is cooked with the addition of a little plantain and ridge gourd during this month. Coconut was not being used earlier as it is not a local ingredient. Of late, some people have started using it in the recipe.*

DAHI MANJA

(Plantain stem steeped in curd and aromatic seasoning)

Plantain is one of the primary vegetables consumed this month. The local markets are inundated with plantain stems, the by-product of harvesting the vegetable. Plantain stems (the core part of it) are considered superior to the banana stems from a culinary perspective, as the former are harvested at an earlier stage, and hence, they are more tender. A common dish prepared during this month is 'Dahi manja', a preparation of finely chopped banana stem steeped in curd and spices.

 **Preparation time: 4-5 hours**

 **Ingredients:**

- 4 inches long Plantain/Banana Stem
- ¼ cup freshly grated coconut
- 1-2 lightly crushed green chillis
- ½ tsp crushed mango ginger
- ½ tsp mustard paste
- 1/5 tsp salt or to taste
- 1 sprig curry leaves
- 1 tsp chopped coriander leaves
- 1 pinch sugar

Preparation:

- Remove the outer fibrous layers and expose the solid core. This is the part that is used in cooking. Cut the banana stem into thin circles.

- After slicing off one circle, one can feel the fibres when one tries to separate it from the remaining stem. Move your fingers in a circular motion to wrap the fibres around it and remove as much of the fibres as you can.

- Chop the circles into small pieces. Crush lightly using a pestle. Transfer to a non-reactive bowl. Mix in mustard paste, coconut, green chilli, curry leaves and mango ginger. Keep it covered in the hot sun for 3-4 hours. The heat of the sun will cook the ingredients.

- After 5-6 hours, add the beaten curd, salt, and sugar. Mix and garnish with chopped coriander leaves.

> *Note – Do not add the salt when putting it under the sun else it will leach excess water.*

KANDHIYA LEMBU PAGAW
(A Green chilli-citrus condiment)

This pagaw is a winter speciality and is traditionally paired with the *arua* bhata and *Habisa Dalma* meal on Mondays. The sour note helps to balance the slightly astringent quality of the Habisa Dalma. The citrus lends a refreshing flavour that lightens the inherently heavy nature of the *'arua-dalma-ghia'* combination.

Kandhiya or citron has a sweet-sour taste profile and is available in winter. However, some varieties yield fruit as early as mid-monsoon. It has medicinal properties and is known to improve gut health and boost immunity.

 **Preparation time – 5 minutes**

 Ingredients:

- 1 citron
- 1-2 green chillis
- 2 tsp sugar
- Salt as per taste
- 1 clove garlic (used only if one is not observing a fast)

 Preparation:

- Peel the outer skin and the white layer that surrounds the flesh.
- Cut it into two halves across the section. Mash it in a bowl with the remaining ingredients. Add 2-3 tsp water and a little more sugar if it is too sour for one's preference.
- Serve with hot rice and Dalma.

India has always had a rich tradition of using leaves or leaf plates for cooking and serving food. While the usage of some leaves is generic, there are specific leaves designated to be used during certain occasions. Jackfruit leaves are used for the *'pinda'* or 'shraddh food offering' to the spirits of the ancestors in the coastal districts while *Palasa* leaves serve the same purpose in parts of Western Odisha. Another example is the use of 'Kurei' leaves for the Nuakhai feasts. These traditions are evident from tribal sayings like in' *palsā patarar danā ār madiā peje bednā'*, which means that the palasa leaf bowls are best suited for drinking a local drink called *Mandiya Pej*.

Another interesting example is the usage of banyan leaves to prepare the Enduri pitha (steamed rice cake) by the Gouda community on Gamha (Gau-Maa) Purnima. This practice underlines the importance of the leaves as an excellent source of fodder for their cattle herds.

Making leaf plates at home was a skill mastered by most women in rural areas in the earlier days. Especially, in the areas close to the forest where the leaves were easy to source. Days before the weddings and other feasts, groups of women congregated in a home and stitched together piles of leaf plates using their deft fingers.

While biodegradability is the major factor powering the adoption of leaf plates in the current scenario, it was the 'purity' aspect that led to such widespread usage of leaf plates in earlier times. Leaf plates can only be used once, and hence, they are free from the taint of 'untouchability', a practice that is fast receding but still evident in some rural pockets. Habisa traditions, which adhere to the highest levels of 'purity', not just in terms of food but also in terms of actions and thought, dictate that the meals should be served only on banana leaves.

Leaves release beneficial compounds during cooking and when hot food is served on them. Studies have discovered that leaves used in cooking and serving are naturally rich in various flavonoids and are known to exhibit wound healing, antibacterial, antimicrobial, antioxidant, anti-inflammatory, and antidiabetic effects. Some of the leaves used for cooking and serving are:

1. Turmeric (*Curcuma longa*)	9. Gaja Pimpali (Scindapsus officinalis)
2. Sal (*Shorea Robusta*)	10. Gambhari (Gmelina Arborea)
3. Teak (*Tectona grandis*)	11. Kendu (Diospyros melanoxylon)
4. Kurei (*Holarrhena antidysenterica*)	12. Bhelua (Semecarpus anacardium)
5. Banyan (*Ficus bengalensis*)	13. Mahua (Madhuca longifolia)
6. Siali (*Phanera Vahlii*)	14. Jackfruit (Artocarpus heterophyllus)
7. Semuli (*Bombax ceiba*)	15. Banana (MusaParadisiaca)
8. Palasa (*Butea Monosperma*)	

MARGASIRA (NOVEMBER – DECEMBER)

The days and nights are bitterly cold this month. But a warmth fills up the farmer's heart as he toils in the fields. Harvesting of paddy is initiated on an auspicious day, decided after consulting the *Dehury* (in Western Odisha) or the *Panji* (in Coastal parts). A small ritual offering is made in the fields before the farmer himself or a family member cuts the first few sheaves of rice. All the standing paddy is pressed in one direction to facilitate cutting. Once the cutting is complete, they are bundled up and transported to the *khala* (threshing ground). In some parts of Odisha, the harvested paddy is carried in a colourful procession to the threshing ground. Paddy being a manifestation of Goddess Lakshmi in Indian culture, any remaining spikelets are also carefully collected. Although much of the process has become mechanized, people still follow most of the rituals and customs that have been associated with paddy cultivation since the olden days.

Manabasa Gurubar is the most important ritual associated with paddy. The Thursdays of this month are dedicated to appeasing Goddess Lakshmi, the Goddess synonymous with both '*dhaw-naw*'(wealth) and '*dhaa-naw*'(rice). Married women express their gratitude to the Goddess of wealth by offering her a variety of dishes prepared with the new harvest. Houses are cleaned and decked up to welcome the Goddess. Beautiful designs made with rice paste called 'Jhunti' or 'Chitta' adorn every house. Even the path leading up to the front door is dotted with these designs which mandatorily feature a pair of dainty feet symbolic of the Goddess herself. The 'Padma Mandali' and '*dhana ghaccha*' are other designs that feature prominently on this occasion. Lakshmi is represented by 'Mana,' a unit of measurement popular in earlier times. It is decorated with rice paste designs, filled to the brim with paddy and draped with a new red cloth. The 'bhoga' prepared on this occasion is not shared with anyone other than family members. Even married daughters cannot partake in the offering.

Another important festival observed this month is *Prathamastami*, a ritual that felicitates the first-born who is expected to take forward the family's legacy. New clothes and ingredients required on this occasion are provided by the maternal uncle of the child. Interestingly, the niece or nephew is eligible to partake in the offerings made on Manabasa Gurubar. This is because of the important role of the child in any events in the maternal family. Unlike the married daughter, the child is eligible to offer the '*pinda*' or offerings to the mother's ancestors. Due to this reason, the Manabasa rituals do not begin until after *Prathamastami* in the coastal parts of Odisha. The speciality of *Prathamastami* is *Enduri Pitha*, a stuffed rice cake steamed in turmeric leaves.

A wide variety of pithas and rice-based dishes are prepared during this month from the newly harvested rice. Seasonal vegetables like radish, flat beans, tomatoes, cauliflowers, cabbage and green peas are available in abundance. Freshwater shrimps, and fish from the paddy fields and rivers are added to the menu.

What's on the menu this month

Prathamastami or the festival of the 'first born.' A unique Odia festival that felicitates the eldest child and grooms him/her for continuing the family name and shouldering the responsibilities that come bundled with it. Folklore points to the sibling rivalry between Lord Jagannath and his elder brother, Lord Balabhadra, behind the origin of this festival. Whether it is true or not is rather debatable, but Odisha's folklore is replete with fables (and miracles) about the celestial siblings. This day is synonymous with the unique aroma of the turmeric leaves as steaming *'Haladi Patra pitha'* or *'Enduri pithas'* are doled out in every household. In the olden days, a new earthen pot called *'Athara'* would be brought out and lined with twigs from various aromatic and medicinal plants to make a bed for steaming the 'Enduri.' Most Brahmin families would continue to make and eat the pitha for seven days and finally, on the eighth day, a special *'Amuhan'* pitha would be prepared and submerged in the river along with the 'Athara.' The repetition was the accepted way to maximize the anti-bacterial and anti-inflammatory properties of the turmeric leaf.

While Odia households all over the state make the pitha using turmeric leaves, a variation is observed in some tracts nearby Angul where Gaja Pippali or Hasti Pippali, commonly known as *Scindapus Officinalis* is used. Given that ayurveda prescribes the fruit as a remedy for a number of ailments like joint pains, fever, cough, intestinal worms and other cold-related ailments, it makes sense to incorporate it into a festival to ensure that it finds a way into our plates. The Gajapimpali enduri is a beautiful example of Odisha's underexplored micro cuisines, a testimony of the diversity that exists within the state.

The day is also considered as 'Nua' for the newly harvested black lentil which is also an important crop. Hence, this festival also marks the beginning of the *'badi paka'* or making of the sun-dried lentil dumplings. The low temperatures with the onset of winter and clear skies create ideal conditions for drying the badi. A very unique ritual called a '*badi bahaghara*' is observed in my mother's family on this day. Two of the freshly-laid dumplings are designated as bride and groom. They are decorated with a dot of vermillion, a few sprigs of 'doob grass' and a few grains of 'arua rice' are sprinkled over them. Perhaps, it is a modification of the ancient practice of offering the first harvest of 'biri' or black lentils to the Gods. Apart from being a source of food during the lean summer months, these sun-dried lentils occupy an important position when it comes to Odia marriage rituals such as the '*Jaee ragada.*'

Sathi Puja is done during the evening on this day. As there is no restriction on non-vegetarian food while worshipping the Goddess, some people prepare mutton or chicken curry with the enduri pitha during dinner.

ENDURI PITHA
(Rice cake steamed in turmeric leaves)

An airy pillow of fermented rice and black lentil batter. A generous heap of nutty fresh coconut laced with jaggery. A hint of cardamom. Maybe a pinch of black pepper too. But the final magic happens when the ingredients are encased in a layer of fragrant turmeric leaves and enveloped in steam. The warmth slowly cooks the batter even as the flavours of the turmeric leaf are released. The aromatic compounds or phenols (more specifically curcuminoids) from the leaf permeate into the pitha, combine with the aromatic rice and lend it that unique flavour.

 **Cooking time: 45 minutes**

 **Ingredients:**

- 1 cup Black gram (skinned)
- 2 cups raw rice (rice flour can also be used)
- 1 coconut (freshly grated)
- ½ cup jaggery
- 1-2 finely powdered green cardamoms
- ¼ tsp freshly crushed peppercorns
- 10 nos. turmeric leaves
- ½ tsp salt
- 1 tbsp ghee

Preparation:

- Soak the rice and black gram for 5-6 hours. Drain the water and grind it into a fine paste.
- Keep overnight or 8-10 hours.

- Grate the coconut or cut it into big pieces and grind it into a coarse paste in a grinder.

Cooking:

- Heat a wok. Add the jaggery along with a few spoons of water. Once it melts and starts bubbling, add the grated coconut and spices. Stir gently for 5 minutes. Remove from the flame and keep aside to cool.

- Heat water in a steamer/pressure cooker. Bring to a boil.

- Wash the turmeric leaves and wipe them dry. Take a little ghee on your fingers and smear it all over each leaf. Take a blob of the batter and spread it evenly on the leaf.

- Spread 2-3 tbsp of the coconut mixture over the batter. Fold the leaf carefully and place it on the steamer stand. If using a pressure cooker, please remember to remove the weight.

- Repeat the process for the remaining batter/leaves. The leaves can be stacked one over the other for 2-3 layers. Close the lid and steam for 15-20 minutes. Remove from the stove.

- Remove the turmeric leaves. Serve the Enduri pitha with ghee and sugar or dalma/ghuguni. Enduri made without the sweet stuffing is very popular with a thin gravy mutton curry.

- *The above recipe makes 8-10 pithas.*

Note - Flaxseed (phesi) is roasted and added to the Enduri pitha stuffing along with the other ingredients in some of the Brahmin 'sasans' near Salepur. It is one of the rare instances of the Flaxseed being used in Odia cooking.

TORANI KANJI
(Fermented rice water soup)

Winters are incomplete without a mention of the *Torani Kanji*. One needs to plan well in advance to prepare this dish. Water discarded from cooked rice is collected over days and stored in an earthenware pot, which allows it to ferment and develop a sour taste. It is a technical process wherein we retain half of the previous day's rice water and mix it with the current day's lot after the latter has been cooled and diluted. It is a slow and elaborate process which is worth the wait. I still get nostalgic remembering the large pots in which my grandmother used to brew and simmer this thing. It has a strong aroma (more like pungent) that is sure to tickle the olfactory ducts of the neighbours. Hence, the generous quantity in which it is prepared.

While one can enjoy various kinds of *Kanji* all around the year, the abundance of vegetables and leafy greens during the winter months adds a wholesome quality to it. There is something very soothing about sipping Kanji from a big bowl while enjoying the wintry sun. So, here is the recipe for the *Torani Kanjee* which I got to learn from my mother, but only after a lot of advice and deliberation. "Keep the torani carefully covered," "Do not let it become too stale and smelly," "Remember to throw away half of the previous lot when you mix in the fresh one," and so on. I guess it is ingrained in a mother's psyche to keep the advice coming even after we have grown up. I still get it every time I mention making this particular dish at home.

 **Preparation time – 40 minutes**

 **Ingredients:**

- 2-3 litres of torani (rice water)
- 1/2 cup radish slices

- 1/2 cup pumpkin pieces
- 1/4 cup green papaya slices
- 1 small eggplant (cut into semi-circles)
- 6-7 okra (cut into inch-long pieces)
- 1 ripe cucumber (*budha kakudi* cut into thick circles)
- 10-12 fat garlic cloves
- 4-5 dry red chilli
- 2 sprigs of curry leaves
- 1 tsp mustard seeds
- 2 pinch nigella seeds
- 1/4 tsp turmeric
- 3 tsp mustard oil
- 3-4 pieces of ambula (dried green mango)
- 1 1/2 tsp salt or to taste

🍽 Preparation:

- Collect the excess water after cooking rice. Dilute it with a cup of water.

- Drop in a piece of ambula and cover the vessel with a thin cloth. Let it stand overnight.

- Again, collect the rice water on the next day. Dilute and allow it to cool down completely.

- Throw away half of the previous day's rice water along with the ambula. Add the fresh lot along with another fresh piece of ambula. Let it stand overnight.

- Repeat this process for 3-4 days. Once the *torani* starts to smell pungent and develops a sour taste, we can proceed to make the kanji.

Cooking:

- Dilute the torani with 2-3 cups water and transfer to a deep saucepan. Add salt to taste and a bit of turmeric. Bring it to a full boil. (One needs to be cautious as it tends to rise and come out of the vessel pretty fast)

- Add the chopped vegetables to the boiling torani. Let it boil on a medium flame until all the vegetables are cooked.

- Check for salt and sourness. If it lacks enough tang, drop in 1-2 pieces of ambula.

- Heat the oil in a tempering pan. Once it starts to smoke, reduce the heat. Add the broken chillis, mustard and nigella seeds. Quickly follow with the crushed garlic and curry leaves. Once the garlic turns slightly brown on the edges, pour the contents of the tempering pan over the boiling kanji and cover with a lid.

- Remove from the flame and serve hot or at room temperature.

Note – It stays good for 2-3 days in the fridge. Remember to bring it to room temperature before consuming.

***In the earlier days, the fresh lot of 'Sukhua' or fermented and dried fish would arrive sometime during the winter months. Enjoying a meal of hot parboiled rice with Torani Kanji and Patharamundi sukhua while sitting in the winter sun and gossiping was something the ladies looked forward to. Especially those living in smaller towns in quarters where the household work was limited and leisure time sacrosanct.*

Manabasa Gurubar

The story behind Manabasa Gurubar is taken from the Laxmi Purana, a 15th-century text that is read in almost every Odia home on Thursdays during the Hindu month of Margasira.

"It is her day and Maa Lakshmi decides to go out and check on her devotees in the disguise of an old woman. She comes across a merchant's house and finds it in disarray. She wakes up the lady of the house and advises her to inculcate discipline. The latter refuses to do so inviting the wrath of the Goddess. The merchant's house is reduced to penury. Next, the goddess chances upon a lower caste household that had been cleaned and beautifully decorated. She forgets social decorum and steps into the house. She blesses the lower caste woman with unimaginable riches.

This episode is witnessed by the brothers Balabhadra and Jaganaath. Balabhadra is incensed at Lakshmi's lack of propriety. He accuses her of polluting the temple by entering it after visiting an untouchable. Jagannath is forced to ask Lakshmi to leave. She leaves and along with her goes away all their riches, for she is the Goddess of prosperity. They are now 'Lakhmichaadaw,' virtually without food and money.

They roam around for food and water until they chance upon a beautiful mansion. This residence represents Lakshmi's 'maya.' They decide to ask the servants of the mansion for food, only to be informed that it is an untouchable's abode. They are forced to look at the irony of the situation and only when they accept the food gracefully, does Lakshmi decide to return to their temple dwelling."

Maa Lakshmi and Sriya Chandaluni. One woman supporting another. In the garb of a Goddess who blesses her disciplined and hardworking devotee irrespective of the latter's social standing. Orderliness is the key to appeasing the Goddess, we are told.

Lord Balabhadra (Jaganaath's elder brother), represents the high handedness of a patriarchal society meting out unjust punishment to a woman for crossing her boundaries by visiting a 'Chandala' or outcaste.

The 'Lakshmi-chadaa' phase of the siblings with the elements of nature conspiring with the Divine Mother to deny them food and water, establishes her all-encompassing role as the centre of the Universe.

The final redemption of the siblings is when they hungrily accept food at another 'Chandala' home (a test devised by Maa Lakshmi). Thereby, completing the cycle and vindicating the Goddess' stand. Food as a common denominator. No one rises above it. Hence, to this date, people from all castes are allowed to partake in the 'mahaprasad' from the same pot at the Jagannath Dham in Puri.

'Chenna,' the major ingredient for making Rasagola, is mentioned in this text among the ten ingredients of the 'pura' or filling used to prepare the manda pitha.

Vegetables listed in this text are eggplant, manja (banana stem), leutia sagaw (kind or amaranthus), aalu (yam), saru (taro), kadali (plantain) and moola (radish).

It also lists a number of dishes that were prevalent during that period, namely – mahura, saga, muga, tikta, kanji, raai, amruta manohi khanda, madhuruchi, khiri, ambilaa, sakara, kadali bhaja, manja, dudha puli, ghruta puli, sara puli, podapitha and panaa.

Dietary restrictions mentioned in the text are: do not eat curd rice at night (causes accumulation of cough), do not cook bottle gourd with any non-vegetarian ingredient (possibly an attempt to curb outside influences, especially those coming from the Bengal region,) do not eat Pakhala (leftovers) on Thursday, do not cut ash gourd (used in sacrifice), do not face South or West while eating.

CHAULA KAKARA PITHA
(Stuffed and deep-fried rice cake)

It's dark outside and the bitter cold does not help. I want to squeeze in another hour of sleep before getting ready for school. But the blowing of the conch refuses to subside. And the primal *'hulu-huli'* accompanied by the ringing of the bells adds to the cacophony. It is a Thursday and the ladies will not risk the wrath of Goddess Lakshmi.

I gingerly get my fingers out from under the blanket to test the air and almost immediately recoil. Although they no longer feel as numb as they did after a marathon 'jhunti/chitta' (rice paste motifs drawn on the floors and sometimes walls too) session late in the night, they are particularly sensitive to the chill in the air. I decided to stay put in bed with my ears attuned to every sound around me. My mom and grandma are in the thick of the action. I hear them rustle the new saree, open the tin box to bring out the Pooja things and break the coconut. The aroma of camphor drifts in the air even as the sweet smell of the *'chenna kadali chakata,'* the first bhoga of the day reaches my nostrils. The whole house comes alive with the recitation of verses from the Lakshmi Purana.

As I wake up and get ready for school, I overhear the conversation about the 'anna bhoga' and pitha planned for the mid-day offering. I remind them to save some for me.

On the occasions when these Thursdays coincided with a holiday, I would be the most bright-eyed assistant to the two ladies. I would keenly watch the rice flour being cooked in boiling water/milk and the dough being kneaded to a smooth mass while still hot. The pitha were shaped while the dough was warm. Otherwise, they would crumble while frying. As a little child, I wondered how they managed to handle the hot mass until I realized that the trick was to keep moving fast and not to let the hot dough touch the skin for a prolonged period. Even today, when I make a batch of these pitha, I am assailed by a wave of nostalgia

Manabasa Gurubar, the Thursday of the Hindu month of Margasira, is an occasion every Odia household welcomes Goddess Lakshmi into the house with much fanfare.

Cooking time Required: 1 hour

Ingredients:

- 1 cup fine rice flour / *chaula chuna*
- 1 ¾ cup water
- 2 cups freshly grated coconut
- ½ cup jaggery
- 1 tsp fennel seeds (1 tsp)
- 1-2 cardamon
- 1 tbsp ghee
- Oil/ghee for frying
- 1 tsp sugar
- ½ tsp salt

Preparation:

- Boil the water in a deep vessel. Add crushed fennel, 1 tsp sugar and ½ tsp salt to the boiling water. Lower the flame, add the rice flour in batches and keep stirring to avoid formation of lumps.

- Switch off the flame once the rice flour soaks up all the water and forms a loose solid mass. Cover the vessel and let it stand for 15 minutes so that the rice flour gets cooked in the residual heat.

- Remove the lid and allow it to cool down to a tolerable temperature. Sprinkle the ghee over the dough. Knead the mixture with your hands into a smooth dough. The kneading should be done when the dough is still hot, else the pitha will crack while frying.

- Melt the jaggery with 2-3 tsp water in another wok. Once it starts foaming, add the grated coconut and cardamon powder to it. Cook for 3-4 minutes. Keep aside until it cools down.

- Divide the dough into small balls. Flatten the balls. Stuff with the coconut mixture. Shape into small discs.

Cooking:

- Heat a wok. Add sufficient oil for frying. When the oil is sufficiently hot, add the stuffed discs. Reduce flame to medium. Fry until the pitha is cooked and turns golden brown.

- Remove from the wok and serve warm.

- Tip to avoid lumps in the dough – Reduce the flame to the lowest. Dissolve 1 tbsp rice flour in cold water and add to the simmering water before adding the rest of the flour.

- *The above recipe makes 10-12 pithas.*

GHURA

(Set rice custard with a sweetened coconut filling)

Odia cuisine is much like the state itself. Unexplored and undiscovered. Except for a few dishes that have been highlighted too much and over-exploited, the rest are not known to the majority of Odia population. One such hyper-local recipe popular in the Sundargarh (specifically Bonei) district is the *Ghura* or *Ghora Manda*. Unlike the other kinds of 'manda pitha' which need to be shaped, this one is just poured out and left to set. It is made by slowly cooking a thin rice batter (not rice flour) for a relatively longer period of time, hence the name 'ghura.' Technically, it is not a manda. It has an amazing texture that it akin to a 'set pudding.' The stuffing or 'pura' can be a mix of coconut, *chenna* (cottage cheese), sesame and groundnuts. Soft and melt-in-the-mouth, this recipe takes a few trials to perfect but is very much worth the effort.

⧗ **Cooking time – 40 minutes**

Ingredients:

- 1 ½ cup raw rice / arwa rice
- 1 freshly grated coconut
- 1 ½ cup chenna (cottage cheese)
- ½ tsp salt
- 1/2 cup jaggery OR 1/3 cup sugar (will be used both for the batter and stuffing)
- 2 tsp ghee
- A pinch of camphor
- 1-2 pinch cardamom powder

🍽 Preparation:

- Wash and soak the rice for 3-4 hours. Drain excess water and grind into a fine paste. Transfer to a bowl. Add salt and water, and adjust the consistency to a flowing liquid (a little thinner than Chittau Pitha batter.) [The ratio of rice to water is roughly 1:5]

- Take the grated coconut, chenna, jaggery/sugar, camphor and cardamom powder in a mixing bowl. Mash everything together.

🍳 Cooking:

- Slowly decant the batter into a large wok taking care to leave behind any solids (residue) at the bottom of the bowl. (If this residue gets into the wok, it makes the pitha grainy and spoils the overall texture.)

- Add salt and 4-5 tsp jaggery to the batter Switch on the flame and keep it low at all times. Keep stirring at regular intervals so that it does not catch at the bottom. Once the mixture thickens to that of a custard-like consistency, switch off the flame.

- Pour ladles of the hot mixture onto a greased steel plate or banana leaf. Gently spread (but not too much) using the back of a spoon. Layer with the stuffing of sweetened coconut and cottage cheese. Seal it by topping it with a spoonful of the hot mixture. (While the more seasoned cooks can afford to touch the hot stuff, the rookies are warned to keep their fingers safe and unscathed.)

- Allow it to rest until it is completely cool.

- Serve cold.

Note – Ghura is also prepared with finger millet or mandiya. The finger millet custard preparation is similar to the method used for making Tikhri. The filling used is either coconut-jaggery or chenna-jaggery.

A very interesting question came up during the research of this book. Why the name 'Manda' for such a wide range of recipes? To decode the name behind this delicacy which is notably mentioned in the Laxmi Purana text, I decided to look beyond the external trappings of each pitha. The word which popped out was 'Mandaw' which refers to starch or even pulp in some cases. The cooking action (heat + water) brings out the starchy properties (thickening and gelatinization) of the rice which helps to mould the pitha or to hold it together. Another possibility is that it is derived from the Sanskrit word 'Manda' which refers to something that has coagulated. It is perhaps a reference to the gradual thickening of the powdered rice powder and water during the cooking process.

BIRI GOJJA

(Steamed rice cake with spicy black lentil filling)

Biri Gojja is one of the few savoury pithas we prepare in Odisha. While most of them are more or less on the sweeter side, some like the *saru chakuli, bhabra, biri poda pitha, sada enduri* and *biri gojja* fall into the category of exceptions. This recipe belongs to a small pocket of Coastal Odisha and was shared by my mother-in-law's sister who prepared it as a part of my 'sadaw khia,' a special meal fed to a pregnant woman during the third trimester. It is not as common as the other pithas like Manda, Kakara, Arissa and Enduri.

The rather interesting name comes from the pinched ends of the pitha. The pointed corners are called 'gojiya' in Odia, and over time it evolved into the much easier on the tongue 'gojja.'

 **Cooking time – 1 hour**

 **Ingredients:**

- 1 1/2 cups rice flour
- 4 cups water
- 1/2 tsp salt
- 1/2 tsp ghee

For the stuffing:

- 2/3 cup black lentil (without skin)
- 1-2 finely chopped green chillis
- 1 sprig of curry leaves (finely chopped)
- 1/4 tsp coarsely crushed black pepper
- 1 tsp finely chopped ginger
- A pinch of cumin (optional)
- Salt to taste

🍽️ Preparation:

- Wash and soak the black lentil for 2-3 hours. Grind into a smooth and thick paste. Season it with salt, pepper, cumin, ginger, curry leaves and green chillis.

🍲 Cooking:

- Bring the water to boil. Add salt and ghee. Add the rice flour in small batches and mix continuously so that no lumps are formed.

- Stir the mixture on a low flame for about 10 minutes or until it starts to form a tight dough. Switch off the flame at this stage.

- Allow the dough to cool down until it is tolerable to touch. Rub ghee all over your hands and knead the dough for 5 minutes to make it smooth.

- Rub more ghee over your hands. Pinch small lumps out of the dough. Roll each lump into a ball and gently pat it to flatten it out into a circle. Put some of the black lentil batter on one half of the circle and fold the other half over it. Press it gently to close on the sides but keep the middle portion slightly open. (This ensures that the batter gets cooked evenly and the pitha does not burst open due to the expanding lentil paste).

- Boil water in a steamer. Spread some banana leaves/thin cloth over the plate. Put 5-6 pieces of *biri gojji* over it (depending on the steamer capacity). Close the lid and steam for 25-30 minutes. Switch off the flame and allow it to stand for 5-10 minutes. Remove from the steamer.

- Serve warm.

MANABASA KHIRI/JAU
(Aromatic rice pudding)

'Jau' is an important part of the Manabasa Gurubar offering and is prepared with the new rice which has an unmistakable stickiness to it due to its higher amylopectin content. The rice lends this 'binding' quality to the dishes prepared with it, but in the case of 'Jau,' it acts as a natural thickening agent.

Manabasa Jau is cooked with a trickle of milk, a dash of sugar and a single *annapurna* (Pandan) leaf. It can be described as a very light 'kheer.' Sugar (Sarkara) is used to retain the pristine white colour which alludes to the 'ocean of milk' where the divine couple Lakshmi -Narayan are said to reside.

 **Cooking Time – 30 minutes**

 **Ingredients:**

- 1 cup new rice (broken aromatic rice is preferred)
- 1/4 cup milk
- 2-3 tbsp sugar
- A pinch of salt
- a hint of edible camphor
- 1-2 pandan leaves
- 5-6 cups water

Cooking:

- Bring the water to a boil in a thick-bottomed vessel. Wash the rice thoroughly and drain it. Add to the boiling water and stir it so that it doesn't catch at the bottom.

- Add the salt. Lower the flame and let it cook until the rice is cooked. Add the Pandan leaves and cook for 15-20 minutes longer so that the grains start to disintegrate. Top with more hot water if required.

- Add 1/4 cup milk, 2-3 tsp sugar and a pinch of salt.

- Remove from flame and serve warm.

Note – Generally, a different version of Jau is prepared during Nuakhai with the addition of jaggery, Indian bay leaf, camphor and chopped coconut. The addition of milk is optional in this case.

Khiri/Payas/Jau

'Khiri' is derived from the Odia word 'Khira,' which again is similar to the Sanskrit word 'Kshira,' meaning milk. It refers to a sweet dish cooked with milk.

Payas is derived from 'Payasa' or 'payasam,' and refers to a dish cooked with milk and sugar/jaggery.

Both the above terms are often used interchangeably.

Jau on the other hand, refers to a rice dish cooked to a porridge-like texture. The usage of milk or a sweetening agent is entirely optional. Even if milk or sugar is used, it is much less than what is used in a 'khiri' or 'payas.' As it is a rather frugal dish, no cardamon or dry fruits are added to it.

DAHI BHATA

(Rice mixed with curd and aromatic seasoning)

Goddess Lakshmi is worshipped by offering her a variety of milk products and dairy-based dishes. Perhaps, this practise is linked to the imagery of the divine couple reclining on the serpent 'Shesha Naga' surrounded by an ocean of milk. Hence, there is a conscious attempt to adhere to the colour palette by keeping out ingredients like red rice, black rice, molasses and jaggery from the list of ingredients used to prepare the offerings. Some of these are even prohibited during the Thursdays of this month (as per the Purana).

Dahi bhata or '*Dadhi Anna*' is among the offerings made on a Manabasa Gurubar. Sometime, a watery version of the same dish is prepared. It is then referred to as 'Dahi Pakhala.' It is distinct from the 'curd rice' eaten in South India in terms of the seasoning used.

 **Cooking time – 15 minutes**

 **Ingredients:**

- 1 cup aromatic small-grained rice
- 1 cup fresh curd
- 2- 3 tsp sugar
- ½ inch mango ginger
- 1 green chilli
- 1-2 sprig of tender curry leaves
- ¼ tsp salt

🍳 Cooking:

- Bring 2 ½ cups of water to a boil. Add the washed rice and let it cook until it turns mushy.

- Remove from the flame and cool it down. Add the beaten curd, crushed mango ginger and green chilli, torn curry leaves, salt and sugar.

- Mix everything.

- The Dadhi anna is ready to be offered to the Goddess.

ATTA SUANLI

(Deep-fried whole wheat cakes)

While Kakara or Manda refers to a pitha with a filling in it, *'sunali'* is made without any filling. The naming is not standard and varies as one travels across the state. The primary ingredient used for making pitha has always been rice and also, wheat in some cases. But the current generation has shifted to using semolina or even 'maida' for preparing this pitha.

 **Cooking time – 40 minutes**

 **Ingredients:**

- 1 cup wheat flour
- 1 cup water
- 1/2 cup jaggery (reduce as per preference)
- 1 tsp fennel seeds
- Oil for deep frying

Preparation:

- Boil the water in a deep vessel. Add crushed fennel and jaggery to the boiling water. Then add the flour in batches and keep stirring to avoid formation of lumps.

- Switch off the flame once the flour soaks up all the water and forms a loose solid mass. Cover the vessel and let it stand for 5 minutes.

- Remove the lid and allow to cool down to a tolerable temperature. Sprinkle the ghee over the dough. Knead the mixture with your hands into a smooth dough. The kneading should be done when the dough is still hot, else the pitha might crack while frying.

- Break the dough into small balls. Roll out the balls into small discs.

Cooking:

- Heat a wok. Add sufficient oil for frying. When the oil is hot, add the discs. Reduce flame to medium. Fry until the pitha are cooked and they turn brown.

- Remove from the wok and serve warm.

- Tip to avoid lumps in the dough – Reduce the flame to the lowest. Dissolve 1 tbsp wheat flour in cold water and add to the simmering water before adding the rest of the flour.

KANDAMULA KHATTA
(Sweet potato relish)

Sweet potato is a delightful winter vegetable that is often roasted and eaten as it is. It is also added to various other preparations like Ghanta and Dalma. However, in Western Odisha, it is turned into a delicious sweet-sour preparation to be enjoyed with rice meals on 'no onion-garlic' days.

The reasons to include sweet potato in one's diet go beyond taste. It is a 'kapha-pacifier' – that tackles accumulation of kapha during winter, has ample fibre – takes care of sluggish bowel movements on cold days, is loaded with vitamin A/Beta-carotene and has a low glycaemic index.

One of the vivid memories from my childhood involves picking up a roasted sweet potato from the embers and giving it a thorough dusting before removing the charred skin. These tubers were usually tossed into the wooden/coal fire towards the end of the lunch preparation when the fire had almost died down. They would be picked up later for a quick afternoon snack.

 **Cooking time – 25 minutes**

 **Ingredients:**

- 2 medium-sized sweet potato
- 2-3 tsp tamarind pulp
- ½ tsp chilli powder (optional)
- 4 tsp jaggery
- 2 dry red chilli
- ½ tsp pancha phutana (use cumin and mustard seeds in a 1:1 ratio if not available)

- ½ tsp turmeric
- ½ tsp salt
- 3 tsp oil
- 2 sprigs of curry leaves

For the masala:

- 2 dry red chilli
- 1 tsp fennel seeds
- 1 tsp fenugreek seeds
- 1tsp cumin seeds

Preparation:

- Peel and cut the sweet potato into small pieces.
- Dry roast the ingredients for masala. Allow it to cool down and then grind it into a coarse powder.

Cooking:

- Take the sweet potato pieces in a saucepan along with 2 cups of water. Add salt and turmeric and boil until the pieces are about 70 per cent cooked.
- Heat a wok. Add the oil and once it starts to smoke, add the broken red chilli and pancha phutana. Add the curry leaves after 30 seconds.
- Add ½ cup water to the wok. Add the tamarind pulp and bring it to a boil. After boiling for 2-3 minutes, add the jaggery. After some time, the jaggery starts to foam.
- Add the cooked sweet potato pieces along with the water used for boiling it. Let it simmer for 5 minutes. Adjust the salt/jaggery/ tamarind/water consistency as per preference.
- Finally, sprinkle a little of the masala prepared earlier and remove it from the flame.
- Serve at room temperature.

There is a certain grammar when it comes to the various dishes created with a vegetable during its lifecycle. The earlier or tender stages of the vegetables usually involve milder preparations with lower spices levels to allow the inherent taste of the vegetables to bloom.

As the vegetables tend to mature, more robust preparations are invoked that work best with their texture. The spice levels also tend to go higher as a certain monotony starts to creep in. At this stage, they can retain their shape better so they are also good for dishes like Ghanta or Dalma, which require a longer cooking time

During the last stages, when the fibres have toughened or the seeds have matured, the vegetables usually become the part of dishes like kanji or a Khatta, where the last dredges of their flavour are extracted.

MULA BHAJA

(Pan-fried roundels of radish)

The first radish of the season is offered to Goddess Lakshmi during Manabasa Gurubar. *This is in-line with the tradition of eating 'Nua' that we observe in different parts of the state.* Hence, it qualifies to be a part of the *anna bhoga* that is offered to the Goddess during mid-day. This is usually done in the form of a *mula bhaja*, a simple stir fry. The radish is cut into rounds and these are pan-fried with a little salt, turmeric and ghee.

However, on other days, the radish is cooked with a hint of mustard paste.

 **Cooking time – 10 minutes**

 **Ingredients:**

- 200 gm white radish
- 2 tsp mustard seeds
- 1 tsp cumin seeds
- 2 dry red chilli
- 5 tsp cooking oil
- Salt to taste
- 1/5 tsp turmeric

Preparation:

- Grind the mustard seeds, cumin seeds and chilli into a fine paste.
- Peel and cut the radish into 6-7 mm thick pieces.

Cooking:

- Take the radish pieces in a wok. Add the mustard seed paste along with salt and turmeric. Add 1 cup water.

- Cook on a medium flame for 5-6 minutes or until the radish is cooked but firm. The mustard paste should form a layer around the pieces.

- Heat a pan. Drizzle a little oil on it.

- Place the boiled radish pieces on the pan. Drizzle a little more oil on the sides.Flip it over and fry on both sides until lightly crisp.

- Serve hot with rice meals.

DAHI MULA RAITA

(Grated radish and yoghurt preparation)

Radish is a much-loved winter vegetable that is added to kanji, ambil, khatta, sagaw and even to mixed vegetable preparations like 'Ghadghadiya tarkari.' Cooked by itself, it is often turned into a bhaja or a refreshing raita.

Cooking time – 15 minutes

Ingredients:

- 2-3 tender radish
- 1 cup freshly grated coconut
- 3/4th cup fresh curd
- 2 tsp sugar
- ¼ tsp mustard seeds
- 1-2 red chillies
- 1 sprig curry leaves
- 1 tsp oil
- Salt to taste
- 2-3 pinch coarsely ground peppercorns

Cooking:

- Grate the radish, squeeze out excess water (if you want to reduce the pungency) and transfer it to a mixing bowl. Add the grated coconut, curd, sugar, ground peppercorn and salt. Mix well and keep aside.

- Heat the oil in a pan. When it starts smoking, add the spices (red chilli and mustard seeds) and a few curry leaves. Pour the spluttering mixture into the bowl and mix.

- Serves as an excellent side dish for any vegetarian meal.

Chunks of tender radish are often crushed and mixed with some lemon juice and coriander leaves and kept aside for a while. Salt is added just before serving. This is one of the few examples of indigenous salads that one finds in Odia cuisine.

BADAM BATA DIA MULA SAAG
(Radish greens cooked with peanut paste)

A common method of cooking bitter greens is to add vegetables and a thickening agent to balance the bitterness, and hold the dish together. While powdered rice or lentils are given preference in the Eastern part of the state, one finds groundnuts and poppy seeds being leveraged for the same purpose in the Western parts.

These preparations still have a bit of liquid left at the end of cooking and hence pair nicely with hot rice. Sometimes, the 'dal' is skipped if there is one or more such dishes on the menu.

 **Cooking time – 20 minutes**

 **Ingredients:**

- 3 cups chopped radish greens
- 1 cup veggies of choice (eggplant/pumpkin/radish/potato)
- 1 medium-sized tomato
- ½ tsp mustard seeds
- 1 dry red chilli
- 1 tsp oil
- Salt to taste
- 10-12 Fried and crushed badi

For the paste:

- ¼ cup pink groundnuts
- 4-5 garlic cloves
- 1-2 green chilli
- A pinch of cumin seeds (optional)

🍽️ **Preparation:**

- Soak the groundnuts for 30 minutes.

- Grind into a medium-fine paste with green chilli, garlic and a pinch of cumin seeds.

- Wash and chop the radish greens into small pieces. Cut the vegetables into appropriate sizes so that both the greens and the veggies can cook together.

🍳 **Cooking:**

- Cook the greens and the veggies in a pressure cooker for 1 whistle on medium-high flame. [This can be done in a pot but it will take a longer time]

- Heat a wok. Add the oil. Once it starts smoking, add the mustard seeds and broken red chilli.

- Once the chilli darkens in colour, add the chopped tomato and cover it until the tomato softens. Mash the tomato lightly with the back of the ladle. Add the groundnut paste and sauté for 2 minutes.

- Add the boiled greens and veggies. Add a little water if required. Mix and cook on a low flame for 5-6 minutes until excess water evaporates and the saag and vegetables turn into a mushy consistency.

- Remove from the flame. Add the fried and crushed badi.

- Serve hot or warm with rice or roti.

Note – Mustard greens are also prepared in the same way.

JHILIYA

(Freshly pressed rice noodles cooked in sweetened milk)

The typical fare from western Odisha is very much frugal and is devoid of spices like cardamom and saffron, and even nuts like cashews, almonds and pistachio. But in our quest to add more flavour or even flaunt a certain social status, we end up skipping the indigenous ingredients and adopting ingredients that seem more trendy or mainstream.

I remember from conversations with my late grandmother that the green cardamom was a very late entrant into her kitchen. Bay leaves, ginger, pandan leaves, peppercorn and fennel were the most popularly used flavouring agents. But over a period of time, cardamom became an integral part of almost every sweet dish and savoury curry. Indigenous nuts like the peanut and *char manji* were overtaken by cashews and almonds. In fact, a lot of ingredients that we use today have slowly crept into our menu over the last five to six decades, and have become firmly rooted in our conscience.

⏳ **Cooking time – 1 hour**

 **Ingredients:**

- 2/3 cup raw rice
- ½ cup cooked rice
- ½ litre milk
- 1 ½ cup powdered jaggery
- Bay leaves for flavouring
- 1 tsp salt (approx.)

 **Preparation:**

- Wash and soak the raw rice for 5-6 hours. Drain the water and transfer it to a mixer jar. Grind into a smooth but thick batter (like

Bara/vada batter or even thicker). Add the cooked rice and grind it again for 1- 2 mins.

🍳 Cooking:

- Take 2 litres of water in a wide-mouthed vessel. Dissolve the jaggery in it and turn the flame to medium high until it gets to the full boil stage. Let it boil for 5-6 minutes.

- Push the batter through a sieve with small holes and let it fall directly into the boiling jaggery water. It will form thin elongated shapes like noodles or globules depending on the size of the holes and the thickness of the batter.

- Let it cook for 1-2 minutes and then, switch off the flame. It should get cooked in the residual heat.

- Boil the milk separately along with the bay leaves for a couple of minutes. Switch off and allow it to cool down until it is just about warm. Add it to the vessel containing the rice noodles and give a gentle stir.

- Serve it warm.

Note – This recipe was earlier prepared during the sugarcane harvest in Western Odisha. The extracted sugarcane juice was put to boil, and once it had reduced to a certain extent, the rice noodles would be directly pressed into the still-liquid. Sugarcane cultivation was phased out in these regions due to scarcity of water and hence, this recipe gradually faded away from public memory. Others like my grandmother preferred to tweak the main ingredient and hold on to it.

***Some people also prepare a paste out of powdered arua and cooked usna rice, instead of using the rice batter as described above. Parboiled rice is used as it considered to be light and better for digestion.*

CHINGUDI SORISA KHATTA

(Prawns cooked in a tangy mustard gravy)

The increased availability of prawns during the winters, which follow closely after their breeding season, adds an interesting dimension to the menu. Prawns are cooked by themselves, added to numerous 'mixed' preparations or turned into a hassle-free 'checcha' by crushing small fried prawns with shallots, garlic, a fiery green chilli and a glug of mustard oil. The tangy mustard version remains my favourite solely for the thin gravy that I love to sip with a makeshift 'ambula spoon.'

This recipe that is usually prepared in the Western parts of the state.

⧖ Cooking time – 30 minutes

 **Ingredients:**

- 200 gm small-sized prawns
- 2 tsp brown mustard seeds (+ ½ tsp for tempering)
- 6-7 garlic pods
- 1-2 hot green chillis
- 3-4 tsp mustard oil
- ¼ tsp turmeric
- 2 tsp rice
- 1-2 pieces dried mango(ambula)
- Salt to taste

 **Preparation:**

- Wash and clean the prawns. Marinate with ¼ tsp turmeric and ¼ tsp salt.
- Grind the mustard seeds and the garlic pods into a fine paste.
- Soak the rice for 2-3 hours. Grind into a fine paste. Soak the ambula and keep it aside.

- Heat a wok. Add 2 tsp oil to it. Add the prawns and stir fry for 3-4 minutes or until the prawns turn red. Remove and keep aside.

- Add the remaining oil to the wok. Once it heats up, add slit green chilli and mustard seeds.

- When the seeds start spluttering, add the mustard paste diluted with two cups of water. Add the prawns along with salt and turmeric and let it boil for 5 minutes. Add the rice paste while stirring the gravy continuously. Let it simmer for 5-6 minutes and then, add the ambula along with any water used for soaking it.

- Cook it for another 5 minutes. Drizzle half a tsp of mustard oil over it. Switch off the flame.

- Serve with rice meals.

Note – Unlike regular gravies that use potato and tomato for thickening, the rice acts as a thickening agent in this case. Rice water(pej) can also be used for thickening. The ambula can be substituted with amchur if the former is not available. But make sure to use a minimal quantity of the rice paste and ambula/ tamarind as this is a relatively thin preparation with just the right note of tanginess.

MACCHA AMBILA

(A sweet-sour fish gravy)

Maccha ambila is best described as a fish preparation that is sweet, sour, spicy and beautifully fragrant. A fine amalgamation of the culinary cultures of Odisha and neighbouring Andhra, the dish represents a region that straddles the two states and yet blends the two into a seamless entity.

The telltale hobnobbing of the two distinctive spice mixes is discernible and yet so discreet. The signature tang could come from anything ranging from 'ambula' to tamarind to ripe tomatoes or even curd. I prefer to stick to tamarind for my version.

⏳ **Preparation time – 20 minutes**

 **Ingredients:**

- 3 pieces of rohu fish
- 1 small onion
- 2-3 garlic cloves
- 1/3 inch ginger
- 1 dry red chilli
- 1/3 tsp cumin
- A pinch of fennel seeds
- 1 tsp mustard paste
- 2 tsp tamarind paste
- 2 tbsp jaggery (one can also use sugar)
- 1/2 tsp turmeric
- 1/3 tsp chilli powder
- Salt to taste
- 4-5 tsp oil

For tempering:

- 4-5 curry leaves
- 2 pinch mustard seeds
- 5-7 fenugreek seeds
- A pinch of asafoetida
- 1 tsp oil

🍽️ Preparation:

- Add a pinch of turmeric and a bit of salt to the fish. Marinate for 10 minutes.
- Take the garlic, ginger, cumin seeds, fennel seeds and dry red chilli in a grinder. Make it into a paste. Add the onion (diced) to the same grinder and buzz for 1 sec to get a coarse paste.
- Dilute the tamarind paste in ½ cup of water.
- Dissolve the mustard paste in 1 cup water. Strain it to separate the solids.

🍲 Cooking:

- Heat the oil in a wok. Add the marinated fish and fry on both sides until lightly browned.
- Remove from wok and keep aside.
- Add 1 tsp of oil to the wok and add the onions. Fry until the onions turn translucent. Add the masala paste to the same wok and fry until the raw smell goes off. Add the strained mustard water to the wok. Add salt, turmeric and red chilli powder. Bring it to a light boil.
- Add the tamarind water. Sprinkle the jaggery and allow it to dissolve.
- Add the fish pieces to the gravy and simmer on medium flame until you get the desired consistency. It will take about 5-6 minutes.

- Heat oil for tempering. Add the mustard and fenugreek seeds. Follow with the asafoetida and curry leaves. Fry the leaves for 4-5 seconds. Pour the tempering over the fish gravy, mix in and remove from the flame.

- Serve at room temperature. Tastes best with rice.

Note - Some versions omit the mustard paste in this preparation. I prefer to use it. The recipe is quite versatile which is the hallmark of 'home cooking'.

MUTTON AMBILA

(A spicy sweet-sour mutton preparation)

An old gem that was usually prepared during weddings. It is another dish that has shades of neighbouring Andhra. Probably, it originated from exposure to the *Pulusu* or an older dish at some point in history but later went on to acquire a distinct character of its own. However, it is still prepared in parts of Koraput and adjoining areas during the winter.

 **Cooking time – 1 hour**

 **Ingredients:**

- 500 gm goat meat (with bones)
- 250 gm chopped onions
- 1-inch ginger
- 0-8 garlic cloves
- 1 tsp coriander seeds
- 1 tsp tamarind paste
- 1-3 tsp jaggery
- 2 bay leaves
- 2-inch cinnamon stick
- 8-10 peppercorns
- 1 star anise
- 5-6 cloves
- 3-4 tbsp mustard oil
- 1 tsp turmeric
- 1 tsp red chilli powder
- Salt to taste

Final tempering:

- 1-3 dry red chilli (use green chilli to make it spicier)
- 1 sprig curry leaves
- ½ tsp cumin + mustard seeds for tempering
- A pinch of asafoetida
- 1 tsp mustard oil

🍽 Preparation:

- Grind 50 gm onions, coriander seeds, ginger and garlic cloves into a fine paste.
- Clean the mutton. Marinate with salt, turmeric and 1 tbsp mustard oil.
- Dissolve the tamarind paste in ¼ cup water.

🍲 Cooking:

- Heat a wok. Add the remaining oil. Once the oil is hot, add the whole spices and fry them for 30 seconds.
- Toss in the onions and fry them on a low flame until they caramelize.
- Add the masala paste at this point and cook for 3-4 minutes.
- Add the turmeric and red chilli powder. Sauté until the oil starts to separate out.
- Now, add the mutton pieces and fry on high until they stop oozing water. Lower the flame and cover with a lid. Stir once every few minutes. Repeat until the mutton is nicely browned.
- Add 3 cups of hot water. Cook on a low flame until the meat is tender. Add the tamarind water and the jaggery. Adjust the amount as per preference.
- Let it simmer for 8-10 minutes.

- Heat 1 tsp oil in a wok. Add the asafoetida, mustard and cumin seeds, dry red chilli and curry leaves. Pour it over the mutton and cover it.

- Serve hot with rice.

> *Note – A few decades back, people used to serve fish during wedding feasts as mutton was expensive and beyond the budget for most families. It was mandatory to invite the entire village to the wedding. So, often there used to be a smaller feast for a close circle of family and friends with mutton being the main attraction. Maccha Ambila would ideally be served at a wedding feast for the entire community and Mutton Ambila prepared on another day for a more intimate celebration. But this was much before people moved on to fancy catering and elaborate menus that feature more than a hundred dishes but fail to do justice to indigenous recipes like this.*

LADAA PITHA
(A slow-cooked rice cake)

A Western Odisha pitha that is generally made and enjoyed in the winter, the cooking process bears a resemblance to the Podaw pitha prepared during Rajaw. However, it is a very frugal version and does not use leaves as an encasing to cook the pitha. The term 'Ladda' generally refers to something that has been dumped on one's shoulder. In this case, it paints an image of the batter being cooked into a dough and then dumped into the same wok for further cooking.

 **Cooking time – 1 hour**

 **Ingredients:**

- 1 cup raw rice
- ¼ cup urad dal
- ½ cup sugar (or as per taste)
- ¼ tsp salt
- 2 tsp oil for greasing the wok
- 1/4 roasted peanuts or char manji (optional)

Preparation:

- Wash and soak the rice and lentils for 5-6 hours.
- Grind into a fine paste. Dilute it to get a batter of thin consistency. Add the sugar and salt to the batter. Mix it until the sugar dissolves.
- Place a thick-bottomed wok on a low flame. Add the oil and spread it all over with the help of a spatula. This will keep the pitha from sticking too much to the sides.
- Transfer the batter to the wok and keep stirring it continuously.

- After some time, it will start to thicken. Add the roasted nuts if using. Keep stirring it until it solidifies into a dough.

- Wet your fingers and flatten out the dough. [*Work fast to avoid burning your fingers.*]

- Cover with a heavy lid and let it cook for 30-40 minutes.

- Switch off the flame and let it continue cooking in the residual heat for another hour.

- Cut into pieces once it cools down.

- Serve with milk, ghee or just by itself.

People in Odisha swear by fresh produce. Hence, the state has a somewhat modest tradition of preserving ingredients to help one tide over the paucity of food resources during a lean period. Since ages, Odia people have used different techniques ranging from sun-drying, salt-drying, pickling or even smoking to preserve various kinds of vegetables and river/sea catch.

'Badi', hand-made and sun-dried lentil dumplings are possibly the most universal among the various kinds of preserved foods we find in Odisha. Most of it is made from black lentil paste. However, the Western parts of the state are known to prepare 'Badi' from popped rice (*'Lia Badi'*) and even cooked rice paste (*'Chaula Badi'*). Even among the black lentil *'Badi'* varieties, one finds quite an intriguing diversity. From adding ash gourd pulp or sugarcane pulp to create varied textures, Badis are also prepared with a variety of seasonings like groundnuts, sesame, charoli, spices and even ash gourd seeds to enhance the taste. And then, there are more ingenious ones where excess seasonal produce like radish or cabbage is grated, squeezed out and incorporated into the batter for making badi.

Dried fish or *Sukhua* comes a close second. Salted, sun-dried and smoked ones are found in different geographies. *'Pita sukhua,'* or small river fish that have been sun-dried without removing the innards, are believed to have medicinal value and are highly prized. Small prawns and shrimp are also preserved frequently. The dried roe of fish like *Khainga*(Mullet) and Hilsa are much loved ingredients. The paddy fish is usually smoked and preserved in the Western parts.

Sula or dried vegetables are an important preserved ingredients in Western Odisha. Vegetables like tomato, eggplant, radish and cabbage are ideal for making *'sula.'*

Preserved seeds like those of jackfruit, flat beans and pumpkin are popularly used during periods of scarcity.

Dried or fermented bamboo shoots, dried mahua flowers, sundried mango or mango leather are other preserved foods that are found in Odisha.

Tribals preserve Sal seeds, Tamarind seeds, mango stones and cook them with preserved mahua during lean periods.

The tribals also store different varieties of yams and tubers by sun-drying and powdering them.

Margasira month is ideal for preserving foods due to the ambient temperatures, uninterrupted sunlight and abundant food resources.

PAUSA (DECEMBER – JANUARY)

It is winter. The days are pleasant and the skies are mostly clear except for the occasional haze. It is an ideal time to harvest the golden paddy stalks and transfer them from the farm to the barn. More crops are ready to be harvested, but paddy must take precedence, for it symbolizes Lakshmi, the Goddess of Prosperity. Black lentils, horse gram, sesame, and sugarcane patiently await their turn. Mango blossoms start showing up in places, heralding a new cycle even as the older one nears completion.

The cold and dry weather is ideal for post-harvest activities like threshing, drying, and parboiling. But the sight of overflowing granaries has elevated the everyone's spirits and the timing is right for celebration. Multiple regional festivities mark this month but it takes the occasion of *Makar Sankranti* to binds the state into one. A unique offering called *Makara Chaula* is prepared with new rice, milk, chenna, jaggery, coconut, ripe banana, popped rice, and warming spices like ginger and black pepper. This dish stems from the Jagannath dham where Goddess Lakshmi returns from her paternal home bearing gifts from the new harvest. Even in Odia homes, it is first offered to Lord Jagannath and then distributed among the family members. But what makes this dish truly intriguing, is the addition of diverse local ingredients in different parts of the state. From sugar palm sprouts in a village near Cuttack to various tubers in Baripada, to pieces of sugarcane and sesame seeds in Western Odisha, pretty much everything that can be tagged as 'new produce' qualifies for this offering. And, perhaps, it is our way of saying that we are the same even though we like doing things a little differently.

The other major festival this month is the *Pausa Purnima*. It is celebrated with much joy and feasting in Western Odisha. As it is quite cold, rich and energy-giving foods are an integral part of this feast. Various kinds of pitha(or rice cakes) like kakara, manda, arisa, ras bara and poda pitha are prepared. Stuffing prepared with jaggery and sesame or groundnut is used in the pitha. Before the Wildlife Act came into being, the annual 'Sikar' ritual for many tribal communities took place during this month. The animals naturally acquire a layer of fat thanks to the cold winter months, and hence, meat consumed during this period is considered to be extra delicious. Goat meat has since replaced game, although it is fondly referred to as *'sikar'* and remains sacrosanct to the *'Pus Puni'* menu.

Since the agricultural year ends, the farm-hands or labourers' contracts also come to an end in Western Odisha. They are paid with food grains and a cash bonus. This festival is a period of hard-earned rest and merriment for them. With the advent of mechanized farming, the role of the 'Haliya' or 'contract-bound farm-hand' is getting increasingly marginalized. Yet this festival retains its significance for the broader farming community.

During this month, the women folk in the coastal parts of the state observe a fast for the long lives of their offspring. The *Ghadaghadiya Tarkari*, a boiling medley of seasonal vegetables like radish, flat beans, taro, sweet potato, local tubers, and freshly made black lentil badi, is integral to the offerings made to the Sun God. On the evening of the same day, another preparation called *Budha Chakuli* is offered to Yama, the God of death. It is a thick pancake prepared with rice, black lentils, coconut, a local variety of cheese, banana, jaggery, and a few spices like black pepper, fennel and ginger.

A lesser-known festival that falls during this month is *Bakula Amabasya*. It is observed in the Jagannath Dham, and in the homes of the coastal districts. On this occasion, a pitha called 'Gaintha' is prepared, and prepped with mango blossoms before being offered to God. This falls in line with the concept of offering the first fruit to the Gods before any earthly creatures consume them. The tribal *Bhuiyans* observe a similar festival called 'Am-nua' around the same time, and the offering is a porridge made with pared rice(arwa) and mango blossoms. However, this festival has no fixed date and it is left to the 'Dehuri,' the non-brahmin priest, to decide an auspicious date after the mango blossoms start showing up.

Note – Dishes like Chakuli and Budha Chakuli are a part of almost all the festivals where prayers are offered for the long life of the family members. Perhaps, it is an attempt to allude to the never ending-ness of the circle, or a hint at the cyclic nature of life and death.

What's on the menu this month

Eons ago, when electronic media was not the chosen mode of distracting a fussy toddler, mothers would recite the tale of the *'Manda khia asuru'* during meal hours. Set in the Mahabharata era, it refers to the period when the Pandavas were in exile. The story revolves around a fearsome demon who had struck a deal with the scared inhabitants of a village. They had agreed to send a bullock cart full of 'Manda pitha' every day to the cave where the demon resided and in exchange, the demon would spare their lives. So, it was decided that every family had to take turns and prepare the pitha for the demon. Every day, a young man from the village would load his cart with 'manda pitha' and drive up to the cave. But the demon being a demon did not keep his side of the bargain. And the poor cart driver would disappear along with his precious cargo on a regular basis. It did not take long time for the villagers to understand that the poor chap ended up becoming a part of the demon's meal and hence, the thought of driving up to the cave struck a chord of terror amongst them.

This continued until it was the turn of the family that hosted the Pandavas to deliver the 'manda pitha' to the demon. Seeing the family in tears, Bhim, the strongest among the Pandavas volunteered to drive the cart to the demon's place. Given his voracious appetite, Bhim ended up devouring the cartload of delicious 'Manda pitha' on the way. Finally, he used his immense strength to vanquish the demon and save the villagers.

The beauty of this folklore lies in the narration. Every time Bhima opened his mouth to swallow a 'manda,' a tiny mouth would pop open on cue, and a morsel of food shoved inside.

PUSA MANDA

(A steamed rice cake)

Manda pitha is, perhaps, the most prolific of all pithas that we have in Odisha. It makes its appearance with unfailing punctuality during the 'Osa' and 'baras' that mark our calendar. Be it *Dasara, Sudasha brata, Manabasa Gurubar*, Pus puni or even the *Manaa Ujhapana*, the manda is omnipresent.

Adding to the beauty of this pitha is the seasonality of the stuffing. While the coconut jaggery stuffing is the most common and is made throughout the year, there are varieties with a coconut and dahi chenna stuffing (*Sudasha brata*), moong and coconut stuffing, horse gram stuffing, popped rice and sesame stuffing (Pus Puni), peanut and sesame stuffing (Nuakhai), and even one with a spicy-savoury black lentil stuffing.

The preparation method also varies. Most mandas are steamed earning it the name of *Sijha Manda* or *Sijhri Manda* but some people prepare it by dunking the balls in boiling hot water. '*Phutla mandas*' as known to rise to the surface once the dough is thoroughly cooked and require a tad more skill to craft as compared to the ones that are steamed. '*Channa mandas*' or fried mandas are also made but these have a limited repertoire when it comes to the stuffing part.

 **Cooking time – 1 hour**

 **Ingredients:**

- 1 ½ cups Rice flour
- 2 cups *khaee or lia* (popped rice)
- ½ cup *rasi (khasa)*/sesame seeds
- ½ cup jaggery
- 1 tbsp ghee

- 4 cups water
- ½ tsp salt

|O| Preparation:

- Toast the sesame seeds lightly. Allow them to cool down and grind them into a coarse powder.
- Take the popped rice in a big bowl. Sprinkle a few teaspoons of water and mash it.

Cooking:

- Bring 3 cups of water to boil in a deep vessel. Add salt and follow it with the rice flour in small batches. Keep stirring continuously while adding the rice flour to prevent the formation of lumps.
- Stir the mixture on a low flame for about 10 minutes until it reaches a sticky dough-like consistency. Cover with a heavy lid and switch off the flame at this stage.
- Allow the dough to stand until it cools down to a tolerable temperature. Remove the dough to a flat surface, rub ghee all over your hands and knead the dough for 5 minutes to make it smoother.
- Melt the jaggery along with a few teaspoons of water in another wok. Once it bubbles, add the mashed *khaee*, mix it and then, add the coarsely powdered sesame. Mix everything thoroughly and cook it for 3-4 minutes. Remove from the flame.
- Rub some more ghee over your hands. Break small balls out of the dough. Flatten them out and put some of the popped rice-sesame stuffing on it. Close and seal the stuffing carefully. Mould into a spherical shape.
- Boil water in a steamer. Spread some banana leaves over the perforated plates. Put the *manda pithas* over it. Close the lid and steam for 20 minutes. Allow to stand with lid covered for 5 minutes.
- Take the steamed 'Mandas' out of the steamer, cool them and serve at room temperature.

Note – In the traditional setup, a cloth would be tied around the mouth of a wide-mouth pot, the manda pitha placed over it and covered with a dome-shaped lid. The boiling water inside generated the steam required to cook the pithas.

The outer layer of Manda pitha is traditionally made from rice dough but in some parts of Western Odisha, the dough is prepared by soaking, grinding and cooking the split yellow moong dal. The latter is generally stuffed with a sweetened mixture of groundnut and sesame, and is referred to as Muga Manda or Muga Kakara. Unlike the steamed variants, this one is always deep fried.

PAUSA KHECHUDI
(A rice and mixed lentils preparation)

Pus Puni celebrations in parts of some parts of Odisha call for a special Khichdi that is a culmination of all the major seasonal produce. *'Pausa Khechudi'* makes use of the parboiled rice prepared from the new harvest and all the dals that have been harvested at the end of the winter and turns it into one celebratory dish. Even the sesame from the Rabi crop finds its way into this dish.

Bursting with flavours and riding high on earthy notes, this is usually served in smaller portions as it is quite heavy to digest.

 **Cooking time – 1.5 hours**

 **Ingredients:**

- 1 cup parboiled rice (Usna Chaula)
- ¼ cup Lobia (rumha dali)
- ¼ cup Green Moong (Gota muga)
- ¼ cup horse gram
- 2-3 tsp black lentil (Gota biri)
- 1-2 bay leaves
- 8-10 peppercorns
- 2-3 tbsp jaggery
- 2 tbsp ghee
- 1 tsp salt

Cooking:

- Dry roast each of the lentils on low heat until it just starts to release a fragrance.
- Wash and soak the lentils for 3-4 hours.

- Discard the water used for soaking and transfer the lentils to a pressure cooker. Add 5 cups of water.

- Cook on a high flame for 2-3 whistles or until half done.

- Transfer to a deep vessel and add the washed rice. Add the bay leaf and peppercorns. Cook on a medium flame until the rice is almost done (90 per cent cooked).

- Add the salt at this stage.

- Once the khichudi is ready, switch off the flame.

- Add the ghee and jaggery. Mix it and it is ready to serve.

Note – Parboiled rice does not turn mushy like raw rice. So, it retains its shape even though it is completely cooked or even overcooked. Check if the lentils are done before switching off the flame. Unlike most khichadis, the rice and lentils retain their shape even after cooking.

MAKARA CHAULA

(Powdered raw rice mixed with dairy and fruits)

Makara Chaula is prepared and offered to the Gods in most parts of the state during Makara Sankranti. The rice used is always sourced from the fresh harvest and mixed with seasonal fruits. There are slight variations in the ingredients depending on the region. For example, some sesame-growing regions sprinkle a little sesame over it while other parts that grow sweet potatoes also add it to this preparation. This dish is never cooked or even warmed in any way.

 **Preparation time Required: 15 minutes**

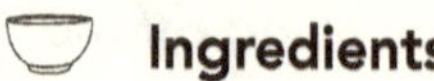 **Ingredients:**

- 1/2 cup small-grained aromatic rice
- 1 cup milk
- 1/2 cup freshly grated coconut
- 1/3 cup small sugarcane pieces
- 1-2 ripe banana
- Jaggery/Sugar to taste
- 1/2 tsp pepper powder
- 1/4 cup cottage cheese (Chenna)
- 1 tsp grated ginger
- 1/2 cup chopped fruits of your choice

🍽 Preparation:

- Soak the rice for 2 hours. Wash and drain the water. Spread out and allow to dry for 1-2 hours.

- Grind into a coarse powder and transfer to a mixing bowl. Add the rest of the ingredients except for the banana and mix well. Peel and crush the banana. Add to the mixing bowl and mix.

- Let it stand for a little time for the flavours to come together before consuming.

- Consume within a day if kept outside the refrigerator. Can be refrigerated for 2-3 days.

***Note – A similar preparation called 'Nabanna' is made on Nuakhai in some parts of western Odisha. A few stalks of ripened paddy are taken from the fields before harvest and they are threshed to separate the husk. This rice is crushed and mixed with milk, curd, ghee, banana and sugar/jaggery and offered to the Gods before being distributed within the household.*

MAKARA JAU

(Rice and sesame seeds porridge)

Yet another recipe that celebrates the new harvest, it is the culmination of two important crops, namely paddy and sesame. The addition of sesame further enhances the soothing and warmth-giving properties of the 'Jau.' However, it is usually consumed in small portions as newly harvested rice is considered 'heavy.'

 **Cooking time – 30 minutes**

Ingredients:

- 1 cup broken raw rice (aromatic rice is preferred)
- ¼ cup black sesame seeds
- 1/3 cup jaggery
- ½ tsp salt

Cooking:

- Soak the sesame seeds for 1-2 hours. Grind into a coarse paste.
- Bring 5 cups of water to boil in a deep vessel. Wash and add the rice. Bring to a boil on a high flame and then lower the flame.
- Let it simmer until the rice is overcooked but the grains have not started to disintegrate. Add the sesame seed paste and mix it.
- Add jaggery and salt and let it simmer for a few minutes while stirring it continuously.
- Switch off the flame. Serve warm.

> Note – a few pieces of toasted coconut add extra flavour to this recipe.

MUAN

(Crunchy snacks made from sweetened cereals)

Muan is best described as a crunchy sphere-shaped (mostly) snack made from popped rice, puffed rice, roasted flattened rice, Huduma and even puffed sorghum (*Gangei* in Western Odisha). These have a long shelf life and are useful to pacify those numerous hunger pangs that strike during the cold winters. A stimulated appetite is nature's way of reminding one to eat food which gets converted into energy (heat) after digestion. This helps maintain the body temperature which tends to dip during the cold weather as we lose the heat to the surroundings.

I'm sharing the basic recipe used for preparing all kinds of Muan.

 **Preparation time – 20 minutes**

 **Ingredients:**

- 1 cup jaggery

- 6 cups puffed rice (*Mudhi*)/Roasted flattened rice (Bhaja Chuda/ *Phuta Chuda*)

- ¼ cup dry roasted peanuts¼ cup dry roasted *char manji* (*Buchanania Lanzan*)

- 2-3 tsp ghee

Cooking:

- Heat the jaggery with 1/3 cup water in a wok. It will melt and then start to foam/bubble. Take care to keep the flame low at all times.

- Gradually, the bubbles will get smaller and now it is time to test for the right consistency of the jaggery. If it gets over-cooked, then the puffed rice will not bind together.

- Take a large bowl with cold water in it. Put a single drop of the jaggery into it. If it dissolves into the water, it needs to be cooked for a longer time. Keep repeating this test at intervals of 1 minute until the moment the jaggery stops dissolving.

- Immediately remove the wok from the flame.

- Add the ingredient of your choice (*mudhi/phuta chuda*) and mix thoroughly to uniformly coat the puffed rice. Add the peanuts/char manji/toasted coconut. Mix everything together.

- Rub ghee on your hands and scoop out a fistful of the mixture as soon as you can handle the heat. Press gently on all sides and mould into a ball shape. Repeat for the remaining mixture.

- Keep aside to cool down for 1-2 hours. One can then store them in an airtight tin for almost a month.

Note – If you find it difficult to shape the muan, grease small steel bowls with a little ghee and press the hot mixture into it. Once cooled, it will easily separate from the steel.

Dhanu Muan is made with Khaee from newly harvested paddy, jaggery from the season's sugarcane crop, fried coconut slices and ghee. It is seasoned with a mix of spices like pepper, cloves, cinnamon, cardamom and fennel. The jaggery and spices provide warmth and help build immunity for the farmers and farmhands as they continue toiling in the cold weather. Post-harvest activities like threshing, milling (manual), parboiling, etc., are all labour-intensive and require a lot of energy. For making Dhanu muan, tweak the above recipe. Increase the quantity of the jaggery, throw in more add-ons like toasted coconut and sprinkle a powdered mix of spices like pepper, cloves, cinnamon, cardamom and fennel over the hot mixture before shaping the muan. Finally, smear a little ghee over the finished muan for that heavenly aroma.

Dhanu Muan bharaw (a gift sent to a married daughter's family) used to be mandatory for families in Coastal parts of Odisha. Therefore, the muan was prepared in huge quantities in homes. But with changing tastes and a decline in the tradition of 'bharaw,' it is rarely made at home. Most people buy a small piece of muan for offering to the Gods on Dhanu Sankranti.

Unlike other kinds of Maun, the Dhanu Muan is given various fancy shapes to make it appear more attractive to the customers.

GHADAGHADIYA TARKARI
(A watery mixed vegetable stew)

'*Samba Dashami*' evokes images of women getting up early to take a bath before the crack of dawn. The kitchens come alive with the clanging of utensils and the heavenly aromas drifting out of them. The rising sun is greeted with a cacophony of sounds like the blowing of the conch shells (sankha), the '*hulu-huli*' (a kind of sound uttered by the tongue) and the ringing of bells. This ritual is observed for the good health and long life of the children and the mother dedicates a dish to the Sun God for each of her children. The *Ghadaghadiya Tarkari*, the speciality of this festival, is offered to the Sun God during the mid-day. The final prasad is offered to Lord Yama in a ritual known as the '*Mahakala Puja.*' This pooja is done in the evening and an offering of '*Budha Chakuli*' is made to the God.

The legend of Samba Dashami is attributed to Samba, the son of Lord Krishna. It is said that Samba, who was afflicted with leprosy, prayed to the Sun God for 12 long years and finally got cured. A small temple dedicated to the Sun God still stands on the Chandrabhaga beach (near Konark temple) as a reminder of his penance. The name 'Konark' is derived from 'Konaditya', which is another name for the Sun God. Interestingly, 'Konark' is also spelled as 'Kona-arka', which literally translates into 'a corner of the land (Arka Khetra) where Sun God is worshipped', further cementing the association of the place with Sun worship.

Since it is offered to the Sun God, 'Ghadaghadiya Tarkari' does not contain any onion or garlic. The vegetables which go into it are supposed to benefit those suffering from cold and cough, both of which are common ailments during the winter months. Samba Dashami is celebrated on the 10th day of the *Shukla Pakhya* (waxing moon) during the Odia month of Pausa.

⏳ **Preparation time – 20-25 minutes (plus extra time required to chop all the vegetables)**

🥣 **Ingredients:**

- 1 cup yam (cubed)
- 1 cup pumpkin (cubed)
- 1/2 cup raw papaya (cubed)
- 1/2 cup sweet potato (cubed)
- 1/2 cup taro (cubed)
- 1/2 cup potato (optional, cubed)
- 1/2 cup radish (cubed)
- 1/2 cup eggplant (cubed)
- 1/2 cup plantain (cubed)
- 1 cup broad beans (inch-long pieces)
- 1 cup yard long beans (inch-long pieces)
- 2-3 medium-sized tomatoes (chopped, optional)
- 1 cup fried urad dal badi (must add)
- 2-3 dry red chillis
- 1-2 tsp cumin seeds
- 1 tsp roasted cumin-chilli powder
- 2 tsp oil
- 2 tsp ghee
- 1/3 tsp freshly crushed black pepper
- 1/2 tsp turmeric powder
- Salt to taste
- A fistful of coriander leaves (optional)

🍽 Preparation:

- Wash and clean all the vegetables. Some of them like plantain and eggplant have a tendency to blacken if left in the open for too long. So, cut them and immerse them in a bowl of water to which a little turmeric has been added.

🍳 Cooking:

- Heat the oil in a large wok. Add the broken red chilli and cumin seeds to it. Once it gets spluttering, add vegetables like yam, potato, sweet potato, plantain, pumpkin, and papaya, which take a relatively longer time to cook.

- Sauté for a few minutes before adding 2 cups of boiling water, salt and turmeric. Cover with a heavy lid and allow it to boil for 3-4 minutes or until half done.

- Add the remaining vegetables and let it boil for another 5-6 minutes or until the veggies are cooked.

- Finally, add the roasted cumin-chilli powder and coriander leaves just before removing from the flame.

- Add the black pepper and badi when serving.

- This curry is always served steaming hot (*'ghadghad'* refers to the sound it makes when it is at full boil, usually in a pot).

SIKAR JHUL

(Goat meat cooked with minimal spices)

Sikar refers to the meat of animals that were hunted rather than reared for consumption. Prior to the enforcement of the Wildlife Act of 1975, hunting wild pigs (*barha*), deer, sambar, kutra, peacock and wild fowls for food was very much the practice in the parts of Odisha. This game meat was highly prized. For the tribals, hunting was something of a much-awaited community event and it was permitted only once or twice during the year.

After the ban, the term Sikar was used to refer to goat meat.

 **Cooking time – 1 hour 20 minutes**

 **Ingredients:**

- 500 gm mutton
- 2 medium-sized potatoes
- 250 gm red onion
- 2 tbsp coarse garlic paste
- 2 tbsp coarsely chopped ginger
- 3-4 dry red chillis
- 1 big cardamom
- 2-3 bay leaf
- 2 2-inch cinnamon sticks
- ½ tsp turmeric
- 1 tbsp peppercorns
- 1 tsp salt (approx.)
- 6-7 tsp mustard oil + 2 tsp for the marination

🍽️ Preparation:

- Wash the mutton pieces and drain away all the water. Add ½ tsp salt, ½ tsp turmeric and 2 tsp mustard oil. Mix well and keep aside for 30 minutes.

- Cut the onions into medium-sized pieces. Crush the ginger and garlic into a coarse paste.

- Cut the potatoes into big chunks.

🍳 Cooking:

- Heat the oil in a pressure cooker.

- Add the potatoes and fry until they turn golden brown. Remove and keep aside.

- Add the broken red chillis followed by all the whole spices to the hot oil. Fry until they turn fragrant.

- Add the onions and fry them on low flame until they start to caramelize. Next, add the crushed ginger and garlic and sauté for 2-3 minutes.

- Add the mutton pieces. Fry them on high until they stop oozing water. Lower the flame and keep the lid on the cooker without completely closing it. Stir once every few minutes. Repeat until the mutton is nicely browned. (*Maillard's reaction at work – This process takes a long time but it is crucial for a great-tasting mutton curry.* No chilli powder is used and the colour of the curry is entirely due to the browning.)

- Add 3 cups of hot water along with the fried potato pieces. Adjust the salt. Close the lid and cook for 2-3 whistles on a low flame. Remove from flame.

- Allow the steam to escape before opening the lid. Check if the mutton is done. Else add another half cup of hot water and cook for another 1-2 whistles.

- Serve hot or warm with *palua* or aromatic white rice.

Note – The recipe yields a mutton curry with a thin gravy. Reduce the water if you want a thicker consistency.

**Both fat and bones are crucial for adding flavour to this curry. Hence, avoid using lean or boneless mutton while cooking with this recipe.

PALAU

(Sweetened rice pilaf)

Before fried rice and biryani became popular in Odisha, Palau was the only 'special rice' to be served during most wedding feasts, picnics and family gatherings. It is prepared with aged *Arua* (aromatic rice) available. Beautifully spiced and slightly on the sweeter side, it pairs nicely with a mutton or chicken curry.

Although it has become one among the many varieties laid out in lavish buffets these days, I enjoy it occasionally at home with a thin mutton gravy, tomato-onion-cucumber salad and a piece of fried *papad* to relive the memories of those winter picnic days. Flashes of the limited-menu meals enjoyed in a clearing by a stream, the winter sun beating down on us and conversation rippling through the group, remind me once again that food goes beyond the ingredients or even the menu for that matter.

 **Preparation time – 20 minutes**

 **Ingredients:**

- 1 cup small-grained aromatic rice (*Macchakanta/Pimpudibasa/ Sitabhoga*)
- 1 ½ tbsp ghee
- 10-12 raisins
- 10-12 cashews
- 1 black cardamon
- 1 green cardamon
- 1/2-inch cinnamon
- 2-3 cloves
- 1/4 of a mace
- 1 big bay leaf

- 2-4 tsp sugar
- ¼ tsp salt
- 1/8 tsp turmeric

🍽 Preparation:

- Wash and soak rice for 1 hour. Drain all water and spread it on a plate.
- Sprinkle the turmeric over the moist rice and mix it gently. Spread it out and allow it to dry for 1-2 hours under the fan.

🥘 Cooking:

- Heat the ghee in a deep and thick-bottomed vessel. Add the raisins and cashews. Fry until cashews swell up but do not burn them. Remove with a slotted spoon and keep aside.
- Add the whole spices and stir for 20 seconds. Add the dried rice and fry it gently for 2-3 minutes. Still better if you can gently toss it instead of stirring as with the latter one might end up with broken rice grains.
- Add enough boiling water (a little more than two cups) to cover the rice. Add salt. Allow to cook on a low to medium flame.
- Stir gently at an interval of 4-5 minutes. Once the rice is almost done, add the sugar, nutmeg powder, cashews and raisins, and mix them gently with the rice. (Keep aside a few cashews and raisins to garnish later.)
- Allow all the water to dry up. Remove from the flame.
- Serve with a thin mutton curry or if vegetarian, pair it with *kakharu buta dali* and *amba khatta*.

Note - *This recipe varies slightly across the state.*

CHUNA RUTI
(A native bread made with rice flour)

A dish probably inspired by some of the tribal preparations in which a layer of rice paste is patted down between two leaf plates and cooked over fire. It is made and enjoyed during winter as it is especially good at mopping up the richer gravies that constitute the meals during the colder months.

It is more popular in the northern parts of the state.

 **Cooking time – 40 minutes**

Ingredients:

- 1 cup rice flour
- 1 ½ cup water
- 1.4 tsp ghee/oil
- ½ tsp salt

Cooking:

- Take the water in a thick-bottomed wok. Add salt and bring it to a boil.

- Lower the flame and add the rice flour while stirring continuously. Cook until the mixture starts to come together like a dough. Switch off the flame

- Cover with a lid and let it stand for 5 minutes to cook in the residual heat.

- Open the lid and let it cool down to a tolerable temperature.

- Transfer to a working surface that has been dusted with rice flour. Rub a little oil or ghee on your hands and knead it nicely for 5-6 minutes while it is still warm.

- Pinch out the dough for making 2-3 rotis and cover the rest.

- Divide the dough and shape it into discs like one would do for making regular wheat rotis.

- Roll out using more rice flour.

- Heat a griddle and cook the roti on both sides until it starts to puff up. No need to cook it on an open flame.

- Remove and keep it covered until serving.

- Repeat the process with the remaining dough.

- Serve with mutton curry or country chicken curry.

Note – The dough needs to be used up the same day. If refrigerated, the dough gets difficult to work with and the rotis tend to crack around the circumference.

CHAUL BARA

(Deep-fried crunchy snacks made with rice)

A trip to the local markets of Sambalpur, Bargarh and Bolangir is never complete without grabbing a *'Dona'* of crunchy *chaul bara* and *tentel jhol.* It can be termed as the quintessential common man's snack as it is priced within every budget. Unlike the expensive ingredients like gram flour, black lentils or fine white rice that constitute the primary component of most street snacks, it is made from the rough parboiled rice that we term *'Bagada'* or *'Balka.'*

While it is available around the year as a street food, winters are the time when usually people make a batch in the comfort of their homes. With friends and family gathering for occasions like pus puni, it is a snack that can easily be made in bulk.

 **Cooking time – 30 minutes**

 **Ingredients:**

- 2 cups parboiled rice
- ¼ cup black lentil (without skin)
- 1 finely minced small onion
- 1 inch ginger (roughly pounded)
- 2-3 garlic cloves (roughly pounded)
- ½ tsp carrom seeds
- ½ tsp salt
- Oil for deep frying

🍽 Preparation:

- Soak the rice for 6-7 hours. The black lentil needs about 2-3 hours of soaking.
- Grind both into a smooth thick batter. Add the remaining ingredients except for the oil and whisk it for 2-3 minutes.

🍲 Cooking:

- Heat sufficient oil in a wok for deep frying.
- Drop small blobs of the batter into the hot oil without crowding it at any point in time.
- Fry the *chaul bara* on a medium flame until it turns brown on all sides. Remove from the wok and keep aside.
- Serve hot with *tetel jhol.*

TETEL JHOL
(A spicy tamarind dip)

Tetel jhol stands out like a sore thumb in a world dominated by store-bought sauces. Tangy and hot, it is as unassuming as the Chaul bara that it accompanies. It does not require any cooking and even the tempering is optional.

 **Preparation time – 5 minutes**

Ingredients:

- 1 lemon-sized tamarind ball
- 2-3 green chilli
- 1-inch ginger
- 2-3 garlic cloves
- 2-3 tsp chopped cilantro
- ¼ tsp cumin seeds
- A sprig of curry leaves
- A pinch of asafoetida
- ½ tsp oil
- Salt to taste

Preparation:

- Soak the tamarind in 1 cup water. Mash it and strain out the liquid. Dilute it with another 2 cups of water.
- Crush the ginger, garlic and green chilli using a mortar and pestle. Add to the tamarind water along with the salt.
- If using a tempering, heat the oil. Add the cumin seeds, asafoetida and curry leaves. Pour the spluttering mix over the *Tetel jhol*.
- Garnish with chopped cilantro.

METHI SAGAW POSTO BATA
(Fenugreek leaves cooked with poppy paste)

Fenugreek leaves are a boon for folks suffering from diabetes and high cholesterol. It is proven to improve fasting blood sugar levels and reduce bad cholesterol deposits. But otherwise, too, these aromatic leaves make for a delicious addition to various curries, stir fries and even breads. From the *Jeera Aloo Methi* to *methi* parathas, North Indians have their share of iconic recipes that make use of these leaves.

While fenugreek leaves were never a dominant ingredient in Odia cuisine, we have successfully adapted them to our style of cooking. The usual preparation is a simple stir fry with some vegetables like ridge gourd, aubergine or even finely chopped potato/tomato and a garnishing of crushed lentil badi (vadi).

This is one of the lesser known from recipes from Deogarh (erstwhile Bamara state).

 **Preparation time – 15-20 minutes**

 **Ingredients:**

- 2 cups Methi/fenugreek leaves (lightly packed)
- 1 medium-sized tomato
- 1 medium-sized potato
- 1 tbsp poppy seeds
- 1 tsp mustard seeds
- 2-3 garlic cloves
- 2 tsp mustard oil
- 1-2 dry red chillis
- 2 pinch pancha-phutana
- Salt to taste
- A pinch of turmeric

🍽 Preparation:

- Wash and drain the fenugreek leaves.
- Bring 4-5 cups of water to a boil in a saucepan. Add a little salt to it.
- Add the fenugreek leaves to the boiling water. Wait for 3-4 minutes. Switch off the flame and strain the leaves.
- Make a fine paste of the poppy seeds, mustard seeds and garlic cloves.
- Chop the potatoes into thin long pieces. Cut the tomato into 4 halves.

🍲 Cooking:

- Heat the oil in a wok.
- Add the pancha phutana and broken red chilli.
- Once they start spluttering, add the finely chopped potatoes. Fry on a low flame.
- When the potatoes are half done, add the tomato. Sprinkle a little salt and turmeric. Cover for 2 minutes.
- As the tomato softens, add the spice paste and cook for 3-4 minutes.
- Finally, add the fenugreek leaves along with a little water. Adjust the salt.
- Cook until the excess water is gone.
- Switch off the flame.
- Serve hot with white rice.

PALANGA SAGAW BAIGANA

(Spinach cooked with eggplant)

While greens like Kosala and Mula dominate the winter menu in most parts of the state, Palanga or spinach is also consumed in parts of Odisha. It is always cooked with another vegetable or two to balance the slight bitterness and provide texture. Powdered lentil or rice is usually added towards the end of cooking as it tends to leach a lot of water.

 **Preparation time – 15 minutes**

 **Ingredients:**

- 4 cups cleaned and chopped spinach
- 1 cup diced eggplant (chopped into small pieces)
- 1 medium-sized onion (chopped into small pieces)
- 2 dry red chillis
- 1/3 tsp pancha phutana
- 2 tsp coarsely powdered rice
- 1-2 tsp oil
- Salt to taste

Cooking:

- Heat the oil in a wok.
- Add the broken red chilli and pancha phutana. Once the seeds start to splutter, add the chopped onion.
- Fry on a low flame until they start to turn red.
- Add the chopped spinach along with the eggplant and cook on medium high for 2-3 minutes.
- Add the salt, mix and cook until the eggplants are almost done.

- Add the powdered rice and cover with a lid. Switch off the flame and let it stand for a few minutes.

- Give it a good stir before serving.

- Serve it warm with rice or roti.

Note – One can also add 1 tsp mustard paste and a medium-sized tomato to the above recipe as a variation.

**If powdered rice or powdered lentil are not readily available, a handful of fried and crushed badi can also be used.*

BUDHA CHAKULI
(Thick rice pancakes)

One of those pithas that one comes across rather frequently in the 'offerings' menu of the Coastal belt of Odisha. And one that is not so surprisingly absent from the Western Odisha menu. The addition of 'dahi chenna' and 'plenty of fresh coconut' is a geo-specific practice that draws from the easy availability of dairy and coconut near the coast.

Just like one would find laddoos made up of charoli or even 'Muan' studded with it in villages near Bonaigarh (an erstwhile princely kingdom of the Garhjat belt), the coastal recipes always have their share of coconut or chenna or even both.

 **Cooking time – 20 minutes**

 **Ingredients:**

- ½ cup split and skinned black lentil
- 1 cup broken raw rice
- 1 small ripe banana (mashed to a puree)
- ½ cup freshly grated coconut
- ½ cup mashed dahi chenna (use regular chenna if not available)
- 3-4 tbsp jaggery
- A pinch of cardamon powder
- 6-7 freshly ground peppercorn
- 1 tsp grated ginger
- 2-3 tsp ghee

Preparation:

- Wash and soak the rice and lentil for 4-5 hours. Discard the water used for soaking and grind it into a smooth paste.

- Let it stand for 1-2 hours before adding the remaining ingredients (except ghee) and giving it a good mix. Leave aside for 30 minutes.

Cooking:

- Heat an iron wok to a medium temperature. The temperature should not be very high as the batter contains ingredients that tend to catch at the bottom rather easily.

- Add ½ tsp ghee. Pour a ladle or two of the batter. No need to spread. Drizzle another half teaspoon of ghee around the circumference.

- Cover with a lid and cook on a low flame. Flip it over when the bottom side is done. Cook both sides to a reddish colour.

- Remove from the pan and allow it to cool down a bit before offering it to the Gods.

- Always serve at room temperature.

Note – A little salt is added to this recipe when it is being made for regular consumption but salt is omitted when it is made for the offering.

Attakali. Gaintha. Ghruta. Tarana.

A group of recipes that are more or less belong to the same category but are named differently by virtue of difference in region or even occasion. Each of them involves using a rice paste or powder to create a dish with custard-like consistency. They are sparingly sweetened and the use of dairy is also kept to a minimum.

Gaintha involves making balls out of the rice dough and then boiling them to a point where some of the dough breaks away and acts as a natural thickening agent.

Attakali or Ghruta on the other hand involve cooking the rice paste directly to a point where it thickens to the desired consistency.

Tarana is the most frugal of these dishes, and in the olden days, it was always made as a by-product of the making of the 'Gaja' (a kind of manda pitha) for Bada Osa festival. It was made from the rice paste sticking to the sides of the vessel used for preparing the dough. This paste was washed down with water and boiled with some jaggery, bay leaves and pepper. It is one of those recipes that remind us of the ingenuity of our ancestors and their pledge to zero wastage.

GAINTHA/ATTAKALI
(A variety of rice custard)

Gaintha. I close my eyes and all of a sudden, I am transported to a small village near Salepur in Coastal Odisha. That's the association my memories have forged. While I have tasted this 'pitha' basically all over the place, this one lingers at the back of my mind. As we sat on the floor of the quaint little house with a low roof, enveloped by the aroma of the food and the warmth emitted by the cooking, I experienced the beauty of minimalism. A half-litre packet of *'Omfed'* milk had been squandered on making the tea for the visitors and the last dredges remaining in the pan were rescued for making the pitha. A pinch of salt. Just enough jaggery to accentuate the natural sweetness of the aromatic rice sourced from the family's fields. A torn bay-leaf. And of course, the fragile rice balls. Sublime. The kind of food that gets to me every time.

This pitha is best described as a rather gloopy dish with a few broken spheres (of rice) swathed in a rice custard. It is on the sweeter side (but lesser than most desserts) with a twinge of salt and was often served warm for dinner in the older days. Especially in the cold weather.

Over time, the 'Gaintha pitha' has morphed into 'Gaintha Khiri', an overtly sweet and intensely milky preparation that is being dished out these days. While some variation can be attributed to the fact that some families were better off than others and hence, had more resources at their disposal, too much of meddling with the recipe has led to a dilution of the original.

Preparation time – 40 minutes

Ingredients:

- 2/3 cup broken aromatic rice
- ¼ tsp coarsely ground pepper

- 1-2 bay leaves (or) 1 green cardamon
- ¼ tsp ghee
- 2/3 cup jaggery (or) ½ cup sugar
- ½ cup milk
- 3-4 tbsp freshly grated coconut (optional)
- A pinch of salt

🍽 Preparation:

- Wash and soak the rice for 1 hour. Drain all water and spread on a plate to dry (preferably in the balcony or under a fan) for 1-2 hours or until surface moisture almost disappears.
- Transfer it to a grinder jar and grind it into a smooth powder.

🍲 Cooking:

- Heat 1 cup water in a wok. Add salt and bring to a boil. After 2 minutes, lower the flame.
- Dissolve 1 tbsp of the rice flour in 3-4 tbsp of water and add to the wok. Give it a stir.
- Add the remaining rice flour to the boiling water. Keep stirring all the time to prevent the formation of lumps.
- Cook the rice flour on low flame until it comes together as a dough. Cover and remove from the flame. Wait for 10 minutes.
- Transfer the rice dough to a plate and let it rest until it is bearable to touch.
- Around the same time, bring the jaggery to a boil along with the spices and 2 cups of water in the same wok in which the dough was prepared. Scrape down the walls to dissolve any rice paste sticking to it. Add the coconut and let it simmer for 7-8 minutes.
- Add the ghee to the dough and knead for 3-4 minutes to smooth/even it out. Take small lumps out of the dough and roll into balls (preferably the size of marbles).

- Lower the flame and add the rice balls to it. Initially, the balls will sink to the bottom but will break slightly and rise to the surface. Add the milk at this stage and switch off the flame. Do not boil any longer or the balls will break completely.

Note – When making this recipe during the festival of Manabasa Gurubar, sugar is preferred instead of jaggery by many people. This is because the white colour is considered to be pure and more appropriate for rituals. Our religious books specifically forbid the usage of red and black rice during Manabasa Gurubar and Kartika Brata.

KOLOTHA DALI
(Tangy horse gram dal)

Life is all about striking the right balance. And somehow, this philosophy permeates into every sphere of our being. This horse gram dal cooked with a profusion of tomatoes is the perfect example in this case. Horse gram is an excellent source of plant protein but it is quite astringent in nature. Ayurveda defines astringent as 'dry' and 'heavy.' Hence, the horse gram needs a countering agent to balance it. In comes the humble tomato to the rescue. An excellent souring agent, it is 'moist' and 'light.' (Here, 'moist' is not a reference to the water content but the effect it has on the tongue. It stimulates the production of saliva which moistens the mouth). Isn't that impressive? Astringent foods are excellent for cleansing the body. It's little wonder that the water in which horse gram has been soaked overnight is prescribed for curing kidney/gall bladder stones and prostate problems.

I love to cook it as a thin soupy dal with loads of tomatoes to balance the astringency, some taro and eggplant are added to give body to the broth and an amazingly aromatic tempering of garlic and garlic chives.

 **Cooking time – 30 minutes**

 **Ingredients:**

- 1 ½ cups roasted and broken horse gram/ *Kolotha*
- 2- medium-sized tomato
- 1 cup taro + eggplant cubes (optional but recommended)
- 1 ambula (or dried green mango slices)
- 2 dry red chilli
- 4-5 fat garlic cloves
- 1/3 tsp pancha phutana (Or else, one can also use a mix of mustard and nigella seeds)

- ½ tsp turmeric

- 2 tsp oil

- Salt to taste

Preparation:

- Wash and cook the dal and vegetables with 3 cups water, salt and turmeric in a pressure cooker. It takes 3-4 whistles or about 15 minutes on a medium-low flame. Keep aside until steam escapes.

- Soak the ambula in 1 cup hot water.

Cooking:

- Heat the oil in a wok. Add the panch phutana and the broken red chillis.

- Add the crushed garlic once it gets spluttering. When the garlic starts turning brown, add the finely chopped tomato and cook until it's mushy.

- Pour the dal into the wok. Bring it to a boil. Allow to boil for 2 minutes before adding the ambula along with the water in which it had been soaked. Simmer for 5-6 minutes.

- Remove from flame and serve hot with rice.

Note – During the winter season, when garlic chives are available, they are chopped and added to the tempering. Also, the dal is much easier to cook and has a creamy texture when it is from the same year's harvest.

Jhunga or Red Lobia is also cooked into a dal using the same method as described in this recipe.

MAGHA (JANUARY – FEBRUARY)

The winter shows signs of abating. Harvest activities continue but post-harvest activities like parboiling of paddy takes up most of the time and energy.

Farm produce and menu are not much different from that of Pausa but one finds some interesting recipes linked with the agricultural practices. Some 'unnamed' delicacies go with activities like parboiling. Rice and lentil paste wrapped in banana or sal leaves are shoved into the embers under the huge pots used for parboiling the paddy. Sweet potatoes, potatoes, and other tubers are skewered onto bamboo sticks and immersed in the boiling paddy. In the earlier days, agriculture was a labour-intensive activity and these dishes were created to feed the additional hands engaged during the period. It also led to maximum utilization of all the firewood that was consumed in the process. However, with the farmwork and processing getting mechanized, such recipes are also on the way out.

Although the summer produce is yet to come, a few transient greens are available this month. Popular greens consumed this month are *rasuna patra, chana saag* and *bahala kadha.*

Magha, which derives its name from the *Magha Nakshatra,* is an auspicious month in the Odia Calendar. As the constellation is presided by the Pitras, this month is considered to be an ideal time for *Pitru Puja* or '*Pitru Tarpana.*'

One of the major festivals that falls during the month is *Magha Saptami,* during which people take a dip in a local water body before sunrise. It is observed as the birth anniversary of the Sun God. A huge crowd of devotees gathers every year for a dip (called 'buda' in Odia) near the Chandrabhaga beach that lies close to the Konark temple. Most of them camp overnight on the beach.

Another ritual that takes place on this day is the offering of cooked meals consisting of rice, dalma and khiri to the *'Pitrus.'* These dishes are cooked on the beach itself, offered to the 'Pitrus' on banana leaves and also consumed by the family members as an offering. Thereafter, the pots are broken and thrown into the *'Handibadia pokhari'* from where they are said to disappear without a trace.

The surprise element of the 'ancestral offerings' made on Magha Saptami, is the offering of Sukhua. While this offering is associated with the highest level of 'purity' in the Great Traditions, the Little traditions emphasize on offering fish and liquor to assuage dissatisfied spirits. Usually, this translates into incorporating the favourite food of the deceased ancestor in the offerings. And 'sukhua' has always been on the list of favourites of the Odia people. This is not a standard practice but is followed by a small section of the population.

Saraswati Puja which falls on *Basanta Panchami*, is celebrated in all educational institutions and offices of the state. The wild jujubes, which have just started to ripen and turn sweet, are offered to the Goddess before they are consumed by people. As Saraswati is the Goddess of Learning, this day is ideal to initiate a child to the written word. Scores of little kids can be seen lining up at the pandals for their 'Khadi-Chuan.' 'Khadi' refers to chalk because, during earlier times, children used to write on slates with a piece of chalk.

Agni Utsava or Agira Purnima, an agricultural festival, is celebrated on the last day of the month as a sign of farewell to the cold winter days. The straws that have piled up from the harvest are offered to the Fire God and a coconut along with winter vegetables like sweet potato, eggplant, wild tubers, etc., is roasted in it. These offerings are subsequently consumed by the people.

What's on the menu this month

PIAJA PATRA DIA MUGA DALI
(Onion chives cooked with split moong)

Onions are cultivated commercially is some parts of Odisha, but earlier, a lot of people used to grow their own supplies for the year in their backyards. The tender leaves with a mildly pungent, onion-like smell are a by-product of this crop. Since over-exploitation of the leaves can lead to a decline in the quality of the bulks, only a few leaves are plucked from each plant. However, there are folks who grow them just for an endless supply of the short-lived greens.

They are usually fried to a crisp by adding some rice batter or cooked with lentils into a semi-liquid preparation.

 **Cooking time – 20 minutes**

 **Ingredients:**

- 1 cup split and skinned moong dal
- 200 gm spring onions/onion chives
- 2-3 dry red chillis
- 1 tsp pancha-phutana
- 5-6 garlic cloves
- ¼ tsp turmeric
- 3 tsp mustard oil
- 1/3 tsp salt

 **Preparation:**

- Wash the spring onions and drain excess water. Cut into inch-long pieces.

Cooking:

- Dry roast the moong dal until it gives off a sweet fragrance.

- Wash and transfer the moong dal to a pressure cooker. Add salt, turmeric and 2 cups of water. Close the lid and cook for 1-2 whistle.

- Remove from the stove and allow the steam to escape. The dal should be 80 per cent cooked and not mushy.

- Add the spring onions to the dal and cook on a medium flame for 4-5 minutes or until the greens are done.

- Heat oil in a wok. Add the pancha phutana and broken red chillis. Crush the garlic

- cloves lightly and add to the spluttering seeds. Fry until the garlic turns light brown.

- Pour the tempering over the contents of the pressure cooker. Close the lid and simmer for 2 minutes.

- Serve hot with white rice/rotis.

RASUNA PATRA PITHAU BHAJA
(Crispy garlic chives)

Just like the onion, garlic was grown by many people to meet their kitchen needs. The leaves are considered a delicacy. They are usually turned into a crisp side dish or used as a tempering for dals.

 **Preparation time – 15 minutes**

 **Ingredients:**

- 2 cups chopped garlic chives/greens (tightly packed)
- 1 small potato (finely chopped)
- Salt to taste
- 3 tsp oil

For the rice paste:

- 1/4 cup raw rice
- 2 pinch cumin seeds
- 1 dry red chilli

Preparation:

- Wash and soak the rice for 3-4 hours. Grind into a smooth paste along with the cumin seeds and red chilli using a little water.
- Crush the garlic greens and potatoes slightly. Transfer to a mixing bowl. Add just enough of the rice paste to bind the greens. Two-thirds of the given quantity should be enough. Sprinkle salt and mix everything.

- Heat a thick-bottomed skillet. Drizzle oil over it.

- Take about two teaspoonfuls of the garlic potato mixture for each fritter and place it on the skillet. Flatten it a bit (about 5-6 mm) but do not spread it too thin, else it will burn too soon. Let it cook on a low flame until it turns a little brown on one side.

- Flip it over. Drizzle a little more oil on top. Cook to a similar brown hue.

- Remove and serve immediately with rice or *Pakhala*.

CHANA SAAG

(Seasonal greens cooked with selected vegetables)

Yet another case of mistaken identity. Although popularly sold as chana saag, these much-coveted greens found in Western Odisha belong to the *Khesari* crop and not the small chickpeas plant. Although they look different and even taste different from each other, they are found in the markets around the same time. The easiest way to differentiate them would be to look out for the flowers. Khesari bears small blue flowers while chana saag bears pink ones. Both are consumed in Odisha but the Khesari greens are easier to find in the local markets.

These short-lived greens are cooked once or twice a year in our urban kitchens as prepping them is time-consuming.

 **Cooking time – 30 minutes**

 **Ingredients:**

- 3 cups prepped chana saag
- 1 medium-sized eggplant
- 1 cup tender flat beans
- 2 medium-sized tomatoes
- 8-10 fried badi
- 2-3 dry red chilli
- ½ tsp mustard seeds for tempering
- 4-5 fat garlic cloves
- 2 tsp mustard oil
- ½ tsp salt or adjust as per taste

🍽 Preparation:

- Wash the greens thoroughly as they tend to contain sand and mud.
- Cut the eggplants into medium-sized chunks. The flat beans are cut into small pieces.
- Chop the tomatoes into small pieces.

Cooking:

- Heat 1 cup water in a pressure cooker. Add the chopped greens, flat beans and eggplants.
- Sprinkle a little salt and close the lid. Cook for 2-3 whistles depending on the greens. Allow the steam to escape.
- Heat the oil in a wok. Add the mustard seeds, garlic and broken red chilli.
- Once the garlic turns light brown, add the chopped tomatoes. Sprinkle a little salt over the tomatoes.
- Cover and cook until tomatoes turn mushy.
- Pour the cooked greens into the same wok. Use the back of a heavy spoon/ladle to mash everything together.
- Let it cook for 3-4 minutes before adding the fried and crushed badi.
- Remove from the flame.
- Serve hot with rice.

HIDIMICHA SAGAW PATUA

(A variety of Bitter greens cooked with potatoes)

One among the many medicinal bitter greens that have always been a part of the everyday Odia diet, the Hidimicha Sagaw (Enhydra Fluctuans) grows in marshy areas and fields. An excellent Kapha and Pitta pacifier, it's availability during the months that bridges the seasons when these two doshas are at their worst, demonstrates Nature's unique method of looking out for us.

These greens can be cooked using the recipes that have been shared for 'Pita sagaw.' But I consider the Patua to be my favourite way of staying connected to my maternal lineage.

Cooking Time – 20 minutes

Ingredients:

- 1 cup cleaned and prepped greens
- 1 medium-sized onion
- 1 medium-sized potato
- 1 tsp mustard seeds
- 6-8 garlic cloves
- 2-3 green chilis
- 1 tbsp mustard oil
- 1/8 tsp turmeric
- 1/4 tsp salt (approx.)

⦿| Preparation:

- Soak the mustard seeds for 2-3 hours.

- Transfer the soaked mustard seeds, garlic, 1 green chilli and a little amount of water to a chutney jar. Grind into a smooth paste.

- Add the greens to the same chutney jar. Grind into a coarse paste.

- Chop the onion into small pieces. The potato should be cut into thin long pieces.

⦿ Cooking:

- Heat the oil in a wok. Add the green chilli and chopped onion. Fry till just translucent.

- Add the potato and give it a quick stir before adding the greens paste along with half a cup of water. Sprinkle the salt and turmeric, give it a mix and close the lid.

- Let it sit on a low flame till the potatoes are done and all liquid is absorbed.

- Serve warm with rice meals.

MULA KANJI

(A tangy soup with radish and other vegetables)

Another version of Kanji that is made with winter vegetables. This one is served as a warming soup during lunchtime. But it is common for people to sample some even before sitting down for lunch as the aroma of the tempering fills up the house and draws everyone like a magnet.

This is the season when people are usually troubled by cough and cold. The *mula kanji* acts as an expectorant and clears the channels. In addition, radish is known to cleanse the digestive organs like the liver and gall bladder. After all the feasting that goes on during Pausa, a recipe like this is our grandmothers' way of detoxing the body before the seasonal changes set in.

⧗ **Cooking time – 20 minutes**

 **Ingredients:**

- 1 cup radish (cut into long pieces)
- ¼ cup Flat beans (cut into long pieces)
- 1 cup brinjal (cut into thick discs)
- 1-2 ripe tomato (diced into four)
- ½ cup taro (cut into thick roundels)
- 2 tsp rice
- 2-3 ambula
- 1 tsp pancha phutana
- 6-7 garlic pods
- 1-2 sprig curry leaves
- 2-3 dry red chilli
- 1 green chilli

- 2 tsp jaggery
- 2 tsp oil
- ½ tsp turmeric
- salt to taste

Preparation:

- Soak the rice for 1-2 hours. Grind into a fine paste and keep aside. Soak the dried green mango pieces for 2-3 hours. Slightly crush the garlic pods.

Cooking:

- Bring 1 ½ litres of water to a boil. Add the cut vegetables along with turmeric and salt. Allow it to cook on a medium flame till the vegetables are 75 per cent done.
- Stir in the rice paste and allow to cook for 3-4 minutes before adding the soaked dried green mango. Throw in the green chilli.
- Let it simmer for 2-3 minutes.
- Heat a pan. Add the oil. Allow it to smoke. Add the pancha phutana, red chilli, crushed garlic pods and curry leaves. Once the chilli darkens in colour, pour the tempering over the boiling kanji. Add the jaggery and let it simmer for 2 minutes.
- Remove and serve warm with rice.

JHUNGA – SAKAR KANDA SIJHA
(Sweet potato and cowpeas side dish)

The menu this month is relatively toned down as compared to the previous month. This is to allow the body to adapt and to ensure a gradual transition between the seasons. Minimally spiced dishes and short-lived greens dominate the menu this month.

Jhunga (or rumha dali), known as lobia in Hindi, is consumed mostly in Western Odisha. Interestingly, it is harvested from the matured pods of '*Barbati*' or '*Jhudunga,*' which is more popular as a vegetable in the Coastal areas. These seeds are cooked into a dal or added to various other preparations.

A somewhat mushy preparation of the *Jhunga* with sweet potato is served as a side dish during the 'no onion garlic' days during the winter months.

 **Cooking time – 20 minutes**

 **Ingredients:**

- ½ cup Jhunga (red lobia)
- 1 cup diced sweet potato
- ¼ tsp pancha phutana
- 1 dry red chilli
- 1 bay leaf
- 2 tsp ghee
- 1/6 tsp turmeric
- Salt as per taste
- 1-2 tsp jaggery (optional)

To be made into a coarse powder:

- 1 tsp cumin seeds
- 2 dry red chillis

Preparation:

- Dry roast the pulses on a low flame for 2-3 minutes. Wash and soak for 2-3 hours.
- Dry roast the cumin seeds and red chillis until fragrant. Allow to cool down before powdering it using a mortar and pestle.

Cooking:

- Transfer the soaked pulses and diced sweet potato to a pressure cooker. Add 1 cup water, turmeric and salt to taste. Cook for 2-3 whistles until the pulses are well cooked.
- Heat the ghee in a wok. Add the torn bay leaf, broken red chilli and pancha phutana. Once the seeds start spluttering, add the contents of the pressure cooker.
- Mix and simmer for 3-4 minutes. Add the coarsely powdered cumin-chilli as per preference.
- Serve warm.

SEM-BAINGAN
(Flat bean eggplant side dish)

Some recipes are as unpretentious as they can get. Just a seasonal ingredient or two with some spices thrown in. Usually what stands out in such dishes in the tried and tested pairing of vegetables (sometimes a non-vegetarian ingredient too) and, of course, a little tweaking of the usual spices. The regular mustard paste is given a makeover in this case with the addition of the 'desi' coriander which is very much in season and skipping the garlic to let the former shine through. The roots and the lower stems of the coriander plant hold the maximum flavour and are a must-add to the spice paste.

Cooking time – 15 minutes

 **Ingredients:**

- 2 cups flat beans (cut into 2-inch long pieces)
- 1/2 cup eggplant (cut into long pieces)
- 1 small tomato (minced)
- 1/2 tsp mustard seeds
- 1/4 tsp cumin
- 1 green chilli
- A handful of coriander plants (including the roots)
- 1/4 tsp turmeric
- 2 tsp mustard oil
- Salt as per taste
- 1/2 tsp mustard seeds for tempering

🍽 **Preparation:**

- Wash the coriander thoroughly, especially the roots.
- Grind the mustard, cumin, coriander and green chilli into a paste.

Cooking:

- Boil 1 cup of water in a sauce pan. Add the flat beans, mustard paste, little salt and turmeric to it.
- Once the beans are half cooked, add the eggplant. Cover and cook until both vegetables are cooked.
- Heat the oil in a wok. Add the mustard seeds and allow it to splutter.
- Add the tomato pieces and cook until mushy. Pour the contents of the saucepan into the wok.
- Simmer for 2-3 minutes before switching off the flame.
- Serve hot with meals.

Note - Add some extra coriander leaves as garnishing.

CHUEIN ALU BHAJA
(Stir-fried drumsticks and potatoes)

The added bonus of having a Moringa tree in the garden is a steady supply of drumsticks around the year. With good amounts of vitamins and minerals, drumsticks are considered to be a powerhouse of nutrition. These are regularly added to various dishes like dalma, santula and ghanta prepared in Odia homes. But they also make a delicious stir fry to be served along with hot rice or pakhala.

⌛ **Cooking time – 15 minutes**

🥣 **Ingredients:**

- 3-4 drumsticks
- 1 large potato
- ½ tsp pancha phutana
- 3 tsp mustard seeds
- 1 tsp cumin seeds
- 2-3 garlic cloves
- 2 dry red chilli
- 3-4 tsp mustard oil
- 1/4 tsp turmeric
- Salt to taste

🍽 **Preparation:**

- Soak for 1 hour and grind the mustard seeds, cumin seeds, garlic cloves and chilli into a fine paste.
- Carefully peel the drumsticks' thin outer layer and cut into 2 ½ inch long pieces. Also, cut the potato into wedges.

- Take the vegetables in a wok. Add the mustard paste along with salt and turmeric. Add 1 cup water.

- Cook on a medium flame for 7-8 minutes or until the vegetables are 90 per cent cooked. The mustard paste should form a thick layer around the pieces.

- Heat a pan. Drizzle a little oil on it.

- Place the boiled vegetables in the pan. Drizzle more oil on the sides. Fry until lightly crisp.

- Serve hot with rice meals.

A light stew like preparation of drumstick is prepared during periods of convalescence. A few pieces of drumstick, potato wedges, tomatoes and eggplant cubes are boiled along with a little cumin-ginger paste, salt and turmeric. It is later finished off with a tempering of pancha phutana and a red chilli(optional). A handful of coriander leaves and a few fried badi are thrown in as the final touch.

KHIRA SANTULA
(A light vegetable stew)

A light stew-like preparation that uses select vegetables and a little milk for that added creamy touch. There are quite a couple of '*Santula*' recipes in Odia cuisine and these are served mostly with rotis for dinner.

A santula is meant to be 'easy on the stomach' and nutritious. It is usually served in a big bowl to fill up the stomach without burdening the digestive system. A heavy meal at night can result in disrupted sleep patterns. So, Roti-Santula is a much-desired dinner combination.

 **Cooking time – 20 minutes**

 **Ingredients:**

- 2 cups Raw papaya pieces
- 1 cup pumpkin pieces
- 2 cups bottle gourd pieces
- 1 cup ridge gourd
- 1 medium-sized eggplant
- 1/2 cup potato pieces
- 2-3 dry red chillis
- 1 small onion
- ½ tsp pancha phutana
- ½ tsp turmeric
- ½ tsp salt
- ½ cup milk
- ¼ tsp *jeera-lanka* powder (roasted cumin chilli powder)
- 1 tsp oil or 1 tsp ghee.

🍽 Preparation:

- Cut the onion into small pieces.

🍲 Cooking:

- Heat a wok. Add 1 cup of water along with the vegetables, turmeric and salt. Close the lid and cook on a medium flame until all the vegetables soften.

- Add the milk and cook for 2 minutes.

- Heat the oil in a pan. Add the pancha phutana and red chillis. When the seeds start spluttering, add the onion pieces. Fry until the onion turns translucent.

- Pour over the boiled vegetables. Sprinkle cumin chilli powder. Mix well.

- Remove from fire after 30 seconds.

- Delicious and healthy santula is ready to eat. Serve with rotis (or rice flour rotis).

Note: One can also add vegetables like sweet potato/ brinjal/ pointed gourd/raw banana according to one's taste. Using ghee instead of oil adds a lovely aroma to the santula. On fasting days this recipe is made without adding the onions.

SUKHUA DALMA

(Lentils cooked with selected vegetables and dried fish)

While Dalma is generally stereotyped as temple food, it is also the food of the masses. Dalma probably owes its origins to the tribals (Sabaras), who were the earliest worshippers of *'Nilamadhaba.'* The addition of meat or fish to Dalma may appear unacceptable from a strictly Brahminical standpoint but it is quite relatable if one thinks of it as a single wholesome accompaniment for rice meals. Hence, it is a staple for the common man. And the practice of adding a little meat or fish to this hearty lentil and vegetable dish to feed a large family points to the practicality and resourcefulness of home cooking.

The novelty of the fresh batch of Sukhua is yet to wear off and one finds it being added to many of the dishes cooked during this month, including Dalma.

 **Cooking time – 30 minutes**

 **Ingredients:**

- 1 cup split pigeon peas (Toor Dal)
- 1 cup red pumpkin (diced)
- 1 cup plantain (diced)
- 1 medium-sized Eggplant (diced)
- 1/2 cup Taro (or) 1/2 cup potato (diced)
- 1 medium-sized onion
- 6-7 cloves of Garlic (coarsely pounded)
- 3-4 dry red chillis
- 1/2 tsp cumin+mustard seeds
- 2 bay leaf
- 2 inch cinnamon

- 2 tsp oil for tempering

- 2-3 pieces of *alana sukhua* (unsalted fermented fish)

- 1/3 tsp turmeric

- Salt to taste

Cooking:

- Wash and soak the lentils for 1-2 hours.

- Wash the dried fish 2-3 times in warm water and keep it aside. Cut the onion into medium-sized pieces

- Bring 2-3 cups of water to a boil. Add the turmeric and the lentils along with all vegetables except eggplant. Once the dal is half cooked, add the eggplant.

- Cook until the lentils and vegetables are soft and starting to turn mushy.

- Heat 1 tsp oil in a pan. Add the dried fish pieces and fry them for 4-5 minutes. Remove and keep aside.

- Heat the remaining oil in a wok. Add the broken red chilli, mustard seeds, cumin seeds, bay leaf and cinnamon stick. Sauté until fragrant.

- Add the onions and sauté until they turn translucent. Add the pounded garlic and cook for another 2-3 minutes.

- Pour the cooked lentils and vegetables into the wok. Bring to a boil and then, lower the flame and let it simmer for 2-3 minutes before adding the fried fish. Cover and switch off the flame.

- Serve warm with rice.

SUKHLA MAACH – PARIBA GHANTA
(Assorted vegetables cooked with smoked fish)

Prepared with assorted winter vegetables, a little smoked fish and minimal spices, this is one wholesome and nutritious side served with meals. Unlike the more elaborate ghanta that is prepared during 'Dwitiya' or *'Garbhana Sankranti,'* this one is more functional and meant to cleanse and 'earth' the body before the seasonal shift.

This recipe can also be prepared without the fish. However, the appeal of freshly smoked or sun-dried fish is too much of a temptation for people who swear by it. And this is very much evident in the dishes prepared during this month.

Preparation time – 30 minutes

 **Ingredients:**

- ½ cup pumpkin
- ½ cup eggplant
- ½ cup flat beans
- ½ cup plantain
- ½ cup taro
- 1 medium-sized tomato
- ½ tsp mustard seeds
- 2 pinch nigella seeds
- 1-2 small pieces of smoked fish
- 1 small onion (chopped into medium-sized pieces)
- ¼ tsp turmeric
- 2 tsp mustard oil
- Salt to taste

For the masala paste:

- ½ tsp coriander seeds
- ½ tsp cumin seeds
- 1 dry red chilli

🍽 Preparation:

- Grind the coriander seeds, cumin seeds and red chilli into a fine paste.
- Wash the sukhua and soak it in water for 1-2 hours.

🍲 Cooking:

- Heat oil in a wok. Add the mustard and nigella seeds.
- Add the onions and fry them until they turn reddish.
- Break the soaked fish into small pieces and add to the wok. Sauté for 2 minutes before adding the masala paste. Keep sautéing it until the raw smell of the masala paste goes away.
- Add the vegetables and mix everything together. Add the salt and turmeric. Mix, add 1/4 cup water, and cover with a lid.
- After every 3 minutes, remove the lid and give it a good mix. Cover and repeat until the vegetables are cooked. [The vegetables will cook in their own juices, but add 3-4 tsp water if the curry starts to look dry]
- Serve warm with rice.

SUKHUA PATALGHANTA
(Smoked fish cooked with tomatoes)

The chill in the air during the month makes one crave something soothing and yet light on the stomach. While a bowl of Kanji is enough to satiate these carvings on most days, a lightly spiced and tangy 'curry' is a welcome change on others. With tomatoes and *sukhua* being easily available and packing a punch when it comes to tantalizing those tastebuds, these two are combined with a dash of mustard to deliver a flavour-bomb.

Preparation time – 20 minutes

 **Ingredients:**

- 2-3 pieces of smoked fish (Niya sukhua)
- 2 ripe tomatoes
- 1 small onion (chopped into long pieces)
- 1 tsp mustard seeds
- 1 green chilli
- 2 tsp mustard oil
- 4-5 garlic cloves
- 2-3 pinch turmeric
- A handful of cilantro leaves
- Salt to taste

Preparation:

- Soak the smoked fish pieces in 1 cup warm water for 1-2 hours.
- Remove the skin and bones. Mash the flesh a bit.
- Grind the mustard seeds, green chilli and 2 garlic cloves into a smooth paste.

 Cooking:

- Heat the oil in a wok. Add the remaining garlic cloves and fry them for 1 minute before adding onions. Sauté the onions until they turn transparent.

- Add the mashed *sukhua*. Mix and sauté for 3-4 minutes.

- Finally, add the chopped tomatoes and sprinkle salt. Cover with a lid for 2-3 minutes.

- Remove the lid and mash the tomatoes lightly with the back of a spoon.

- Add the mustard paste along with 1 cup water, adjust the salt and let it simmer for 5-6 minutes. Do not let it dry out completely.

- Sprinkle chopped cilantro just before removing it from the flame.

- Serve warm with rice meals.

Note – this dish can also be prepared with the 'Jhuri' sukhua.

BAHAL KADHA/ BAHAL SAAG BHAJA
(Tender buds of glue berry cooked with buttermilk)

Bahal Kadha are the tender buds of the Glue Berry (*Cordia dichotoma*) and are usually available for a very short period in late winter or spring. They are mostly consumed in areas on the Western borders of Odisha. There are various recipes for preparing this saag.

While it is made into a tangy tomato mustard-based preparation in Sambalpur, it is cooked with buttermilk in Kalahandi district. Sometimes, it is also made into a 'pithau bhaja.'

I'm sharing a recipe for the 'buttermilk' version, which is a must-try.

 **Preparation time – 20 minutes**

 **Ingredients:**

- 2-3 cup prepped and cleaned *bahal saag*
- 1 medium-sized onion (chopped into medium-sized pieces)
- 1 cup buttermilk
- 2 tsp rice powder (optional)
- 1/4 cup fried kakharu badi
- 2 dry red chilli
- 1/2 tsp mustard seeds
- 2 tsp oil
- Salt to taste

Cooking:

- Heat the oil in a wok. Add the broken red chilli and mustard seeds.
- Once the seeds start spluttering, add the chopped onions and sauté them until they turn reddish.

- Add the buttermilk and bring it to a boil while stirring regularly.

- Add the bahal saag and let it simmer on a low-medium flame until the greens are just covered by a layer of the liquid.

- At this stage, add the salt and the rice flour. Mix and cover it. Cook on a low flame until all the liquid is absorbed.

- Add the crushed badi and serve immediately with rice meals.

MACCHA PUDA

(Paddy field or freshwater fish cooked with a thick mustard paste)

One of the Odia recipes that has always been close to my heart is the *'Maccha Daba Puda.'* The name itself is a misnomer of sorts as the fish is hardly exposed to direct flames. Instead, it is prepared by first marinating the fish in mustard paste, putting it in a small container and cooking it over low heat in such a way that it cooks in its own juices.

It is a modification of the *'purga'* in which the marinated fish is cooked by wrapping it up in *'sala patra'* or sal leaves and popping it in the dying embers of a wood/charcoal fire. As people stopped going to the jungle every day to collect firewood, the availability of fresh leaves went down and at the same time, new utensils started entering the kitchens. They started putting all the ingredients together in a small 'silver' bowl and cooking it on the embers. While this variation of the 'Purga' is delicious, the authentic version flavoured with the smoky scent of the Sal leaves just happens to be out of this world. The 'daba puda' is one of the best examples of how recipes have evolved organically over the last decades.

I happen to have a rather emotional connection with this dish. My grandmother absolutely loved it and did a brilliant job of preparing it. In fact, I haven't tasted a better one. Although it is quite easy to prepare, one has to get the proportion of the ingredients right and use the right quantity of spice/oil. The prime candidate for this recipe would be the fish belly. The fatty almost jelly-like layer studded with a few large bones has a texture and flavour that makes this dish worth dying for.

⧗ **Cooking time – 40 minutes (including standby time)**

◡ **Ingredients:**

- 3 pieces of rohu/*bhakura* fish
- 2 tsp mustard seeds

- 7 garlic cloves

- 1 dry red chilli

- 2 green chillis

- 2 pinch turmeric

- Salt to taste

- 1 1/2 tsp mustard oil

- 1 tsp chopped coriander leaves

🍽 Preparation:

- Wash the fish pieces. Marinate with a pinch of salt and turmeric. Let it sit for 5 minutes.

- First, grind the mustard seeds and dry red chilli. Then add 1 green chilli and 4 garlic cloves along with a little water. Grind again into a fine paste.

- Add the mustard paste to the marinated fish. Also add the slit green chilli, crushed garlic cloves, salt, turmeric, 1 tsp mustard oil and about 1/4 cup of water. Mix everything and let it sit for 15-20 minutes.

🍲 Cooking:

- Take everything in a thick-bottomed pan. Cover it and let it cook for about 10-15 minutes on a very low flame until the mustard paste forms a thick layer around the fish. Remove from the flame.

- Drizzle the mustard oil and sprinkle chopped cilantro before serving (hot). Tastes best with steaming hot rice and dal.

Note – 'Silver' refers to the aluminium utensils that are used in most rural homes. They are preferred as they are light-weight, and being a good conductor of heat, ensure even and efficient cooking. Thin-walled aluminium bowls are best suited for cooking small quantities of food on the embers.

SIMBA RAEE

(Flat beans cooked with a dash of mustard paste)

A constant fixture on the Odia menu, the vegetables used in a 'raee' vary from season to season. Cooked with just enough mustard paste to tease those tastebuds without setting them on fire, it is usually prepared when one wants to keep the menu simple and yet interesting. The key to nailing this dish is to pick tender vegetables, chop them into very small pieces, and allow them to cook in their own juices.

 **Cooking time – 10-15 minutes**

Ingredients:

- 200 gm tender flat beans
- 1-2 red chillis (I prefer using green chillis)
- 1 tsp mustard-garlic paste
- ¼ tsp pancha phutana
- A pinch of turmeric
- 1/5 tsp salt
- 2 tsp mustard oil

Preparation:

- Clean and de-vein the flat beans. Cut into very small pieces.

🍳 Cooking:

- Heat the oil in a wok. Once it is hot, add the pancha phutana and broken chilli.

- Once the spices release their fragrance, add the chopped flat beans and give it a quick stir.

- Add mustard-garlic paste, salt and just sufficient water to cover the beans.

- Close with a lid and cook for 7-8 minutes or until beans are tender. Add a little water during the cooking if it starts to look very dry. The cooked beans should still retain a little liquid.

- Remove from flame.

- Serve warm or cold with rice meals.

PHALGUNA (FEBRUARY – MARCH)

Spring comes knocking. It is the season when Mother Nature is at her resplendent best. Verdant landscapes, punctuated with splotches of colour, greet the eye on the open countryside. As winter beats a retreat, the days start to get longer and warmer. There is a nip in the morning air, heavy with the scent of the blooming trees. The sheer joy of spring is mirrored in the mellifluous song of the cuckoo as it calls out for a mate. On the agricultural front, the fields are mostly barren except for crops like Bengal gram and Khesari. Greens like Hidimicha saag and Muthi saag grow wild in the paddy fields. Planting of groundnuts is underway in some regions.

The menu starts to reflect the changed season. Heavier curries make way for lighter preparations like raee, batibasa, and puda-chikta. Drinks like panaa (a sweetened concoction of jaggery, fruits, spices, and dairy) make their presence felt. Tender jackfruits and mangoes show up on the menu along with different kinds of gourds, cucumber and okra. Greens like bahala kadha (unopened buds of Cordia Dichotoma or glueberry), khadaa saag and leutia saag replace the winter favourites like *kosala* saag, *bathua* saag and *palanga* saag.

This month hosts two important festivals, *Dolo Jatra* and *Shivratri*. Unlike the Northern states, where Holi is a one-and-a-half-day event that includes *Holika Dahan*, Dolo is a community festival that brings the entire village together for week. Even in the towns, localities, and neighbourhoods take turns to welcome Lord Krishna and his divine consort into their homes. The sounds of cymbals, drums, and conch shells accompany the 'Vimana'(chariot) of the Gods as they go on the rounds. *Amba Panaa* (a jaggery drink with mango pieces), *amba chana* (tiny green mangoes) and roasted Bengal gram are some of the foods offered to the Gods during this festival. Most communities lift the ban on eating mangoes after Dolo Jatra as the first fruits have been offered to the Gods.

Parts of Western Odisha observe 'Gundikhai' on the full moon day of this month and offerings of newly harvested gram (chana), mahua flowers, palash flowers, green mango and 'char koli' are made to the local deity (For example, Maa Samaleswari in Sambalpur). The ritual is done to appease the Gods for keeping aliments like chickenpox and measles at bay.

Unlike Dolo Jatra, Shivratri is marked by an entire day of fasting and immersing oneself in prayers. While some people observe a *'Nirjala'* fast and abstain from drinking water, others take *Panaa* during the fast. The *Jhara Panaa* made with finger millet, curd, and rock sugar is prepared on this occasion by the Aghria community of Western Odisha.

What's on the menu this month

Beginning with the day the first blossoms were spotted on the mango trees to the day when the last fruit of the season was plucked (or brought down by the rains), a period of sheer madness would descend on the household. The mornings would begin with a round of close inspection, wherein each and every branch was inspected for the tiny fruits (amba chaana) that emerged slowly amidst the masses of sweet-smelling flowers. Multiple sighs would follow each tiny fruit that was found lying on the ground. And since a lot of them actually drop off, one can easily imagine the plight of the poor family member who did the inspection and broke the news to the others.

An agonizing period of waiting followed until the tiny mangoes turned somewhat bigger and plumper. They hadn't ripened. But one could still savour them raw in the form of many chutneys, an occasional pickle or the most awaited combination with some salt and red chilli powder. Such simple bliss. Sadly, it would easily turn into sheer agony when one went overboard with the mangoes or the red chilli powder. And when such occurrences turned frequent, the elders would take turns ensuring that we did not venture too close to the mango trees.

But the elders were not the only ones who kept the kids in check. In keeping with the tradition of offering seasonal produce to the Gods before consuming it, the first mango of the season had to be offered to Lord Krishna and his consort when they visited people's homes during Dolo Jatra in Odisha. A rather strict grandmother ensured that the mischievous kids fell in line with that diktat of hers. The stories concocted by her seem dubious in hindsight but at a young age, they instilled enough fear in our mind to quell any lingering notions of mischief.

However, once the curfew on the green mangoes got lifted, they would lose their charm all too rapidly. Everyone looked forward to relishing the sweet flesh of the ripe yellow ones.

AMBA PANAA

(Sweetened drink with tender mango pieces)

When it comes offering the first of the green mangoes to the Gods, some people offer the tender mangoes as it is while others prefer to make a sweet drink or *panaa* out of it. As it is made primarily for offering to God, it is a rather simple drink without too many ingredients. And the green mangoes are neither roasted nor boiled like they do it for the 'Aam Panna' consumed in northern parts of India.

 **Preparation time – 10 minutes**

 **Ingredients:**

- 3 tsp crushed raw mango (or finely chopped pieces)
- 3 tsp powdered jaggery
- 2 pinch pepper powder
- 250 ml water

Preparation:

- Take the crushed raw mango, jaggery and pepper powder in a mixing bowl.
- Add water and stir it to dissolve the jaggery.
- Serve.

AMBA CHATANI
(A sweet-sour mango chutney)

Tender green mangoes can be gobbled by the kids with just a dash of salt and chilli powder. But the elders need to have their quota of seasonal goodness too. A chutney with a dash of sugar is the easiest solution to it.

Every household has its own version(s) of this dish. I'm sharing the one made frequently at my place.

 **Preparation time – 10 minutes**

 **Ingredients:**

- 1 green mango (peeled and chopped)
- 1 dry red chilli
- 3 tsp sugar
- 3-4 shallots
- 1/6 tsp salt

Preparation:

- Take the green mango and crush it into small pieces with a mortar and pestle. Add the shallots and crush them along with the mango.
- Add the red chilli, sugar and salt. Pound it to mix the ingredients into a coarse paste.
- Serve with rice meals.

Note – This recipe suits the tender green mangoes that fall during the early stages before the seed is formed completely.

KASI PANASA MUGA DALI

(Tender jackfruit cooked with split moong dal)

The first batch of the jackfruits that arrive in the markets do not have the fibrous meaty texture which earns it the moniker of 'Vegan meat.' The tender jackfruit is rather mellow and is usually cooked as fries or made into a mild flavoured curry with yellow moong dal. The heavier dishes are reserved for the later stages when the fibres and seeds have fully formed.

Cutting and prepping the jackfruit is tedious and requires a certain level of skill. We use an instrument called *'Paniki'* in the Odia households to cut the thick prickly skin of the jackfruit but it can also be done with the help of a well-sharpened knife. Just remember to douse the cutting instrument with a good amount of mustard oil and spread a newspaper on the working surface. Do not forget to smear some on your hands too. It saves a lot of time while cleaning up.

This is a no onion-garlic recipe.

 **Cooking time – 20 minutes**

 **Ingredients:**

- 400 g raw jackfruit
- ½ cup moong dal (lightly dry roasted)
- 1 medium-sized potato
- 1-inch cinnamon
- 1-2 green cardamon
- 2 bay leaves
- ½ inch ginger
- 1 tsp cumin seeds
- 1 tsp coriander seeds
- 2-3 dry red chillis

- ½ cup freshly grated coconut
- 1/3 tsp salt
- ½ tsp turmeric
- 3 tsp ghee

🍽 Preparation:

- Peel and cut the potato into medium cubes. Grind the ginger, 1 dry red chilli, coriander seeds, ½ tsp cumin seeds, cardamom, and cinnamon into a smooth paste with a little water.

🍲 Cooking:

- Wash and transfer the moong dal to a pressure cooker.
- Cut the jackfruit into small cubes. Add to the pressure cooker with the potatoes, 1 1/2 cup water, salt and turmeric.
- Cook for 1-2 whistles. The lentil and jackfruit should be 75-80 per cent done.
- Heat a wok. Add the ghee. Just before it starts to smoke, add broken red chillis, bay leaves and cumin seeds. Once the seeds start spluttering, add the masala paste. Fry for 5 minutes on low flame until the raw smell goes off.
- Add the contents of the pressure cooker to the wok.
- Bring to a boil and let it simmer for 5-6 mins.
- Add the coconut, mix once and remove from the flame. Serve warm.

KASI PANASA BHAJA

(Batter fried tender jackfruit)

Mildly spiced and fried to a crisp, *panasa bhaja* is the first among the many dishes that are made during the jackfruit season which lasts through the better part of the year. But the natives' association with the jackfruit tree itself is a never-ending one. Very much like the mango tree and the mahua tree, the jackfruit tree is a part of the ecosystem and makes its presence felt in life and sometimes, death, too. The leaves are used during the *Shraddh* or ritual offerings to the dead ancestors beginning in October. The tree is good enough to build a house and more. A fully mature jackfruit tree can feed an entire village and it actually did in those days when such trees mostly grew wild.

 **Cooking time – 20-25 minutes**

 **Ingredients:**

- 200 gm tender jackfruit pieces
- ¼ cup raw rice
- ½ inch ginger
- ½ tsp cumin seeds
- 2 dry red chilli
- 1/8 tsp turmeric
- ¼ tsp salt
- 3-4 tbsp oil

Preparation:

- The jackfruit should be cut into rectangles of 5-6 mm thickness.
- Soak the rice for 1-2 hours. Grind into a thick paste with the ginger, cumin, dry red chilli and a little amount of water. Add a little salt to this batter and adjust the water. It should be of flowing but not very thin consistency.

Cooking:

- Boil the jackfruit pieces in a pressure cooker with salt and turmeric until it is 75-80 per cent cooked. It should be firm. Drain excess water.

- Let the jackfruit pieces cool down a bit.

- Heat 3-4 tsp oil in a frying pan. Dip the boiled jackfruit pieces into the rice paste and place it on the frying pan, a few pieces at a time.

- Cook on low flame until it turns reddish brown. Flip over and cook on the other side until it turns reddish brown. Remove and keep aside.

- Repeat for the remaining pieces.

- Serve hot/warm with rice meals or even as a snack.

KAKHARU PHULA JANHI BATIBASA
(Pumpkin blossoms and ridge gourd cooked with mustard paste)

Pumpkin flowers are a seasonal delicacy available during early summer. The usual recipe prepared with these flowers is a pan fry with rice batter(pithau). But when these flowers bloom in profusion, a lip-smacking raee is made by adding some ridge gourd and a little potato to bulk it up. It has a texture similar to a *'chattu besara'* or mushroom curry.

 **Cooking time – 15 minutes**

Ingredients:

- 20 pumpkin flowers
- 1 small tender ridge gourd
- 1 small potato
- 1 small tomato
- 1 small onion
- 1 tsp mustard-garlic paste
- 1 green chilli
- 2-3 tsp mustard oil
- 1/6 tsp salt
- 2 pinch turmeric

Preparation:

- Clean and wash the flowers removing the stamens. Chop into big pieces.
- Peel and chop the ridge gourd and potato into small pieces.

- Heat the oil in a wok.

- Add the slit green chilli and fry for 30 seconds before adding the diced tomato. Cover and cook until the tomatoes turn mushy.

- Add the chopped vegetables, mustard-garlic paste, 1/4 cup water, turmeric and salt. Drizzle a little mustard oil on top. Mix and cover. Cook undisturbed on a low flame until the potatoes are done.

- Serve warm with rice meals.

PANI KAKHARU RAEE

(Tender ash gourd cooked with a dash of mustard paste)

Pani Kakharu aka *Kushmanda* is one of those vegetables that one usually finds in a 'herd.' It is always cooked with a bunch of others or turned into 'badis' once it is past its prime. The *raee* is one of those rare preparations where it is handed the opportunity to stand out and shine.

The watery ash gourd is a highly-rated detoxifier of the digestive system. Additionally, it is one of those 'cooling' vegetables and hence, included in the summer menu. The variation made in our village is somewhat different from that in the coastal parts. It eschews turmeric in a bid to preserve the pristine whiteness of the flesh.

 **Cooking time – 15 minutes**

 **Ingredients:**

- 2 cups of chopped ash gourd (small pieces)
- 1 ½ tsp mustard oil
- 1 green chilli
- 1 tsp mustard garlic paste
- 2-3 pinch panch-phutana
- 1/5 tsp salt

Cooking:

- Heat the oil in a wok. Add the slit green chilli and pancha phutana. Let it splutter.
- Add the ash gourd, mustard paste, 1/3 cup water and salt. Mix and cover.

- Lower the flame and let it cook until the ash gourd pieces are just soft (not mushy).

- Serve at room temperature with rice meals.

Note – In the coastal version, vegetables like taro, eggplant, tomatoes, ridge gourd and potatoes are added to this dish. It is also garnished with fresh coconut.

The flavour of ash gourd decreases at it ages and the flesh turns hard, giving it a certain firm sponge-like texture which can soak up the flavours very well. This suits the robust Ambula-Budha Bhendi-Pani Kakharu Khatta prepared around the months of Bhadraba-Aswina, and especially on the occasion of Bhagabata Janma. It is made by sourcing mature ash gourd the and rainy season okra crop that is already past it's prime. Pieces of dried green mango, jaggery and the right touch of dried red chilis is all it needs. (Please refer to the recipe of Kandamula Khatta for the method.)

JANHI PODA/CHIKTA
(Roasted and mashed ridge gourd)

Ridge gourd is another summer vegetable which is cooling in nature. It promotes weight loss, detoxifies the body and aids skin/eye health. A local variety of ridge gourd called *'pentha janhi'* grows in bunches and is available during this time of the year. These are much smaller than the regular ridge gourd. They are the perfect candidate for making the *Janhi Poda*.

 **Cooking time – 10 minutes**

 **Ingredients:**

- 4-5 small ridge gourd
- 1 medium-sized onion
- 1-2 green chilli
- 1 tsp mustard oil
- 2-3 pinch salt

Cooking:

- Roast the ridge gourd over a low flame until the outer skin is almost blackened.
- Remove the blackened skin and put it in a bowl. Add the chopped onions, green chilli, mustard oil and salt. Mash everything together.
- Serve it hot or warm with rice/roti meals.

Note – In earlier times, these veggies were thrown into the embers of the wood fire while another dish was cooking. It saved time and maximized fuel efficiency. Plus, the wood/coal fire added that smoky note to the roasted flesh.

KAKHARU DUNKA RAEE

(Tender Pumpkin stems cooked in a mustard gravy)

Every single part of the pumpkin is edible but the tender stems are coveted for their exceptional taste. They are usually cooked with a bunch of other vegetables and a dash of mustard paste into a mushy and somewhat watery preparation.

The stems need to be peeled to get rid of the fuzzy layer on them. The mature stems cannot be eaten because they are very fibrous. Yet, they are chopped and added to the curry to extract every bit of flavour from them.

The tender stems are treated as a vegetable as they need to cook for longer. The leaves are usually added a little later when the vegetables are half done.

⏳ **Cooking time – 30-35 minutes**

🥣 **Ingredients:**

- 2 cups chopped *Kakharu dunka* (pumpkin stems)
- 2 cups chopped Kakharu sagaw (tender pumpkin leaves)
- ½ cup pumpkin cubes
- ½ cup potato cubes
- 1/3 cup colocassia/saru
- ½ cup brinjal cubes
- 2 large tomatoes
- ½ cup ridge gourd
- 1 small onion
- 10-12 garlic pods
- 2-3 red chilli
- 2 tsp mustard seeds

- 1 tsp cumin seeds
- ½ tsp pancha phutana
- 3-4 tsp oil
- ½ tsp turmeric
- ½ tsp salt (or) to taste.

🍽 Preparation:

- Grind the mustard seeds, cumin, 2 red chillis and 7-8 garlic pods into a fine paste.

🍲 Cooking:

- Heat the oil in a wok. Add the red chilli and pancha phutana. Allow it to splutter.
- Add all chopped onion and fry until translucent. Add the chopped vegetables except for the pumpkin leaves and tomato. Add turmeric.
- Stir fry the vegetables for 5-7 minutes. Add the pumpkin leaves and tomatoes and mix well. Sprinkle salt and cover with lid for 3-4 minutes.
- Add the mustard-cumin paste. Pour 1/2 to 1 cup water and cover with a lid.
- Bring to a boil and allow to simmer for 10 minutes or until done.
- Crush and add the remaining garlic cloves just before removing the wok from the flame.
- Serve hot with rice meals.

> *Note – One can also add some fried badi to the above preparation for texture.*

BITALU DANKA CHINGUDI CHUDCHUDA
(Pumpkin stems cooked with freshwater shrimp)

Unlike the previous preparation, this one uses the most tender stems that can be eaten with ease. With fewer ingredients, the recipe allows the flavour of the pumpkin shoot and freshwater shrimps to shine through. The tender pumpkin holds the dish together without making it overtly sweet.

 **Cooking time – 20 minutes**

 **Ingredients:**

- 4 cups tender pumpkin stems and leaves (Bitalu dunka)
- ½ cup tender pumpkin (cut into small pieces)
- 1 cup fresh shrimp (*thunti chingudi/bhusi chingudi*)
- 5 garlic pods
- 2-3 red chilli
- 2 + ½ tsp mustard seeds
- 4-5 tsp oil
- ½ tsp turmeric
- ½ tsp salt (or) to taste

Preparation:

- Grind 2 tsp mustard seeds, 1 red chilli and garlic pods into a fine paste.
- Clean and marinate the shrimp with 2 pinches of turmeric and a little salt.

- Heat 1-2 tsp oil in a wok. Add the marinated shrimp and sauté for 3-4 minutes. Remove and keep aside.

- Add the remaining oil, and once it heats up, add broken red chilli and mustard seeds. Allow it to splutter. Add pumpkin pieces and the stalks. Add a little salt and turmeric, and cover it for 2-3 minutes.

- Add the chopped pumpkin leaves and mix well. Cover with a lid for 3-4 minutes.

- Dilute the mustard paste with 1/2 cup water. Carefully pour the mustard water into the wok taking care to retain the black residue at the bottom of the cup. Bring to a boil and then lower the flame.

- Let it simmer for 5 minutes before adding the fried shrimp. Let it simmer for 2-3 minutes before removing the wok from the stove.

- Serve hot with rice meals.

PIAJA SANDHA BHAJA

(Stir fried onion flower stalks)

Piaja sandha or onion flower stalks is an ingredient that is available twice a year in most local markets of Odisha. Coinciding with the flowering of the onion plants, these delicacies are available during early winter and late spring. A quick stir fry with potatoes is the best way to enjoy this mild-flavoured vegetable.

 **Cooking time – 15 minutes**

 **Ingredients:**

- 250 gm Onion flower stalks
- 1 medium-sized potato
- 2-3 dry red chillis
- ½ tsp pancha phutana
- 2-3 pinch turmeric
- 1/5 tsp salt (approx.)
- 3 tsp mustard oil
- ¼ roasted cumin-chilli powder (optional)

Preparation:

- Wash and cut the onion flower stalks into inch-sized pieces.
- Wash and cut the potato into small pieces so that both vegetables take the same time to cook.

Cooking:

- Heat a wok. Add the oil. Turn the flame to high.
- Add the broken red chilli and pancha-phutana. Allow seeds to crackle.
- Add the potato and onion stalk pieces. Sprinkle turmeric and salt. Mix well and cook
- covered for 8-10 minutes on a low flame. Stir occasionally so that the vegetables do not stick to the pan.
- Sprinkle the chilli-cumin powder (if using), mix once and remove from the stove.
- Serve hot with rice or rotis.

Note - In a slight variation of this recipe, swap the pancha phutana with mustard seeds and add 1 tsp of mustard paste (diluted with 1-2 tbsp of water) when the veggies are 80 per cent done. Once this liquid is absorbed, swap the roasted cumin chilli powder with fried and crushed urad dal badis. Remove from the flame and serve immediately to retain the crunch provided by the badi.

PANASA TARKARI
(Jackfruit curry)

By March, most jackfruits have grown to their maximum size and the seeds are fully formed although the flesh is still tender. The fibre resembles meat in terms of texture. This stage is ideal for making the *Panasa Tarkari*, a rich preparation that becomes the highlight of every meal. Little wonder it is being branded the faux mutton curry these days.

⧗ **Cooking time – 40 minutes**

🥣 **Ingredients:**

- 500 gms raw jackfruit (cut into cubes)
- 1 medium-sized onion
- 1 medium-sized tomato
- 1 large potato
- 7-8 garlic cloves
- 1-inch ginger
- 2-3 green cardamon
- 2 inch cinnamon
- 2-3 bay leaves
- ½ tsp red chilli powder
- ¼ tsp garam masala
- 1-2 dry red chillis
- ½ tsp cumin seeds
- ½ tsp turmeric
- 3-4 tbsp mustard oil
- 1 tsp salt (or) to taste
- 1/3 tsp sugar

🍽️ Preparation:

- Peel and cut the onion into cubes. Grind the onion cubes, garlic, ginger, cardamom, and cinnamon into a smooth paste.

🍲 Cooking:

- Cut the jackfruit into medium sized cubes. Add to boiling water for 2 minutes and drain the water.

- Heat the oil in a wok. Add cubed potatoes and fry until they start to brown. Remove and keep aside.

- Add broken red chilli, cumin seeds and bay leaf. When the seeds start spluttering, add the ground spices. Fry until the paste starts to turn a light brown. Add turmeric powder and chilli powder. Fry for 1-2 minutes.

- Add the jackfruit pieces and mix them with all the spices. Cover with a lid for 2-3 minutes. Remove the lid and stir it again. Cover it again and keep stirring at regular intervals till the jackfruit starts to brown.

- Add the chopped tomatoes and cover for 2-3 minutes until they start turning mushy. Add the fried potatoes and mix. Cover for 2 mins.

- Transfer the contents of the wok to a pressure cooker and add 2 cups of water. Sprinkle garam masala, and sugar and adjust the salt. Close the lid and allow for 2 whistles on high or until the jackfruit is done.

- Remove from the stove.

- Serve hot with rice or rotis.

It all began with three simple ingredients. Semolina, fresh coconut and a sweetener like sugar/jaggery. A whiff of an aromatic spice. That is if you please. All was good until Milkmaid appeared on the screen.

Add a little for the sake of taste they pushed. It felt better most agreed.

Next packaged cow ghee appeared on the shelves.

Add a little for the sake of good health they said. Once a humble *laddoo*, it was elevated to a decadent delight.

It is true what they say. Human greed knows no bounds.

Add nuts for the sake of texture, they said. Too much of a good thing it became.

Then came the vegans gatecrashing their way. "Can we have a dairy-free version, please?" they said.

And it was back to the three simple ingredients once again!

SUJI-NADIA KORA LADDU
(Coconut and semolina dessert balls)

A popular preparation during the months when the coconuts used in various offerings pile up. The recipe was made to use up the coconuts which could not be used for cooking (restrictions associated with 'bhoga') and to extend their shelf-life (sugar acts as a preservative).

 **Cooking time – 40 minutes**

 **Ingredients:**

- 1 medium-sized coconut
- 1 1/2 cups bombay rawa/suji
- 2-3 tsp ghee
- 1 ¼ cup sugar
- 1 cup water
- 2 pinch green cardamom powder
- 1/3 cup dry fruits (cashews + raisins, optional)

Preparation:

- Grate the coconut.

Cooking:

- Heat 2 tsp ghee on a pan. Add the cashews and sauté until they turn golden. Remove and keep aside. Next, add the raisins and sauté until they puff up. Remove from the pan with the help of a slotted spoon.

- Add another tsp of ghee to the pan. Add the suji and roast for 3-4 minutes on medium heat. Remove from pan when it reaches a light brown colour (*khoya* colour).

- Now add the grated coconut and roast for 3-4 minutes on medium heat. Remove from pan and keep aside.

- Add the sugar and water to a wok, and bring it to a boil. Let it boil until the sugar reaches a stringy consistency. (Test this by taking a little of the liquid, cooling it to a tolerable temperature and keeping a drop of it between the thumb and forefinger. When you try to separate the fingers, a fine thread of the liquid should appear. This indicates that the syrup is ready.)

- Add the cardamom powder and coconut to the sugar syrup. Reduce the flame and mix it for 2 minutes. Now add the suji in small batches and stir continuously to mix all the ingredients. Remove from the flame once the all ingredients are mixed (this mixture further solidifies on cooling so one needs to work fast).

- Let it cool a bit so that it becomes tolerable to work with the mixture using your fingers.

- Spread a nice amount of ghee on your palm and fingers. Take a little amount of the mixture and shape it into round balls.

- Spread a little ghee on your hands after making every 2-3 laddus as it prevents the mixture from sticking to your fingers. The specified quantity makes 20 medium-sized laddus.

- Store in an airtight container when completely cool. Keeps fresh for 1 week.

> *Note: Adding more ghee while roasting the semolina adds to the flavour of the laddu.*

BAIGANA CHUTNEY
(Eggplant chutney)

A Deogarh speciality, this is a dish with a flavour profile that belies the effort that goes into its making. For people who have a problem consuming roasted eggplant, this is one amazing must-try recipe. And it is super healthy too!

 **Cooking time – 12 minutes**

 **Ingredients:**

- 1 cup diced eggplant (cut into small pieces)
- 2-3 fat garlic cloves
- 1-2 hot green chillis
- ½ cup chopped cilantro
- 2 tsp oil
- 1 small tomato
- ¼ tsp tamarind pulp (raw tamarind is used if available)
- Salt to taste

Preparation:

- Heat the oil in a wok. Once it is hot, add the diced eggplants and cook on medium flame until they are soft but not mushy. Switch off the flame and allow it to cool down a bit.
- Transfer to a grinder jar. Add the crushed garlic cloves, slit green chillis, cilantro, diced tomato, tamarind pulp and a little salt. Grind it to a smooth chutney.
- Serve warm with a drizzle of mustard oil.
- Pairs nicely both with rice and rotis.

On the Tuesdays of the month of 'Chaitra', women come together to worship Maa Mangala (a manifestation of Goddess Durga). The story behind it features an untouchable woman who invoked the wrath of the childless king who punished her by having her sons crushed to death. Due to the woman's sheer devotion, the Goddess miraculously brought her deceased sons back to life. With this month being marked by seasonal changes, women invoke the Goddess for the well-being of their family. A hole is dug in the ground, cleaned with turmeric water, decorated with flowers and 'Muruja', and filled with the 'panna'. The ritual of pouring 'panna' into the ground is symbolic of quenching the thirst of the earth which is parched with the arrival of the hot summer days.

What goes into the Panaa in Coastal Odisha:

Raw milk, Curd, Chenna, Jaggery, Mishri, Ginger, Ripe Banana, Black pepper, Cardamom, Camphor, Seasonal fruits

What goes into the Panaa in Western Odisha:

Jaggery, Tender green mango/Chenna/Dahi, Black pepper (sometimes), Khai or Ukhuda (sometimes)

In the older days, the rituals in Western Odisha were carried out in the cowshed or 'Guhal'. But as most homes do not have a cowshed these days, the ritual is mostly carried out by the roadside. Even the frugal panaa has been replaced with a heavier blend of milk, seasonal fruits, black pepper and jaggery.

CHAITRA (MARCH – APRIL)

The initial exuberance of spring wears off, and it almost feels like summer. The blooms have lost their splendour, but the glorious notes of the jasmine's fragrance in the evening air help prolong the utopia. The farm lands are mostly brown, with little sowing taking place in some pockets of the state. Ploughing/tilling of the land is carried out when there are occasional showers. Manuring the paddy fields, and mending the walls keep the farmers busy. This month is characterized by a day breeze which is referred to as the *'Basanta pabana.'* Although pleasant, this breeze is an indication of seasonal change and the diseases that are triggered by it. Little wonder *Chaitra* is earmarked for an annual cleansing ritual or a 'bitter fest' in most Odia households.

The older generations were very particular about ensuring that everyone consumed their daily dose of neem buds and tender leaves during this month. And they made sure everyone remembered this cardinal rule by referring to it in numerous folk songs and poems. During Chaitra, a slew of bitter-tasting dishes is added to the everyday menu. Some of the bitter ingredients cooked in Odia homes during this month are neem flowers/buds, tender neem leaves, bitter gourds, bitter greens like pita saag, and pea eggplants (*bheji baigana*).

There are more changes to the menu this month. Dishes like *Pakhala* and 'aam kanji' cater to the need for increased hydration. And it is not just humans who experience increased thirst during this period. *Chaitra Mangalbara* rituals involve pouring a sweetened drink (Panna) into a hole dug in the earth for creatures like birds, dogs and cows. Women do it in the belief that it will protect their family from the diseases prevalent during this season. It is a primal yet beautiful practice that connects to the philosophy of *'Vasudhaiva Kutumbakam.'* There are subtle differences between the panaa prepared in different parts of the state. While the former is a rich concoction of dairy and fruits, the latter is more like a light South Indian *'Panakam'* with raw mango pieces.

Also, the coastal ritual is more of a *'pantha'* (roadside) puja whereas the western Odisha ritual is more of a *'guhal'* (cowshed) puja.

Important festivals like *Chaitra Navratri, Ashokastami, Ram Navami,* and *Rukuna Ratha Jatra* (Lingaraj temple) fall during this month. Shakti temples like Kakatpur Mangala and Tara Tarini observe Chaitra Navratri in a grand manner. Thousands of devotees visit these temples during the nine days and the atmosphere is one of frenzied devotion. In small villages, primitive and powerful feminine forces are invoked with conch blowing, burning of Indian frankincense, and the primal sounds of the 'hulu-huli.' Animal sacrifices are carried out in most of these shrines during Navratri to appease the Goddesses. The *Chaitra Mela* of *Maa Basuli,* a three-century-old fair, is held in Bonaigarh during this month. *'Danda nrutya,'* a highly energetic dance featuring martial arts moves, is a major attraction of this festival.

This month is vital for the tribal communities. Wild mangoes contribute considerably to their diet and income during the summer months. They prepare and sell several preserved products like *Ambula* (early summer to mid-summer), *Champuta* (mid-summer) and *Aam sadha* (late summer) in the local markets, along with the ripened wild mangoes. During this time of the year, tribal women trudge to the forests before dawn to collect the prized *Mahula (Bassia Latifolia)* flowers. These are either consumed fresh or dried and preserved for later months. Some sell these flowers to supplement their income. Other noteworthy forest produce foraged this month are Kendu (*Diospyros melanoxylon, used for rolling beedi*), Chara (*Buchanania lanzan*) and tamarind.

Some tribal and non-tribal communities observe the Chaitra Nuakhai, a ritual of offering the first fruits and flowers of Mango, *Kendu, Chara, Mahula,* etc., to the local deity.

What's on the menu this month

NIMA KADHA BAIGANA BHAJA
(Neem blossoms stir-fried with eggplant)

Neem blossoms are available for a short period of time. But the sheer abundance of this hyper-seasonal ingredient makes it possible to dry and store some for the latter months. Buds are preferred to the flowers as the latter attract a lot of tiny nectar-seeking insects.

In my home, the fresh flowers are primarily made into a *nima kadha baigana* and a *nima-kadha-pithau bhaja* (the recipe is the same as that for *rasuna patra pithau bhaja,* and is highly recommended for those who find it difficult to eat bitter foods)

 **Preparation time – 15 minutes**

 **Ingredients:**

- 1 ½ cup eggplant (cut into small cubes)
- 2 tbsp fresh or dried neem blossoms
- 1 large onion (cut into long strips)
- 1-2 green chilli
- 3-4 garlic cloves
- 3 tsp mustard oil
- 1/5 tsp salt
- ¼ cup sundried tomatoes (the Western Odisha Addition)

Preparation:

- Soak the sun-dried tomatoes in warm water for 10-15 minutes. Drain and discard the water.

- Heat 1 tsp oil in the wok. Add the cleaned neem blossoms and stir on a low flame until fragrant and crisp. Remove and keep aside

- Add crushed garlic and slit green chilli. Saute for 1 minute before adding the onions. Fry on low flame until onions start to caramelize.

- Add the eggplants and turn up the heat. Sprinkle salt and turmeric. Stir once every 1-2 minutes. Once eggplants have started to soften, add the sundried tomatoes. Stir fry for 3-4 minutes.

- Add the fried neem blossoms. Mix and switch off the flame.

- Serve hot with rice meals.

> *Note – Another bitter green called 'pita sagaw' is also prepared using the same recipe.*

NIMA KADHA PAGAW
(Spicy fried neem blossoms)

The dried neem flowers are primarily used as a tempering over kanji and sometimes even over boiled potatoes and roasted eggplants. But sometimes, it is also made into a bitter pagaw (an exception).

 **Preparation time – 5 minutes**

Ingredients:

- 2 tbsp dried neem blossoms
- 1 small onion
- 1 green chilli
- 1-2 garlic cloves
- ½ tsp mustard oil
- A little salt

Preparation:

- Heat the oil in a wok. Add the dried neem blossoms and stir on a low flame until fragrant and crisp.
- Remove and add to a bowl. Add chopped onion, green chilli, crushed garlic and salt. Mash or pound it gently.
- This can be enjoyed with Pakhala or even hot rice.

Note – One needs to have a higher tolerance for bitter foods to appreciate this recipe.

Growing up in a house surrounded by trees, I developed this uncanny habit of associating seasons with the fragrance of the flowers that bloomed during that time of the year. So, 'Gangashiuli' or Coral jasmine beckoned the arrival of Aswina, 'Amba baula' or Mango blossoms hinted at Pausa/Magha, the fragrant lot of 'Baula,' 'Jui,' 'Malli' and 'Madhumalati' screamed Baisakha and the heady Rajanigandha signalled a parched earth soaking up in the glory of the rains of 'Asadha-Shrabana.' While I would actually look forward to each one of them, the only fragrance that struck terror in my heart was that of the neem or Margosa blossoms. And there is no way one could miss their scent which hung heavy in the air, signalling the arrival of Chaitra masa.

AMBA SORISA KHATTA

(Mango relish with a dash of mustard)

Raw mangoes are cooked into a sweet-sour preparation with a dash of mustard paste to add the right amount of pungency. As appetites are on the wane this month, a little sour food on the menu is more than welcome to stimulate those taste buds. And with mango being the most conspicuous souring agent available around this time, it is made into various chutney and *khatta* to go with the meals.

 **Cooking time – 20 minutes**

 **Ingredients:**

- 1 cup diced green mango
- 2 sprigs of curry leaves
- 2-3 garlic pods
- ½ tsp cumin seeds (optional)
- 2 tsp mustard seeds (half the quantity if less pungency is preferred)
- ½ cup jaggery (will vary with the sourness of the mango)
- ½ tsp pancha-phutana
- 2 dry red chillis
- ¼ tsp roasted cumin-chilli powder (jeera-lanka gunda, optional)
- 1/5 tsp turmeric powder
- 2 tsp oil
- Salt to taste

Preparation:

- Grind the garlic, mustard and cumin seeds into a fine paste.

🍳 Cooking:

- Heat 2 tsp of oil in a wok, add the broken red chillis, pancha-phutana and curry leaves. Stir for about 30 seconds or until the chillis start to darken.

- Add the mango pieces and stir fry on high flame for 1-2 minutes. Lower the flame, sprinkle a little salt and cover with a lid. Check after every 3-4 minutes until mangoes start turning soft.

- Add the mustard paste diluted with 3-4 cups water. Sprinkle turmeric and salt. Bring it to a boil and allow it to simmer.

- When the water reduces to about 2/3rd, add jaggery and boil for 3-4 minutes. Sprinkle jeera-lanka powder (if using) and remove from the fire.

- Serve at room temperature with rice meals.

Note – One can also use sugar instead of jaggery.

*** The longer one cooks the green mangoes, the more intense will be the sourness. Hence, it requires balancing of the amount of water used for cooking and the duration of cooking to get the right consistency and sourness as per one's preference.*

AMBA KANJI

(Soupy dish prepared with raw mangoes)

Unlike the Khatta which needs to be mixed into the rice, the kanji is meant to be slurped like a soup. The ingredients and the nature of the kanji change with the season. While the winter ones are served warm, the summer version is always served cold.

Cooking time – 20 minutes

 **Ingredients:**

- 1-2 green mango (cut into long pieces)
- 3-4 sprigs of curry leaves
- 7-8 garlic pods
- 3-4 tsp jaggery (will vary with the sourness of the mango)
- 1 tsp mustard seeds
- ½ tsp pancha-phutana
- 2 dry red chillis
- 1/4 tsp turmeric powder
- 2-3 tsp mustard oil
- 3 tsp rice
- salt to taste

 **Preparation:**

- Soak the rice for 2 hours. Grind into a smooth paste with a little water.

- Bring 5-6 cups of water to a boil in a deep vessel. Add salt and turmeric.

- Add the mango pieces and let them boil until just cooked. Add the rice paste while stirring continuously and boil for another 3-4 minutes. Add the jaggery and boil for 2 minutes.

- Heat a wok to prepare the tempering. Add the oil. Once it starts to smoke, add the mustard seeds, pancha phutana, crushed garlic and curry leaves. Wait for a few seconds until the garlic turns light brown.

- Pour this tempering over the kanji and cover it with a lid.

- Serve at room temperature.

POEE SAGAW BARA

(Pan-fried Malabar spinach fritters)

Just like the amaranth, the Malabar spinach is one plant that requires minimal care and thrives during the spring-summer season and even during the monsoon months. A few seeds dispersed carelessly in a corner of the kitchen garden ensure a guaranteed supply of greens during the lean period.

 **Cooking time – 15-20 minutes**

Ingredients:

- 2 cup Malabar spinach leaves
- 3 tbsp rice
- 2 tbsp gram flour/besan
- ½ tsp cumin
- 2 red chillis
- Salt to taste
- 3-4 tsp oil

Preparation:

- Soak the rice for 1-2 hours and grind it into a smooth paste along with the cumin and chilli. Add the gram flour. Adjust the consistency of the batter.

- Wash and air dry the Malabar spinach leaves. Cut into thin long strips. Transfer to a mixing bowl. Add some of the batter and mix it. It should be just enough to coat the greens. Add a little salt.

Cooking:

- Heat a griddle. Season with a little oil.

- Add little portions of the mixture and spread it into a thin layer of 2-3 mm thickness. Drizzle a little oil and cook on a low flame until it develops a reddish crust on the bottom. Flip it over and cook on the other side. Remove from the griddle once done.

- Repeat for the remaining mixture.

- Serve it immediately with meals. Can also be enjoyed as a snack.

> *Note – The discarded stems can be cooked with shrimps, ridge gourd, baby potatoes, shallots and a dash of mustard-garlic paste into a semi-dry side dish.*

BADI PHULA

(Sun-dried lentil dumplings cooked with a thin gravy)

Badi-based dishes are a regular feature during the summer months when the vegetable supplies dry up. The lentil dumplings are prepared during the winter months in anticipation of the scarcity during the summers. And involves a lot of work. Right from soaking a batch of black lentils to rubbing off their peels, grinding them on a stone, leavening them to incorporate air and finally laying out the dumplings, the whole process lasts the entire morning. There are quite a few varieties of badi but the *'Kakharu Badi'* (ones made by the addition of ash gourd pulp) is best suited for this preparation.

 **Cooking time – 15 minutes**

Ingredients:

- 10-12 Kakharu Badi
- 1-2 dry red chillies
- 1 dry red chilli
- 2 tsp mustard seeds
- 4 garlic cloves
- 4 tsp mustard oil
- 1-2 pinch turmeric
- ¼ tsp salt to taste
- 1 ambula (dried green mango)

Pre-cooking:

- Keep aside 2 garlic pods and 1/4 tsp mustard seeds. Grind the rest into a fine paste along with the dry red chilli.
- Slightly crush the remaining garlic pods.

🍽 Preparation:

- Heat 2 tsp oil in a wok. Fry the Badi to a light brown colour. Keep aside.

- Add the remaining oil to the wok. When it starts smoking, reduce the flame and add the mustard seeds, pounded garlic pods and broken red chillies.

- Once the seeds start spluttering, add 1/2 cup water to the wok. Add salt and turmeric and bring to a boil.

- Add the mustard paste diluted with 2 cups water. Boil for 5-6 minutes.

- Add the fried Badi and the ambula. Simmer for 2 minutes.

- Take off the fire and let it stand for a while.

- Serve at room temperature with rice meals.

Note – There is a popular variation of this recipe made with milk instead of mustard paste and dried green mango. No turmeric is used in this version.

BADI TARKARI
(Sun-dried lentil dumplings curry)

A semi-dry preparation of badi with baby potatoes, shallots and a few sprigs of garlic leaves (lightly fried) which lend it a unique flavour. Depending on the quantity of gravy retained, the curry can be consumed either with 'pakhala' or hot rice.

⏳ **Cooking time Required – 15-20 minutes**

🥣 **Ingredients:**

- ½ cup baby potatoes
- 9-12 shallots
- 1 medium-sized country tomato (optional)
- 1 cup kakharu badi
- 2 dry red chillis
- 1/4 tsp pancha phutana
- 2 tsp mustard seeds
- 3-4 garlic flakes
- 2 tsp oil
- A pinch of turmeric
- Salt to taste

🍽 **Preparation:**

- Cut the baby potato into half. Peel the shallots. Keep aside.
- Grind the mustard seeds along with the garlic flakes and red chillis into a fine paste. Dissolve in 1 cup of water and let it stand aside.
- Roast the badis with a little oil and crush them lightly.

🍳 Cooking:

- Heat a wok. Add 1 tsp oil. Add pancha phutana and broken red chilli. Allow to splutter for 5-10 seconds.

- Add the shallots and stir fry until translucent. Add the potatoes at this stage and stir fry for 2 minutes.

- Cut the tomato into 4 parts and add to the wok. Cover with a lid and allow it to soften a bit.

- Carefully pour the mustard water into the wok taking care to retain the black residue at the bottom of the cup. Add the fried onion, potatoes, salt and turmeric.

- Cover with a lid and cook for 10 minutes or until the potato is almost done. Add the crushed badi at this stage. Cook for 1-2 minutes more.

- Remove from fire and allow it to stand for 5 minutes.

- Serve with rice and dal or pakhala.

KADALI MANJA RAEE

(Banana stem cooked with a dash of mustard paste)

Banana stem happens to be one of those delicious vegetables that are extremely low in calories and also loaded with fibres. It is highly recommended for those suffering from kidney/gallbladder stones, diabetes, hyperacidity and constipation. For ladies, who are usually prone to infections of the urinary tract, banana stem juice is considered to be an excellent home remedy. Cooking banana stems is a rather cumbersome process. Given today's busy lifestyle, I have adapted the original recipe to reduce the cooking time as one cannot take any shortcuts with the prepping process.

Read on for the recipe.

 **Cooking time Required – 30 minutes**

 **Ingredients:**

- 7-8 inches long banana stem
- 1 medium-sized tomato
- 2-3 slit green chillis
- 2 tsp thick mustard-garlic paste
- 6-7 crushed garlic flakes
- 1/4 tsp turmeric
- 1/6 tsp salt or to taste
- 2 tsp mustard oil for cooking
- 1 tbsp cut coriander leaves
- 1/2 tsp mustard oil for drizzling

🍽 Preparation:

- Remove the outer fibrous layers and expose the solid core. This is the part that is used in cooking. Cut the banana stem into thin circles.

- After slicing off one circle, one can feel the fibres when one tries to separate it from the remaining stem. Move your fingers in a circular motion to wrap the fibres around it and remove as much of the fibres as you can.

- Chop the circles into small pieces. Mix salt and turmeric and keep aside for half an hour.

- After half an hour, squeeze out all the water from the banana stem pieces using both hands. Crush the pieces gently using the bottom part of a heavy steel glass or a pestle.

- Cut the tomato into small pieces and remove the seeds.

🍲 Cooking:

- Take all the ingredients (except coriander leaves) into a pressure cooker. Add 1/4 cup water and close the lid. Cook for 1-2 whistles on a medium flame.

- Remove and keep aside until the steam escapes. Open the lid and add the chopped coriander and 1/2 tsp raw mustard oil. Mix.

- Serve at room temperature with rice meals.

Note – At times, when there is only a handful of tiny fresh shrimp available and too many mouths to feed, they are lightly stir-fried and added to the above preparation.

BHENDI SORISA KHATTA
(Okra cooked in a tangy gravy)

Okra used to be one of those much-loved summer vegetables before hybrid varieties robbed its seasonal charm. Among the multiple dishes that we make in Odia homes, this is one of the most underrated yet sensational dishes.

Cooking time – 15 minutes

 **Ingredients:**

- 10-12 tender okra
- 2 tsp mustard garlic paste
- 1-2 dried green mangoes (ambula)
- 2 slit green chillis
- 1 tbsp fresh yoghurt (optional)
- ¼ tsp pancha phutana
- 2 sprig curry leaves
- 1/8 tsp turmeric
- ¼ tsp salt
- 4 tsp mustard oil

Cooking:

- Cut the okra into 1.5-inch pieces. Soak the green mango in ¼ cup water.
- Heat 2 tsp oil in a wok. Add the okra pieces and sprinkle a little salt. Stir fry until the okra is ¾th cooked. Remove from wok and keep aside.
- Heat the remaining oil in a wok. Add the pancha phutana, slit green chilli and curry leaves.

- Dilute the mustard paste with 1 cup water and add to the wok. Add salt, turmeric and a few drops of mustard oil. Bring to a boil.

- Reduce the flame and add the fried okra. Let it simmer for 5 minutes before adding the soaked green mango along with the water used for soaking. Simmer for 2 minutes before removing from the flame.

- Stir in the beaten yoghurt. Serve at room temperature.

ALU PITHA

(A thin crisp crepe made from baby potatoes)

During the harvest of potatoes, the larger ones fetch a higher price. But in Odisha, it is the smaller ones that are most prized as they make a great side with pakhala. They are usually pan-fried with a slathering of spicy mustard paste, sometimes with drumsticks, or made into a delectable side dish with 'sukhua' or dried fish.

Even the tiniest of them do not go to waste as they are turned into an incredible 'pitha' or 'chakuli' if one may call it so.

 **Cooking time – 15 minutes**

 **Ingredients:**

- 1 cup baby potatoes (use the tiny one)
- 2 tsp raw rice
- 1 dry red chilli
- 2 pinch cumin
- A pinch of turmeric
- Salt to taste
- 2-3 tsp oil for frying

Preparation:

- Soak the rice for 1 hour.
- Grind into a slightly coarse paste with the potato, red chilli and cumin seeds.

Cooking:

- Heat a griddle. Season with a few drops of oil.
- Take half of the above mixture and spread it out into a layer about 3-4 mm thick. Drizzle oil around the circumference.
- Cook on a low flame until it starts to turn brown.
- Flip and cook on the other side as well.
- Serve hot with Pakhala.

GUANR DIBA PUDA

(Cluster beans cooked with mustard paste)

Cluster beans are one of the most underrated vegetables. The texture and taste both take a little time to get used to but the health benefits are many. They are rich in plant proteins, possess a good fibre content and are a good source of minerals. It a pitta-pacifying ingredient but longer duration cooking helps to balance its vata-aggravating nature.

 **Cooking time – 20-25 minutes**

Ingredients:

- 1 cup chopped cluster beans (cut into small pieces)
- 6-7 fat garlic cloves (minced)
- 1 green chilli (chopped)
- 1-2 tsp mustard paste
- 1 ½ tsp mustard oil
- Salt to taste

Cooking:

- Mix all the ingredients together with 2-3 tsp water and transfer it to a thick-bottomed wok.
- Cover and cook on a low flame for 15 minutes. Add a little water if it tends to catch at the bottom.
- Serve it warm with a drizzle of mustard oil.

Note – The term 'Diba puda' or 'bati basa' is used to refer to a dish that is cooked in a small aluminium bowl placed on embers. All ingredients are mixed and cooked together and there is no intervention required. But this kind of utensil doesn't suit the gas stove flame that we have in most kitchens as it tends to catch at the bottom pretty quickly. Use a thick-bottomed vessel instead.

MUGA DALI

(Moong Dal)

The only one considered as *'sattvik'* among all the lentils and pulses consumed in Odisha, *Muga* or *Mung* is light and easy on the stomach. Inevitably, it is the 'dal' of choice during the hot summer months. The dal is always roasted a little before cooking which releases the fragrance and makes it even easier to digest.

Cooking time – 15 minutes

 **Ingredients:**

- 1/2 cup moong dal
- 2 ½ cups water
- 3-4 garlic cloves (lightly crushed)
- 1 small onion (chopped into medium-sized pieces)
- ½ tsp pancha phutana
- 1-2 dry red chilli (we prefer green chilli at home)
- 1 tsp mustard oil
- 1/3 tsp salt
- 1/8 tsp turmeric

 **Preparation:**

- Dry roast the moong dal on a low flame until it starts to give off a fragrance.

Cooking:

- Wash and transfer the dal into a pressure cooker. Add water, salt and turmeric.
- Cook for 1 whistle.

- Once the steam escapes, open the lid and let it simmer for a while.

- Heat the oil in a medium-sized wok until smoking point. Add the broken chilli and pancha phutana. Add the garlic and allow it to turn light brown. Add the onions next and sauté until the edges caramelize.

- Pour over the dal into the wok and simmer for 1-2 minutes.

- Serve warm.

Chakuli. or *Chakel* if you are in the Western fringes of the state. The unfermented/ever-so-lightly fermented Odia counterpart of the South Indian *dosa*. A somewhat portly mofussil cousin of the crisp pancake. Laced with the aroma of mustard oil. Along with the numerous gravies that it has mopped up, the chakuli has also imbibed quite a bit of the typical Odia psyche. It lies contented, basking in the beauty of its own wholesome being without bothering about the rather hallowed status of the 'dosa.'

But then Chakuli is not just 'one dish.' It is a term used for an entire legion of recipes. Some of them have rice as the primary ingredient, for others it is a mere appendage. We have numerous examples of another ingredient assuming centre stage while rice just acts as a binding agent or solely adds a note of crispness to the dish. In other words, 'Chakuli' is no longer a noun, it is transformed into a verb. *Tala Chakuli, Panasa Chakuli, Nimba Chakuli, Mahula Chakuli* and the list just keeps getting longer.

Chakuli, which is derived from the word 'Chaka' or round, is also a favourite of the 'Chaka Akhi' or 'Chakadola' as the inhabitants of Odisha call him. His gaze is all-encompassing. And so is the Chakuli.

MAHULA CHAKEL

(Crepes made with mahua flowers)

Mahula or *Madhuca Indica* is known more for the intoxicating drink prepared by using it than for any of its medicinal properties. The tribal women go to the forest areas early morning to gather the flowers. They use some of it in everyday cooking and store the rest, which is used throughout the year as a natural sweetener in some of their preparations like pitha, letha, etc.

But the fresh flower is also used by other communities. The Mahula Chakel is a mandatory breakfast in Western Odisha homes during the tree's flowering season in late spring.

 **Preparation time – 30 minutes**

 **Ingredients:**

- 1 cup raw rice
- ½ cup fresh mahula flowers (rehydrated ones will also do)
- 1/3 tsp salt
- Oil for cooking the Chakuli

Preparation:

- Wash and soak the rice for 4 hours. Drain and transfer to a grinder jar.
- Clean the flowers and add them to the same jar. Add a little water and grind into a fine paste. Adjust the consistency and add salt. Let it sit for 2-3 hours to ferment.

- Heat a griddle. Take a ladle of the batter and spread it out like a thick dosa. Drizzle oil around the circumference and let it cook on a low flame.

- Flip it around and cook on the other side as well. These will remain soft and won't turn crispy.

- Remove from the wok. Serve hot with liquid jaggery or molasses.

NADIA BARA TARKARI

A preparation made with coconut and chana dal dumplings in the coastal belt where coconut grows in abundance. While it can be prepared throughout the year, it is the preferred dish during the no-onion-garlic days during this month as coconut has a cooling and nourishing effect on the body. Also, it is excellent for pacifying pitta dosha which tends to aggravate around this time of the year.

 **Cooking Time – 45 minutes**

 **Ingredients:**

For the dumplings:

- 1 ½ cup freshly grated coconut
- 1 cup split Bengal gram (soaked for 3-4 hours, washed and drained)
- 1-inch ginger
- ½ tsp cumin seeds
- 1-2 green chilis

For the curry:

- 1 large boiled potato
- 1 large tomato
- 1-inch ginger
- 1/2 tsp cumin seeds
- 1 tsp coriander seeds
- 1 tsp poppy seeds
- 1 dry red chilli
- 1 green cardamom

- 1-inch cinnamon

- 5-6 black peppercorns

- 2-3 cloves

- 2 bay leaves

- Turmeric

- ½ tsp sugar

- Salt

- Oil

🍽 Preparation:

- Grind the soaked lentils, cumin, ginger and chilli into a thick and coarse paste. Mix it with the grated coconut to make a dough.

- Peel and chop the potato into large chunks.

- Make a paste out of ginger, cumin seeds, coriander seeds, poppy seeds, red chilli, cardamom, cinnamon, cloves, black pepper, one bay leaf and tomato.

🍲 Cooking:

- Heat oil in a pan for shallow frying.

- Pinch small portions of the dough. Shape them into 1 cm thick discs. Slide 4-5 discs into the hot oil per batch.

- Fry on medium heat until it has light brown on one side, flip and repeat for the other side. Remove and keep aside.

- Add the potato cubes and fry until they turn golden. Remove and keep aside.

- Add 3-4 tsp oil in another wok. Add the bay leaf and the masala paste and cook for 3-4 minutes until the raw smell goes away.

- Add turmeric and sauté on a low flame until the oil starts to separate.

- Add 2 cups of hot water, fried potatoes and salt. Bring to a boil and allow it to simmer for 3-4 minutes.

- Add the discs along with the sugar and cook on a medium flame for 5 minutes. Do not stir vigorously as they might break. Cover and switch off the flame. Let it rest for 5 minutes before serving.

- Serve with rice or roti.

Note – Some households substitute the Bengal gram with an aromatic rice

A 'Pakhala meal' showcasing the various sides served with Odisha's most ubiquitous dish. It features batter fried pumpkin flowers, batter fried ash gourd leaves, drumsticks and potatoes fried with a dash of mustard paste, neem buds stir fried with eggplant, the signature 'Keonjhar badi' and batter fried freshwater fish. Green chilis, onions and cucumbers are a staple in every summer meal.

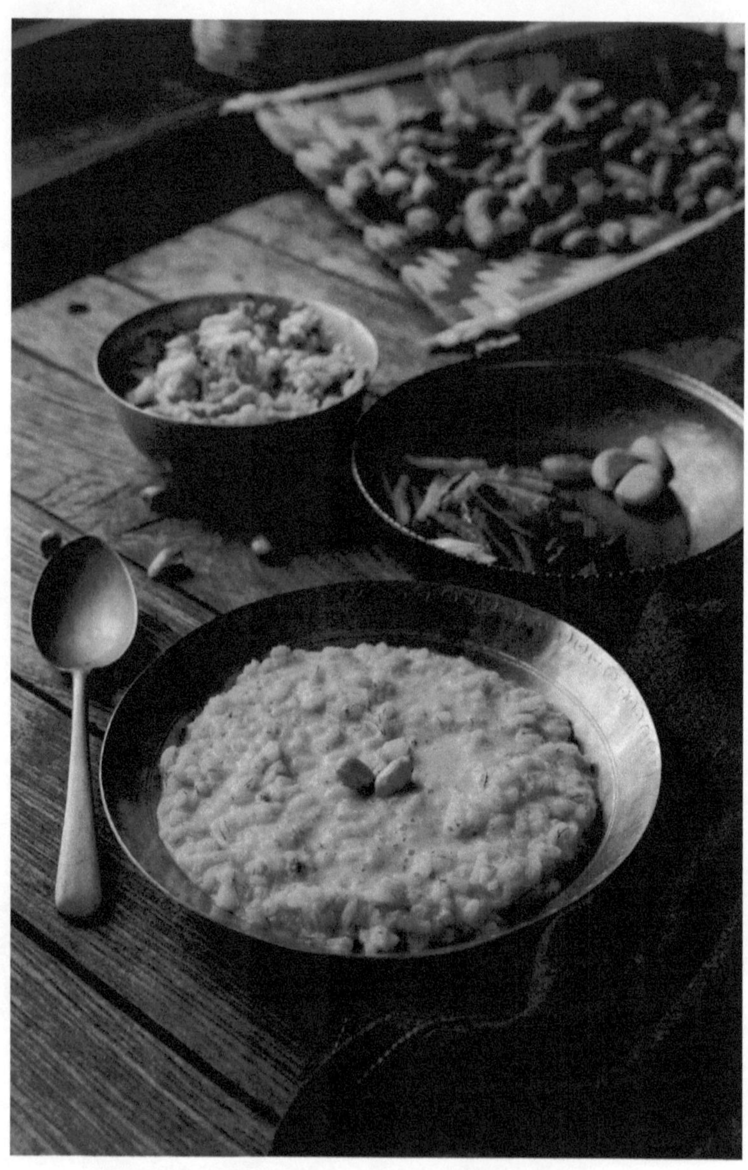

A monsoon meal consisting of *Chinabadam jukha*, stir fried potatoes, and roasted and mashed eggplant.

An 'arrival of spring' meal from the Western parts of the state. Moong Dal cooked with onion chives, last lot of tomatoes boiled with mustard paste, mature flat bean seeds tossed with mustard paste and tomatoes, and stir fried tender okra served with fine rice.

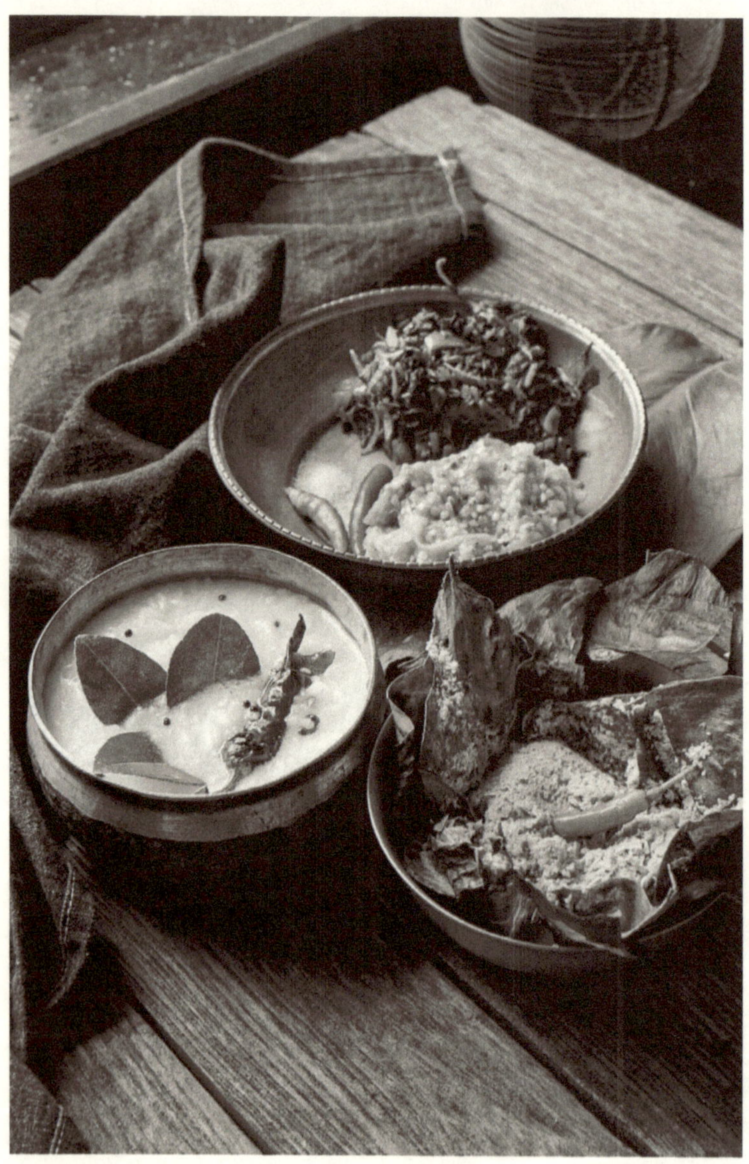

A winter Pakhala meal with Kosala sagaw bhaja, baigana bharta and patua

A celebratory 'end of winter' meal from Mayurbhanj featuring *Chaula ruti*, country chicken curry, *Kakara pitha*, sesame laddu and *Mudhi.*

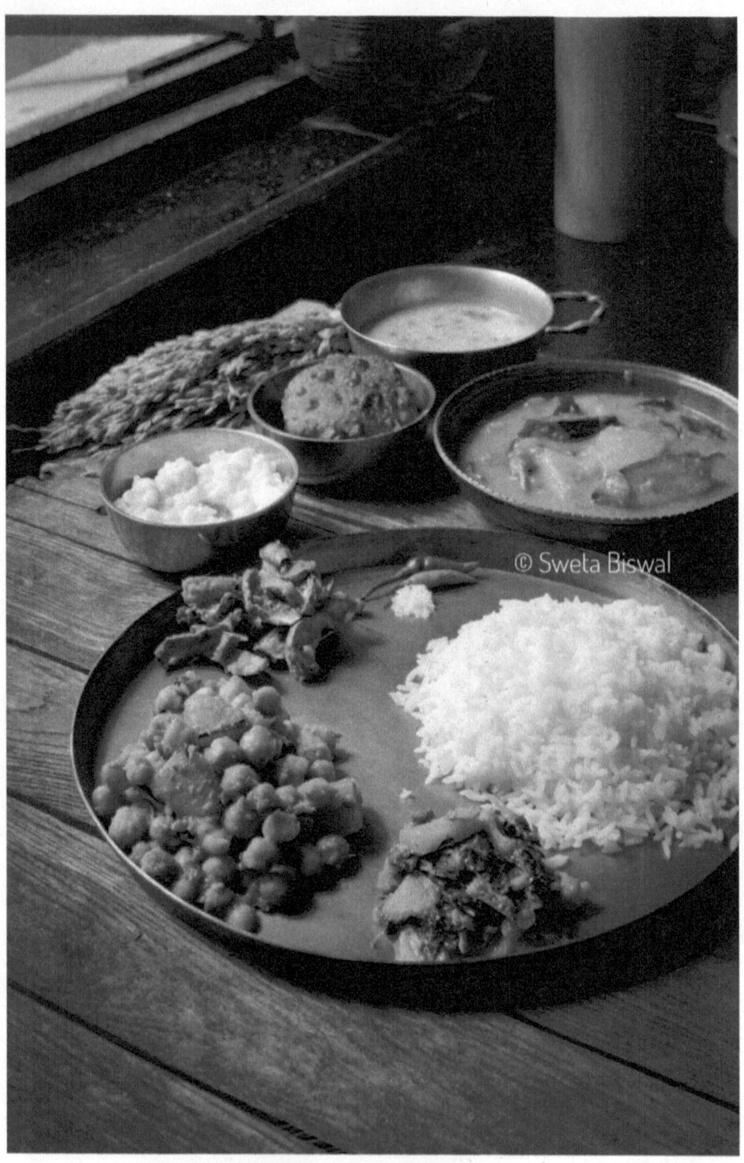

A celebratory Western Odisha meal during Nuakhai featuring *Makhan saag*, *Ambil*, chickpeas curry, fried spine gourd, dal, Kakara and Jau.

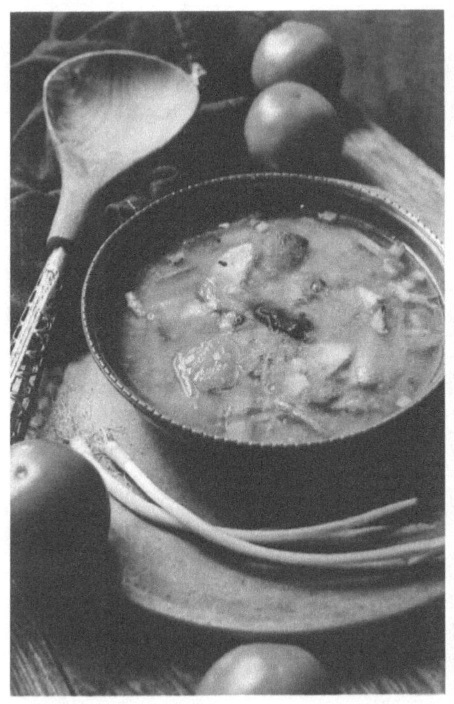

A hearty *Kolotha Dali* (horsegram dal) prepared during winter with taro, eggplant and profusion of local tomatoes.

A warming *Biri Dali* (black lentil dal) cooked during monsoon with a garlic and red chili tempering.

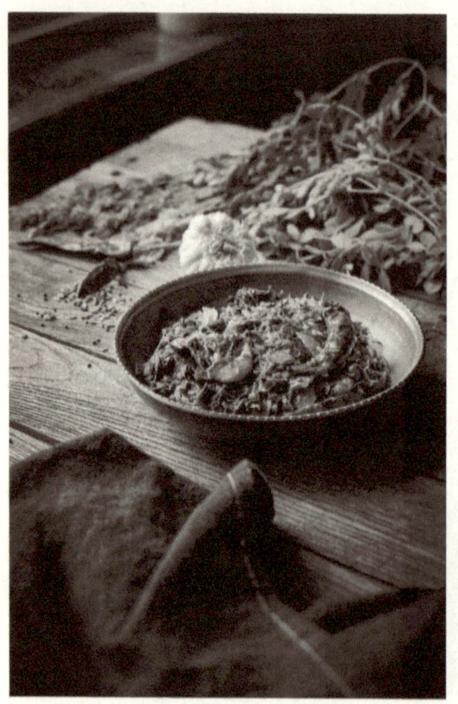

Sajana Sagaw (Moringa) cooked with moong dal is a much-repeated dish during summer and early monsoon.

Barada Sagaw (Bauhinia) leaves cooked with fried and crushed badi is an early summer delicacy.

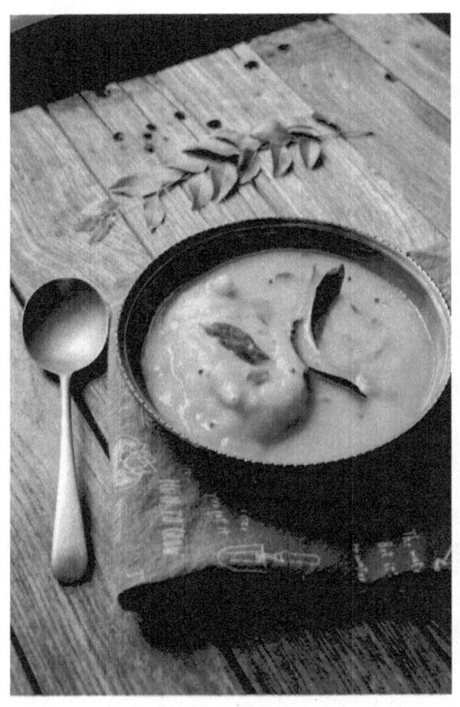

Ripe 'desi' mangoes cooked into a sweet-sour luscious Amba kanji

Tala Kakara made by deep frying a 'pre-cooked' dough of rice flour, jaggery and ripe sugar palm pulp.

A spread of Manda pitha, Biri Gojja and Dalma prepared during festive occasions in the Coastal districts.

Rajaw Poda Pitha is the signature dish prepared during the agrarian festival of Rajaw. It involves baking a 'pre-cooked' rice dough on embers for a long time resulting in a distinctive charred crust.

Makara Chaula is the primary offering made on the occasion of Makara Sankranti. It incorporates rice from the new harvest and various seasonal produce.

Habisa Dalma, a seasonal delicacy prepared with split green gram and a select vegetables during the Hindu month of Kartika is an extremely nourishing dish.

A snapshot of some vegetables available during winters in Odisha – Radish, *Kaintha*, arrowroot tubers and sweet potatoes.

A snapshot of some vegetables available during late monsoon in Odisha – Tender ash gourd, pumpkin vines, ash gourd leaves, elephant apple, teasel gourd and taro leaves.

SEASONAL HAVE'S AND NOT HAVES

Have you ever wondered if certain foods were created around certain festivals or was it the other way around? On how many occasions have we witnessed a continuation of the pagan practice of returning the first few grains of the season's produce to the earth's womb? Was the process a part of a systemic reminder set by our ancestors to nudge us to include seasonal produce on our menu? Or, was it a mnemonic to be grateful to Nature for bestowing us with its bounty? Either way, it succeeded in bolstering the immune systems and buffering the bodies of our ancestors against the cyclic upheavals of nature. And, perhaps, that is why these festivals and rituals have continued through centuries.

There is a deeper symbolism hidden beneath those layers of rituals. Quite a few of them seem obscure to the point of being obsolete. Perhaps, the cryptic nature of these rituals was intentional. It might have been a parallel attempt at recording bits and pieces of our history. It is widely acknowledged that the written word was under constant threat by marauding armies. Hence, it is possible that the folklore woven around the numerous festivals that dot our calendar may conceal more than what they reveal. Sadly, when we take words too literally, often the hidden meaning is lost in translation. Most festivals today have adapted and morphed to a point wherein the older rituals have been taken over by a new set. The ones that exist are followed almost mechanically without any attempt to decipher the truth behind them. While it falls beyond the scope of this book to uncover all the layers of history concealed beneath our rituals and practices, I have attempted to list the seasonal foods recommended in some of the texts (katha) and to uncover the offerings made during the various 'parba' and 'osa' observed in Odisha.

A. Recommended and Prohibited list of Ingredients

Month	Recommended	Prohibited/ Restricted	Season of Aggravation
Pausa/Pushya	Radish, *mudhi, muan,* sesame seeds, jaggery, sugarcane, horse gram, black lentils, game meat, fish, freshly made *badi,* rice		Winter (Kapha)
Magha	Fresh curd, Flat beans, radish		Winter (Kapha)
Phalguna	Roasted chana, *Ukhuda, Chuda, Sakkara*		Spring (Kapha)
Chaitra	Nimba(neem), nimba kadha(neem blossoms), green mango, coconut, chenna, *Bela*(wood apple fruit), sweet drinks like *Panaa*	Onion and Garlic. Go easy on grains (relatable to Navratri food restrictions)	Spring (Kapha)
Baisakha	*Panna*	Sour and spicy foods in general	Summer (Pitta)
Jyesta	Ripe mango, ripe jackfruit, *Kendu,* wild berries, Chebula, Terminalia bellirica, tender sugar palm	Sour and spicy foods in general	Summer (Pitta)
Asadha	Teasel gourd, black plums	Greens like kalama sagaw (Ipomoea aquatica), drinking water from rivers	Monsoon (Pitta)
Shrabana	Ripened sugar palm fruit, beaten rice, local corn	Greens like kalama sagaw (Ipomoea aquatica), drinking water from rivers	Monsoon (Pitta)
Bhadraba	Bamboo shoots, tender pumpkin leaves,	Curds, fermented foods	Monsoon (Vatta)

Month	Recommended	Prohibited/ Restricted	Season of Aggravation
Aswina	*Arisa pitha*, Sprouts, taro, yam, sweet potato, *kaintha*		Autumn (Vatta season)
Kartika	Plantain, green moong, taro, agasti leaves, cucumber, arrowroot, elephant apple, popped rice(*khai*), dairy products	Non-vegetarian food, Horse gram, Red lentils, black lentils, red rice, black rice, leafy green except for Agasti leaves, ash gourd, citrus fruits	Autumn (Vatta season)
Margasira	Radish, rice and lentils from the new harvest, *kanji*, *sukhua*, turmeric leaves/*Gajapimpali* leaves used for preparing enduri pitha	Bitter foods	Winter (vatta season)

B. Offerings in the Various Osa's observed in Odisha

A series of rituals called 'Osa' are a part of the Odia Calendar. Most of them are concentrated in the six-month period beginning at the end of monsoon. There is a close correlation between the observance of these rituals and the prevalence of diseases and illnesses like malaria, diarrhoea, and typhoid fever which had a high mortality rate in earlier times. Cold weather is also known to increase mortality rates as it aggravates some of the existing medical conditions. Hence, in the older days, people used to observe fasts or make offerings to the Gods like Yama (God of Death) and powerful Goddess like Goddess Mangala, Maa Sathi (or her various avatars like Maa Sathi, Maa Khurukuni, Budhei Bamana) for the protection and general well-being of their family.

Each 'Osa' calls for a particular ingredient or a class of ingredients/ recipes that are closely entwined with the seasonal produce. Here is a list of some of those:

Name	Month	Offering	Health / medicinal property
Sathi Osa	Bhadraba [two days after Ganesh Chaturthi]	Six Leafy vegetables are *Khada, Koshala(amaranthus varieties), Kanasiri (Commelina benghalensis), Bana Chakunda (Cassia Tora), Purunimundi, Saru (Taro)* Six fruits are *Dudura(Datura), Kaniari(Oleander), Chaulia(guava), Nadia(coconut), Janhi(ridge gourd), Kakudi(cucumber)* Additionally, the branches of six plants are offered *Bana Saru, Amara Jui, Dhana, Barakoli, Apamaranga(Achyranthes Aspera)* and *Bajramuli(Sida Cordifolia*	The leafy vegetables are consumed in most rural homes. *Dudura, Kaniara, Apamaranga* are medicinal plants and parts are used for external application for a range of ailments. ***Datra and Oleander fruits are highly toxic.*** *Bajramuli* is used orally for dysentery and fever.
Buddhei Osa	Bhadrab [every Wednesday]	Different types of pitha	Energy giving foods
Danda Panhara Osa	Pausa [2nd day of Sukhala Pakshya]	Sugarcane, radish, banana, *budha chakuli, dudha gainthala, mula kanji, muga manda, muga paiti,* fish cooked with black pepper, etc. are mentioned in the same book; A branch of *bajramuli(Sida Cordifolia)* for sweeping the floor	Sugarcane and radish are seasonal ingredients. Bajramuli is used orally for dysentery and fever.
Kanji Anla Osa	9th day of Margasira	The offering is *Sukhua*(dried fish), *kanji*, gooseberry, radish, Malabar spinach, *balunga* (rice plant without the rice spikelet)	Gooseberry and radish are seasonal ingredients. Pita sukhua (dried fish that has a bitter taste as bile is not removed) is rich in protein and mineral content

Name	Month	Offering	Health / medicinal property
Nisa Mangala bara	Shukla Pakhya Aswina masa	*Harida* (Terminalia Chebula), *Kanta Koli*, Plantain stem, Ripe banana, Coconut, *Tandula*(rice), tender jackfruit(probably a very late variety), *Khaee, Muan, Khiri, Khechudi*, Pitha, sweets	Seasonal ingredients mostly. Harida or Chebula is a very useful medicinal ingredient
Dwitiya Osa	Krushna Pakhya Bhadraba	Jambila/naranga (kinds of citrus fruits), *kerandi koli*, Lotus seeds	Increases agni, balances vata, boots immunity
Khudurukuni Osa	Bhadraba [Sundays]	Khudakunda pitha – khudatandula pura (pitha made with broken rice and rice bran)	Khuda and kunda (broken rice and bran) have a better nutritional profile than rice as the essential oils and nutrients are retained
Samba Dasami	Pausa (10th day of Shukla Paksha)	*Ghadaghadiya Tarkari*	Is supposed to clear up the cough and phlegm
Chaitra Mangalabara	Chaitra [Tuesdays]	*Panaa*	Cooling and hydrating
Pua Jiuntia	Aswina (8th day of Krushna pakhya)	Various seasonal vegetables, *Tikhri, Muan*	Seasonal ingredients, nourishing and energy-giving

DECODING THE KITCHEN EQUIPMENT

Kitchen Equipment	Description and Usage
Chakki	Milling Stone; most households had two of these back in the PDS days; a bigger one for wheat and a smaller one for lentils. The bigger one is rarely seen after packaged flour became available at every *Tejarati dokan* (odia term for *Kirana* store). Although split lentils are available easily, the smaller one is still retained at homes as it is an integral part of the Odia wedding celebration. *[Every Odia wedding starts with Jaee ragada, a ceremony where seven married women grind the lentils in a milling stone. The lentils are later turned into badi and placed in the Bahaghara bedi (wedding mandap)]*
Chaluni	Seive; used to separate particles of different diameters. But one can use it every day to seive flours/semolina for small bugs/stones. It is usually made of iron and later steel/plastic
Chimuta	Tongs for holding hot utensils. The older ones were usually made up of iron or brass but steel ones have long replaced them.
Dalaa	Tray; Used for holding fruits and vegetables and even the offerings during the religious ceremonies. It is made up of bamboo and woven by tribal communities.
Gara	These narrow-mouthed brass vessels were once used for ferrying and storing water in the house/kitchen when running tap water was not available. Is used in marriage ceremonies to hold the blessed water in which the bride or groom takes a bath.
Hemadasta	Mostar and pestle; It is used for powdering ingredients in smaller quantities. It is usually made up of iron.
Katuri	A curved knife is used for husking and breaking coconuts. It is made up of iron.

Kitchen Equipment	Description and Usage
Korani	Grater; most of the coastal Odia recipes and pithas call for freshly grated coconut, making this an indispensable tool in the kitchen. The most traditional ones are similar to the paniki in design except for a small serrated head on the front and one usually has to crouch or sit on the floor to use it. At times, a small serrated disc is mounted on the paniki itself making it a multi-purpose tool. But I have not seen the latter design a lot. Utensils or tools used for making pitha for religious ceremonies cannot be used for handling onions, garlic or fish so that kinds of limits the scope of such a modification.
Kula	Winnow; usually the grains or lentils retain some of the husk after being processed manually. Since they have a different density, they are easily blown off while winnowing. Big ones are employed in the barns where rice is milled to remove the husk (*kunda*) from the grains. It is also made up of bamboo and woven by tribal communities. *[The Kula is an integral part of the Osa baras as the offerings are usually placed on a new Kula]*
Pachiya	Colander; used for washing and straining vegetables, rice, lentils, vegetables. It is usually made from bamboo and woven by tribal communities. [They are stackable and have different shapes for different uses. For example, the Pachiya that is used for making the rice liquor or Handiya was a conical base which allows for more efficient drainage.
Paniki	A tool used for peeling, mincing and chopping or cutting vegetables and fish while being crouched/seated on the floor. It is made up of iron. The size varies depending on the usage.
Pesani	Vertical grinding stone more suited for grinding black lentils or a mixture of black lentils and rice.
Sila Pua	Horizontal grinding stone for rice, masalas and chutneys. Made from specific kinds of stone. Unlike a grinder/mixer, this does not heat up the spices/condiments while grinding and hence the aroma and taste are much better as the volatile oils are retained. *[It represents the feminine power and it is decked up and worshipped during some of the Osa Bara's like Buddhei Osa, Sabitri brata, Basundhara Snana]*

LIST OF VEGETABLES USED IN ODIA COOKING

1. Amrutabhanda/Bhanda (Paraya)
2. Asadua (Capparis Zeylanica)
3. bantala Kadali (Plantain)
4. Sanai Kadha (Sun hemp flowers)
5. Mati Alu (Yam)
6. Baigana (Eggplant)
7. Patalghanta/Bilati (Tomato)
8. Kakharu (Pumpkin)
9. Pani Kakharu/Kushmanda (Ash gourd)
10. Lau (Bottle gourd)
11. Janhi (Ridge gourd)
12. Chachindra (Snake gourd)
13. Kannkada (Teasel gourd)
14. Potola (Pointed gourd)
15. Kunduri (Ivy gourd)
16. Simba (Flat beans)
17. Mahunada (Lotus stem)
18. Mahuka Simba (Sword beans)
19. Bhendi (Ladies finger)
20. Khada (Amaranthus)
21. Phula Kobi (Cauliflower)
22. Bandha Kobi (Cabbage)
23. Ganthi Kobi (Kholrabi)
24. Bhejri Baigana (Pea eggplant)
25. Chuein (Drumsticks)
26. Kancha Amba (Green mango)

27. Kandamula (Sweet potato)

28. Panasa Katha (Tender Jackfruit)

29. Palua Kanda (Arrowroots tubers)

30. Mula (Radish)

31. Karamanga (Star fruit)

32. Ambada (Indian hog plum)

33. Oou (Elephant apple)

34. Alu (Potato)

35. Piaja (Onion)

36. Uli Piaja (Shallot)

37. Chattu (Mushrooms)

38. Girel Phul

39. Kakharu Phula (Pumpkin blossoms)

40. Nima Kadha (Margosa buds)

41. Pothi Saru (A kind of Taro)

42. Sankha Saru (A large variety of Taro)

43. Agasti Phula (Vegetable hummingbird flower)

44. Kanchan Phula (Bauhinia flower)

45. Sajana Chuein Phula (Moringa flower)

46. Kadali Bhanda (Banana inflorescence)

47. Kadali Manja (Banana Stem - core)

48. Tol (Mahua fruit)

49. Kaintha (Wood apple)

50. Kandhiya (Citron)

51. Guanr (Cluster bean)

52. Jhudunga (Yard long beans)

53. Tarada (Sponge gourd)

54. Olua Phul (Elephant yam flower)

LIST OF POPULAR GREENS USED IN ODIA COOKING

1. Khada sagaw (Tall variety of amaranthus growing during summer)
2. Kosala sagaw (A variety of amaranthus growing during winter)
3. Leutia sagaw (Variety of amaranthus growing during summer)
4. Mitha Nalita /Nalita sagaw (Hibiscus Cannabinus)
5. Madaranga sagaw (Alternanthera sessilis)
6. Sajana Sagaw (Moringa)
7. Barada sagaw (A variety of Bauhinia)
8. Kuliari sagaw (A variety of Bauhinia)
9. Bahal sagaw
10. Nima patra (Neem leaves)
11. Pita sagaw (Glinus oppositifolius)
12. Kalara patra sagaw (Bitter gourd leaves)
13. Kakharu sagaw (Pumpkin leaves)
14. Pani Kakharu sagaw (Ash gourd leaves)
15. Saru patra (taro leaves)
16. Alu patra (potato leaves)
17. Kandamula patra (sweet potato leaves)
18. Kenna/Kansiri sagaw (Commelina benghalensis)
19. Methi sagaw (fenugreek leaves)
20. Palanga sagaw (Spinach)
21. Khatta Palanga Sagaw (Rumex vesicarius)
22. Kalama Sagaw (Ipomoea aquatica)
23. Mula Sagaw (Radish leaves)
24. Rasuna patra(Garlic chives)
25. Piaja Patra (Onion leaves)
26. Piaja Sandha (Onion flower stalk)

27. Prasaruni (Skunk vine)

28. Jhumpuri sagaw (Streblus taxoides)

29. Agasti sagaw (Sesbania grandiflora)

30. Puruni sagaw (Boerhavia diffusa)

31. Nuni Sagaw (Portulaca oleracea)

32. Muthi sagaw (Polygonum plebeium)

33. Sunsunia Sagaw (Marsilea quadrifolia)

34. Lau Patra (Bottle gourd leaves)

35. Ambiliti sagaw (Oxalis corniculate)

36. Chakunda saag (Cassia Tora)

37. Leper Saag (Chlorophytum Tuberosum)

38. Hidimicha Sagaw (Enhydra Fluctuans)

EDIBLE FATS USED IN ODIA COOKING

Mustard oil is mostly widely used with cow ghee being used on special occasions. However, other oils are also used in specific geographic locations and by certain communities. Also, some of these oils are used sparingly and mainly to derive medicinal benefits for them. The practice of blending oils like raee mustard, groundnut and sesame was once practiced in Western parts but is now obsolete.

Some of them are:

- Buffalo Ghee (used but not preferred)
- Raee mustard oil (milder in flavour)
- Sesame oil
- Mahua Oil
- Flaxseed oil
- Castor oil
- Niger (jatangi) oil
- Groundnut oil
- Black mustard oil
- Coconut oil (Only by Brahmin families in Coastal parts)

RECIPES BY CATEGORY

Breakfast/Snacks
Chaul Bara
Chuda Ghasa
Chuda Kadali Chakata
Jhiliya
Makara Chaula
Mandia Jau
Mandia Pej
Muan
Muga Sijha
Tetel Jhol
Thethri
Huduma

Lentils
Biri Dali
Habisa Dalma
Kakharu Buta Dali
Kandula Dali
Kasi Panasa Muga Dali
Kolatha Dali
Muga Dali (normal)
Mutton Dalma
Sukhua Dalma

Rice/Roti
Chinabadam Jukha
Chuna Ruti
Dahi Bhata
Janta Ruti
Makara Jau
Palau
Pausa Khechudi

Pitha
Biri Gojja
Buddha Chakuli
Chaula kakara Pitha
Chittau Pitha
Enduri Pitha
Gaintha / Attakali
Ghura
Khudaw Pitha
Ladaa Pitha
Lau Pitha
Mahul Chakel
Pej Pitha
Pusa Manda
Rajaw Podo Pitha
Sala Patra Enduri
Tala Kakara
Usna Chakuli
Dudura Pitha
Chunchipatra pitha

Bhaja/bara
Chotta Alu Uli Piaj Bhaja
Alu Pitha
Badi Chura
Chachindra Pura Dia
Chuein Alu Bhaja
Gota Kalara Bhaja
Kasi Panasa Bhaja
Mati Alu Bhaja
Mula Bhaja
Nima Kadha Baigana Bhaja
Nima Kadha Pagaw

Pala Chattu Bara
Palua Kanda Bhaja
Maka Bara

Batibasa/Dibapuda/Patua/Raee
Guanr Daba Puda
Jandi Poda
Kadali Bhanda patua
Kadali Manja Raee
Kakharu Dunka Raee
Kakharu Phula Janhi Batibasa
Lau Chopa Patua
Mahuka Simba Raee
Pani Kakharu Raee
Simba Raee
Hidimicha Sagaw Patua

Kanji
Pachila Amba- Khudaw Kanji
Amba Kanji
Ambil
Charu Pani
Mula Kanji
Torani Kanji

On a sweeter note
Char Manji Ladu
Gahama Khiri
Muga Bara
Mugri Laddoo
Suji-Nadia Kora Laddu
Tala Bara
Tampa
Panasa Bara
Mandiya Tikhri

Mung Tikhri
Palua Khiri

Khatta/Pagaw
Amba Sorisa khatta
Ambil/Letha
Ambula Puda
Bhendi Sorisa Khatta
Champuta
Chingudi Sorisa Khatta
Kandamula Khatta
Oou Khatta
Patalghanta Bhendi Hendua
Saru Patalghanta Khatta
Saru patra Khatta
Sukhua Ambula Pagaw
Karadi Lembu Pagaw
Kandhiya LembuPagaw

Chutney/Raita
Amba Chutney
Baigana Chutney
Dahi Manja
Dahi Mula Raita
Kaintha Chutney
Khatta Palanga Chutney

Sagaw
Bahal Kadha Bhaja
Barada Sagaw Bhaja
Chakunda Saag
Chana Saag
Jukjukia Sajana Saag
Kanjer Saag
Karadi Makhan Saag

Khada Sagaw Bhaja
Kosala Saga-Badi
Madranga Sagaw Raee
Methi Sagaw Posto Bata
Misamusi Sagaw
Mula Sagaw Badam Bata
Paija Sandha Bhaja
Pani Kakharu Patra Pithau Bhaja
Pani Kakharu Patra Pura Bhaja
Prasaruni Patra Bara
Prasaruni Patra Chakuli
Piaja Patra Dia Muga Dali
Pita Saga Bara
Pita Sagaw Batibasa
Poee Sagaw Bara
Rasuna Patra Pitha Bhaja
Sajana Sajaw Bhaja
Sajana Sajaw Muga
Sunsunia Sagaw
Palanga Sagaw Baigana

Non-vegetarian Recipes
Bitalu Danka Chingudi
Chudchuda
Illishi Bihana Sukhua Bara
Jhuri Purga
Karadi Maccha Chudchuda
Macch Puda
Maccha Ambila
Maccha Bihana Bara
Maccha Bihana Patua
Mutton Ambila
Niya Sukhua Tarkari (Smoked
Fish curry)

Poee Chenchedda
Seula Macha Ambula Tarkari
Sikar Jhul
Sukhila Maach Panas Manji
Tarkari
Sukhila Machha Pariba Ghanta
Sukhua Patalghanta

Tarkari/Ghanta/Santula/Patua
Badi Phulaa
Badi Tarkari
Dwitiya Osa/Garbhana Sankranti
Ghanta
Ghadaghadiya Tarkari
Jhunga Kanda Sijha
Khada Tarkari
Khira Santula
Lau Santula
Panasa Tarkari
Pani Santula
Prasaruni Patra Jholo
Puda Dia Kankada Tarkari
Rukta/Rugda Chattu Tarkari
Sankha Saru BaiganTarkari
Saru Magura
Simba Manji Sula Tarkari
Sem Baingan
Nadia Bara Tarkari

Panaa
Amba Panaa
Bela Panaa
Chattua Panaa
Palua Jhara

BIBLIOGRAPHY AND OTHER SOURCES

1. J.Troisi - Tribal Religion: Religious Beliefs and Practices among the Santals

2. Uwe Skoda - The Aghria: A Peasant caste on a Tribal Frontier

3. Burkhard Schnepel - The Jungle Kings: Ethnohistorical Aspects of Politics and Ritual in Odisha

4. Pradeep Kumar Panda - Maritime History of Ancient India: A Primer

5. Jagannath Rath - Tribal Folklore: A Study of Kuvis(Kandhas) of Koraput

6. Dr. N.K. Sahu, Dr. P.K. Mishra, Dr. J.K. Sahu – History of Orissa

7. Kartikeswar Patra – Ports in Orissa: A Study of Maritime History

8. Andrew Stirling – Orissa: Its Geography, Statistics, History, Religion and Antiquities

9. W. W. Hunter – History of Orissa

10. Nakul Seth - Tribes of Western Odisha

11. Manmatha Nath Das – Glimpses of Kalinga History

12. Truptirekha Sahoo - Fairs and Festival of Mayurbhanj: An Overview

13. Pratap Kumar Dash - The Perishing Tradition of Osha, Brata and Mela in Odisha: An Overview

14. Colonel JC Mahanti (Retired) – Fading Festivals of Odisha

15. Uwe Skoda, Rashmi Pramanik – Chronicles of the Royal Family of Bonai (Odisha)

16. L.K. Mahapatra - Tribal Peasantry in Bonai Hills

17. Tribes of Odisha (SC & ST Research Institute of Orissa)

18. Sabitri Brata Katha (Odia)

19. Kartika Mahatmaya (Odia)

20. Bata Osa Katha (Odia)

21. Buddhei Osa (Odia)

22. Danda Pahanra Osa (Odia)

23. Khudurukuni Osa (Odia)

24. Manabasa Lakshmi Purana (Odia)

25. Dr. Krushnabihari Dash - Odia Loka Kahani (Odia)

26. Shrimati Sarojini Chaudhry -Gruhani Sarbaswa (1928) (Odia)

27. Festivals-of-the-bhuinyas-of-Orissa (www.etribaltribune.com)

28. Aruna Jyothi Kora - Leaves as dining plates, food wraps and food packing material: Importance of renewable resources in Indian culture

29. Sidney W. Mintz, Daniela Schlettwein-Gsell - Food Patterns in Agrarian Societies: The "Core-Fringe-Legume Hypothesis" A Dialogue